P9-DED-861

SWITCHING TIME

SWITCHING TIME

A Doctor's Harrowing Story of Treating a Woman with 17 Personalities

Richard K. Baer, M.D.

CROWN PUBLISHERS ▪ NEW YORK

Copyright © 2007 by Richard Baer

All rights reserved.
Published in the United States by Crown Publishers, an imprint of
the Crown Publishing Group, a division of Random House, Inc., New York.
www.crownpublishing.com

Crown is a trademark and the Crown colophon is a registered trademark of
Random House, Inc.

Library of Congress Cataloging-in-Publication Data
Baer, Richard K.
  Switching time / Richard K. Baer.—1st ed.
  1. Overhill, Karen—Mental health.   2. Multiple personality—Patients—
Biography   3. Multiple personality—Case studies.   I. Title.
RC569.5.M8B34 2007
616.85'2360092—dc22
[B]   2007003882

ISBN 978-0-307-38266-5

Printed in the United States of America

10 9 8 7 6 5 4 3 2 1

First Edition

To Rick and Francesca and all of our children . . .

CONTENTS

PROLOGUE

The nurse kept calling me Karen, so I thought that must be my name. I knew I was in the hospital, but I didn't know why. I had bandages over my abdomen and my chest hurt when I breathed. I lay in the bed for a while—quiet, frightened, and feeling alone in a world I couldn't explain. I was afraid I'd lost my mind.

I was transferred to another room. I figured I must have given birth because of the bandages on my abdomen and all the mothers and newborns on the floor. A nurse came in and looked under the bandage. There was a six-inch scar, just above my pubic bone, that, with the stitches, looked like an angry smile.

A man came in, tall and skinny, smelling of beer, with a goofy smile and a crew cut, and told me we'd just had a baby girl. I smiled back at him. He must be the father, I thought, but I had no idea who he was.

"Karen, we have our beautiful Sara," he said. "When are you coming home?"

I didn't know where home was, or who else might be there.

"You'll need to ask the doctors," I said, smiling weakly. "Sara is her name?"

"Sara, of course!" he said. "Did you change your mind?"

"Oh, no, Sara is beautiful," I said. I was so muddled and scared, but I thought I should keep all this confusion secret. How could I ask this man, Who are you? They'd say I was crazy, I thought. I hoped I wasn't. I was sure if they found out I couldn't remember anything, they'd lock me away.

I began to recall images from before the birth—being pushed along a green corridor toward the elevator, the water pipes careening along the ceiling, and glancing at the talking, upside-down faces above me. I remember the nurses strapping me down—first my legs, then my arms. A memory triggered. . . . I can't move! Please don't hurt me! I struggled against the straps. I couldn't see the doctor past the drapes. He was poised over my belly, then I felt his surgeon's knife, and a fire seared into my belly.

I kicked with my legs and tried to scream, but no sound came. My mouth was sour and rancid, and my throat was filled with vomit. I gasped for breath. The doctor saw my legs move and barked something to the nurse. A mask was put over my face. Then I disappeared.

During the first few days after Sara's birth, I learned I had a two-year-old son at home, James, who had wavy blond hair and the bluest eyes I'd ever seen. I saw him in a picture my mother brought. I figured it was my mother. She talked about what she went through when she gave birth to me. "You were the first; you were the hardest. I was in labor forever with you. We didn't have all the fancy pain medicine you have now. I remember how much you tore me up and all the stitches I had." She didn't really let me speak; all I needed to do was listen. After a while, I became annoyed by this woman who dressed in gaudy animal prints and always turned the conversation toward herself. Her husband, Martin, my father, was a big, grim, brooding man who stopped in briefly, asked how I was doing but didn't wait for an answer. After watching my television for a few minutes, he left.

Strangely, I accepted these newly discovered facts about myself and my family without alarm or surprise. Although it was all bewildering, I vaguely sensed I'd been in similar situations before. It felt familiar to pretend and gather information about what I couldn't remember, and somehow I knew it was best to keep my mouth shut.

Sometimes when my family visited, I pretended to be asleep so I could overhear their conversations and secretly familiarize myself with my husband, my brothers, their families, and our friends. I heard my mother call my husband Josh, and him call her Katrina.

Josh worked as a foreman at a moving company. He made sure the trucks got loaded with the correct cargo and left on time. He came in to visit during lunch sometimes, but visiting was hard for him with going to work and taking care of our son.

My hospital stay was extended because whenever I took a deep breath, I had a shooting, stabbing pain along the entire right side of my chest. Eventually my internist told me I had "aspiration pneumonia" from inhaling vomit during my C-section. I went on intravenous antibiotics and stayed in the hospital for three more weeks.

My fever went up and down, but never fully returned to normal. Later, a surgeon was called in. I finally had an operation where they took out part of my right lung because the doctors said I'd formed an "abscess." There were periods of time while I was in the hospital for which I couldn't account; I think I may have been in a coma off and on.

Once I got home, although my right side continually ached, I worked to understand the person I was supposed to be. People called and visited to see the new baby. I'd talk in generalities until I could glean from the other person the nature of our relationship. I pored over the many photo albums I found; it was as if somebody had left them there for me. I studied each page and found much detail written below the pictures. Gradually, I became the person in the pictures.

My husband grew increasingly mean: yelling at me because I'd stayed in the hospital for six weeks and wasn't able to help at home. He cursed me when my pain and fatigue limited what I could do around the house. I didn't want to have sex with Josh; I didn't even know him, so instead I complained about the pain in my side. Worst of all, my son, who at first was a total stranger to me, knew I wasn't his mom, and it took months to gain his trust and acceptance.

But life went on. I adjusted to the routines of our house, became accustomed to the demands of Josh and my mother, and fit back into a busy schedule of volunteering, doing errands for friends, and taking care of my kids. But after more than three years of this, I was despairing. I went from doctor to doctor seeking a remedy for the constant nagging stitch in my chest from my lung surgery, but no one could find the cause. Besides my pain, deep down inside, I knew I was living a lie. I'd become accustomed to my family, but there were still periods of time, off and on, for which I couldn't account. I wouldn't remember getting *dressed, or I'd find a book at my bedside I didn't remember reading. I thought there must be something terribly wrong with me. I feared I was losing my mind. Whom could I talk to? Things were out of control. Finally, I called the crisis line at the hospital and they referred me to Dr. Rosa Gonzalez, a psychiatrist. When I called her office, the receptionist said Dr. Gonzalez was booked, but she'd give me an appointment to see Gonzalez's partner, Dr. Richard Baer.*

STAYING ALIVE

PART ONE

1

FALSE START

*It's January 11, 1989, and I walk down the narrow corri-*dor, past the two other therapists' offices, to the waiting room to fetch Karen. She sits in the corner with her head bent, fidgeting with her purse strap. She's twenty-nine years old but looks older; she's overweight, with a round face, unkempt short brown hair that curls at the ends, brown eyes, gold-rimmed glasses, and a jagged, semicircular scar running up the middle of her forehead. Her clothes are tidy, but her black cotton pants and brown top don't ask to be noticed. She wears no makeup or jewelry except a wedding band. She looks up as I approach. Her eyes say, *Hi, I'm sorry, I give up.*

"Come right in," I say, and she walks past me in a way that is slow, self-effacing, apologetic, and helpless. There's a physical and emotional heaviness about her, an inertia that seems old and solid.

I'm a young psychiatrist; thirty-seven is young in this business. I'm a little over six feet tall, with sprinkles of gray in my formerly dark brown hair, and I once had a gay patient who described me as having boyish good looks. I've been in practice for seven years, practicing part of the time in a working-class suburb south of Chicago. The patients I see here are mainly housewives who are depressed or anxious, a few middle-age manic-depressives, and several elderly patients with what used to be called involutional melancholia, the depressive illness that is common in old age. I also see a few high-functioning schizophrenics and a couple of people in religious life. This is a good place to practice because of the wide variety of psychiatric illnesses I get to observe—and almost all the patients are covered by generous union medical insurance. I also have an office in downtown Chicago where I work the other half of the time, seeing my psychoanalytic patients and a handful of others.

This suburban office, which I share on alternate days with Dr. Gonzalez, is in a brown-brick, three-story 1970s office building situated between strip malls, car dealerships, and fast-food restaurants. The office is sparely appointed. It has a large oak desk with two chairs facing it and a small corner table with a modest arrangement of artificial silk flowers, a gift from my wife. A window spanning most of one wall gives a view of the traffic on 95th Street. The walls are off-white, and the carpeting and furniture are a mixture of browns. Except for the window, there are few distractions.

Karen settles in the chair facing my desk and sighs.

"What brings you to see me?" I ask. I use this standard opening line because it encourages the person to begin confiding their troubles without putting them on the defensive. Nearly all the alternatives—*What do you want? What's wrong with you? I understand you're depressed . . .*—are off-putting.

Karen shifts uneasily, trying to find a comfortable position. She's too big for the chair, although her posture, compact and turned slightly to the side, makes her look smaller.

"I've been . . . depressed . . . for the past three and a half years," she says. Before she speaks, she takes a quick breath, which gives the impression of hesitation, and her speech is full of effort and reluctance. She pauses.

"Never depressed before that?" I ask.

She shrugs, but shakes her head.

"Any problems with depression growing up?"

Another head shake.

"No, I had no problems until the birth of my second child, my daughter, by cesarean section." She briefly describes her hospital stay. "I still have pain." Karen sighs again, gathering strength.

"The doctors ended up taking out part of my lung through an incision on my back." She points along a line from her right breast to her spine. "I was sick for a long time and I couldn't be with my baby right away." Moisture appears in Karen's eyes. "I couldn't breast-feed, and my two-and-a-half-year-old son rejected me when I finally came home."

She tells me she'd been put on antidepressant medication and painkillers, although the painkillers made her more depressed. I know that for patients with chronic pain, depression is common. The rest of her life must be suffering, too.

"How are things going at home, now?" I ask. She shrugs again, apologetic and helpless. She talks to me as if each word has to be urged out, as if an internal force is interfering with her telling me what's wrong. Her words come out so slowly that I almost lose my concentration waiting for them.

"My marriage has crumbled since the baby. My husband and I aren't getting along." Karen's speech is halting now and she looks humiliated. "I've gained a hundred pounds since the baby was born. People walk all over me; I can't say no to them." She pauses and looks to me for a response, but I don't yet know enough to make any comments, so I just wait for more. Karen shifts again and continues.

"I cry all the time and I've stopped working because of the pain. When I'm home, my pain is worse, but when I'm outside, the pain is better." She looks away, then back at me. "I feel guilty about being sick, and I feel I owe my family for helping me."

"You owe them?"

"Because they've had to help me . . ." She turns her head away again to escape my looking at her.

She goes on to say she wakes during the night and can't get back to sleep, and doesn't care anymore. She has no energy, she cries, she can't concentrate, and she stopped taking the medication she was on. . . .

As I listen, I see a woman unable to help herself. She presents herself as a victim, almost insisting on the role, and I feel a twinge of impatience. I know she has depression, with symptoms that can be helped by medication, but I also sense she possesses character traits that contribute to her depression and will make treating her illness more difficult.

After listening to her story, I ask my standard list of mental-status questions. It's clear she has significant depression, but she denies having any suicidal thoughts. I decide to treat her depressive symptoms with medication and leave the character traits alone. I ask her to come back to see me next week. She accepts the prescription obediently and leaves the office. My spirits raise a little as I see her go.

I don't think about Karen again until she returns the next week. She says she feels better, sleeps better, although she still feels sad.

"I've had some light-headedness from the medication," she says, picking at some lint on her slacks. "I'm not sure I like the idea of pills."

"I think they can help you," I say. "I recommend we continue with them."

"Okay," she says softly.

"How else have you been feeling?"

"I still have pain, which starts at my neck and goes down my back and around under my breast, here." She points to her chest. Karen repeats the complaints of our previous session. *I can't say no to people. I feel guilty because my mother helped me when I was sick, and now I owe her. I try to satisfy everybody. My marriage hasn't recovered from my illness. . . .*

With all of these things I feel I can offer only limited help. She never offers a hint of what she herself is doing to solve her problems—she simply suffers. I listen to her with that twinge of annoyance growing inside me again. It's important for a therapist to be aware of his or her own reaction to a patient and try to learn from it. Is this irritation felt by the other people in Karen's life? I wonder. I suggest to Karen that she can change her life if she wants to and that she needn't be as helpless as she now feels. I give her several examples using situations she's mentioned, and suggest how she might make more assertive choices to alter the self-defeating patterns she's following. She offers excuses why that's not possible and I realize I'm talking to a stone. I double her medication and ask her to come back in two weeks.

When Karen returns, her hands are trembling. She's dressed as before; she has on different clothes, but the drab, tidy impression is the same. Her forehead is creased with lines down the middle. She shifts in her chair and looks at me; her eyes are sad.

"I can't sleep . . . at night," she says softly, tentatively, beginning a litany of complaints that I'm familiar with from our last two sessions.

"Do you think about hurting yourself?" I ask. Anyone who's this depressed and helpless must think about it. Karen starts to cry a little.

"Occasionally I think about killing myself," she says, but quickly adds, "I don't think I'd really do anything."

As I listen to her talk about the things that weigh on her but that she makes no effort to rid herself of, I feel my irritation with her grow. She talks in a reluctant monotone and resists my interruptions, and when I make a suggestion, she nods dutifully but goes right on as if I'd said nothing. I feel as if, in her passive way, she's walking all over me. She seems determined to wallow and rut around in these self-defeating emotions. In my own mind, I try to separate the symptoms of her major depressive episode from her passive, self-defeating personality traits. I want to focus on treating the depression, which should be a short-term task. I don't really want to intervene with the personality traits; they're a very long-term task. I feel she's benefiting from the medication, but her response to it has been modest. I triple her dose from her original starting dose and ask her to return in a month.

Karen is my last patient of the day, and I'm eager to get home. I have a wife, a four-year-old son, and an eight-month-old baby girl waiting for me there. After a day of listening to people's problems, I know it will raise my spirits to see them.

Four weeks later I go to the waiting room and look for Karen, but she's not there. I return to my office and scan the notes I'd made during her previous visits. It's my routine, when a patient comes in for their appointment, to review the notes I made from our last session to remind myself of the course of their thoughts and emotions. Patients always pick up where they left off, perhaps not in the subject matter, but always in the trail of their emotional associations. Though the topics may change, the thread of their emotions will be the same or, hopefully, show some progress.

At first, while sitting and waiting for Karen to arrive, I begin to wonder why she might be arriving late. Had I touched on some sensitive topic or trait that she might be reluctant to explore in herself? Is she afraid of getting close to me, and so by being late, is trying to dilute the therapeutic encounter by decreasing the minutes we'll spend together? After ten minutes, I go out and look for her again; she's still not there.

As the minutes tick by, it dawns on me she isn't late—she's missed the session altogether. Karen has been difficult to help, so I look over my notes again to try to find some clue why she didn't return. As I read over what she told me and as I recall my feelings about her, it's easy to see the several ways I failed to understand and empathize with her. Sometimes I get lost in the details of a person's life, and my own reactions to them, and I lose track of the big picture. I see now that she was trying to please me by taking medication she didn't think was working for her, and that I was feeling irritation she wasn't getting better, and thought the way she was acting was wrong. Clearly, my irritation had prevented me from really listening to her, with the result being she'd decided I couldn't help her.

In thinking about my failure, I reflect on the tendency of depressed patients to make psychiatrists feel anxious. Behind every burst of a therapist's annoyance is an anxiety. But anxiety about what? That the depression will be contagious. And it is. When you sit with a depressed person, you feel you're being fed upon: that they're sucking the life out of you, and it makes you depressed, too. That was my problem with Karen and why it was hard to sit with her. Over the years I've worked with many, many depressed patients, but none got to me the way Karen did.

About a month later, my secretary tells me she's received three checks from Karen, one for each session. Each check bounces. She calls Karen to say she has to bring the payment in cash. Karen finally does. If she is trying to engender anger in her psychiatrist, she knows how to go about it.

Another three months pass, it's a balmy spring day in late May, and I see Karen's name on my list of patients for the afternoon. When she comes in, she looks unchanged, dressed in dark slacks and a short-sleeve faded green top, trembling a little, and as depressed as before. I ask her why she stopped coming. She says she was afraid to come back because of the bounced checks. She was reluctant to submit my bills to her husband's insurer, because she feared everyone at his work would know she was coming here.

I think her explanation is just a rationalization for the underlying emotional uncertainty she had about me—that she's come back to give me a second chance. I hope to use it wisely. I reassure her and discuss the rules of confidentiality companies need to follow, pointing out that people at her husband's work won't know she's seeing me. She resists using the insurance, but is worried about keeping up with my bill, so I suggest we start again by meeting once a month. She is relieved and agrees. The problem is, I worry that a half hour once a month will not be enough time to locate and treat what is ailing her.

When Karen comes in next, on June 19, I remind myself to focus and try to empathize with her hopelessness and helplessness, and really understand her, no matter how much her manner pushes me away. I resolve to do better.

"I don't know what to do, Dr. Baer. I feel so shaky and down." She pouts her lower lip, and it trembles. "I don't even want to live anymore." I ask pointed questions aimed at coaxing out of her some specifics. After a few minutes of teeth pulling on my part, she seems to gather herself.

"I have more problems with my husband than I told you."

"Uh-huh." I wait.

"He hits me. If I don't please him and do what he says, he says he has no use for me." She pauses and waits for me to say something, but I wait longer.

"He wakes me up in the middle of the night by punching me and sends me out for McDonald's, or if his basketball team loses on television, he'll beat me and blame me for it—and mean it!" She looks up at me to see if I understand this.

"You make the team lose," I say. She nods.

"How long has this kind of thing been going on?"

"Since my daughter Sara's birth, I think. He drinks a few beers and is in a good mood, then he drinks several more and gets quiet, then he's mean." She *thinks*? Why doesn't she *know*? I wonder.

Shortly before her next appointment, she calls and cancels. Two weeks later I receive the following letter.

11/12/89

Dear Dr. Baer,

It is 1:30 a.m. and I can't sleep. I don't know how much longer I can go on this way. I really want to die. I hate myself and my life. I can't stop crying. I am just waiting for the right moment to die. I don't know how or when, but I feel it will be soon. I am numb. I want to sleep forever. Please help me before it is too late.

Your patient
Karen Overhill

P.S. Do you really care what happens to me? I don't.

My main concern as I read the letter is Karen's risk for suicide. I'm quite attentive to the danger she's in. She seems much more desperate and determined to die than she's ever led me to believe. I call her right away.

"Karen?"

"Yes." Her voice is small and distant on the phone.

"It's Dr. Baer. I got the letter you sent."

"Oh."

We talk for a few minutes, during which I learn that Karen's truly bent on killing herself, possibly by taking an overdose of the pills I prescribed her. At that point I realize there is only one realistic option.

"The most important thing right now is to make sure you're safe," I say emphatically. "And the best place for that is in the hospital." I say this with conviction, because getting someone to agree to be admitted to a psychiatric hospital can be extremely difficult. Karen is quiet for several moments.

"If you think that's best."

2.

ROLLER COASTER

Karen enters the hospital on November 19 and stays for a month. When I visit her, she hands me some of her memories she had written down. She seems embarrassed to give them to me. As I begin to read, I'm introduced to a life of cruelty, terror, damage, and survival.

The handwriting, misspellings, and casual punctuation suggest her words were written quickly, as if pressured.

About Dad

My dad is disgusting, immature, lazy, sloppy, user, kleptomaniac, no sense, moocher, no personality, not dependable, pervert. All he thinks about is sex. He always made passes at my girlfriends. He used to give my friends a dime and tell them to call him in ten years for lessons in love. I hate him. He abused me constantly physically and mentally. He made me feel ugly, unwanted, insecure, useless. He always called me slut, whore, cunt, bitch, etc. He never told me he loved me never hugged me and I didn't want him to. He whines about everything. Depended on my grandparents for everything. Blamed me for all his money problems. The man is sick, and there's no changing him. He always tells me "I owe him my life." He never cared about anyone, except himself he treats my mother like a maid and a sex machine. My mother still puts his socks on for him every morning.

My dad used to make us take our clothes off and lie down on the bed. He tied our hands to the headboard with electrical cords, and beat us with his belt, the buckle side. The more we cried the more he beat us. I had to learn to control my feelings and not cry. I had to survive. Then he would go into the front room, turn on the projector and watch porno flicks. My dad and mom would argue constantly about these movies, my dad telling my mom he's going to teach her the right way to make love. They both disgust me. How could they do this with us listening in the next room? All my life from age 5 to about 16, I was beaten 3 to 5 times a week. I always seemed to feel bruised and hurt. I wished my parents dead. I prayed to God, asking Him to help, but nothing worked. I couldn't trust anyone. I wished I would die. I wanted to run away, but I was afraid if they found me they would kill me.

In addition to these pages, she gave me another, in print handwriting much different than the cursive one of the other pages. It's addressed to me and asks:

Can I trust him?
What should I tell him?
Will he abandon me?
Will he betray me?
Will I ever get better?
Will the pain ever go away?
What if I lose control and snap?
How can he help me through it?
I am scared of Dr. Baer.

One dreary evening while Karen is in the hospital, I've just finished with my last patient of the day in my part-time suburban office when suddenly, I don't know why, I have a twinge of panic. I'm watching the traffic crawl down 95th Street from my office window, as I have for the past seven years, and I think: If I don't get out of here, I'm going to be looking at this same traffic in twenty years. I decide right then to try to move my practice to downtown Chicago full-time. I've always felt more comfortable among the downtown psychoanalysts, but in starting my practice, it was much more practical to work in the suburbs. Downtown, the psychiatrists, psychologists, and clinical social workers are crawling all over one another, and although I'm well trained, my inexperience then made it hard to stand out. In the suburbs, especially the south suburbs, someone with my training is rare, and getting patients is much easier. Besides, a greater percentage of suburban patients have good medical insurance, or at least better than what the HMOs offer most of the white-collar workers downtown.

Now feeling I'm ready to prosper in the city, I visit a few colleagues at the university teaching hospitals downtown to see if there are any part-time positions available. I land one working with the fellow who was the head of the inpatient service where I did my residency training. I hope this position will lead to referrals into my private office practice, so I can sustain myself without referrals from Dr. Gonzalez.

My downtown office is much different from my south-side one. A long green velvet couch dominates one wall, with my Eames chair at one end of it. There I can sit out of sight as my patients discuss their problems. Over the couch are four Chinese prints of birds and butterflies. Facing my chair is a wingback chair in a green-and-white floral print. Behind that chair is a Queen Anne desk, and next to that a credenza on which I can see, by looking just past the head of the patient I'm talking to, my Jefferson Golden Hour electric clock. This is a clock whose hands seem to be floating in air. My analyst had one, and I've seen one in most of the analysts' offices I've been in. I don't know where this little tradition got started, but I feel obligated to follow it. The Oriental rug on the floor echoes the colors of the room. A bookcase with cut-glass doors dominates the wall next to the couch, and on the opposite wall, next to my chair, are floor-to-ceiling windows that look out from my fortieth-floor perch to the parks along the lakefront.

Some of my patients who make the transition from the south-side office to the downtown office are intimidated by the change in surroundings. But it's where I now feel comfortable. Karen readily agrees to follow me to my new location.

It's the day after Christmas 1989, and Karen and I have been seeing each other for almost a year. She says that since we've been talking about her past, some memories have been bothering her.

"Once, my father was mad at me," she says apologetically, "and he threw a meat fork at me and it stuck in my thigh. I just stood there and looked at it sticking out of my leg. I don't remember what happened after that. I don't remember it being taken out."

"Uh-huh." I wait.

"I've had constant suicidal thoughts since childhood." She continues, "I've never attempted suicide, but I've always made plans for it."

"Have you hurt yourself in nonsuicidal ways, just to hurt yourself?" Karen turns away, and I can see her neck flush crimson. She goes silent. Uh-oh, I pried too hard. I shouldn't have interfered with what she was saying by asking that question. I try to recover by changing the subject. "Has the medication been helping?" I ask. She shrugs, but her eyes tell me no.

I change her to a different antidepressant, and we talk about the purpose of the medicine. I suggest that after my vacation we start to meet once per week to help her more. She smiles and says she'll submit the bill to her husband's insurance to cover the additional sessions. As she leaves, she stops at the door and turns to say, "I'm not sure this is important, but I fainted three times at the altar when I got married."

It's January 1990, and I haven't seen Karen since Christmas- time. We're starting our second year together, and I find I worry about her a lot, especially when I'm away.

"I had a bad couple weeks," she says, looking around at the new office before slumping in her chair like an exhausted prizefighter after the tenth round.

"Tell me about it."

"I don't think I can go on," she says, her face collapsing. "I can't do anything. I keep thinking about killing myself." She looks as if she might say more, but she falls farther back into the chair.

"Have you thought about how you might kill yourself?" By

now, my routine with Karen is not to ask *if* she is suicidal, but to assess how close she is to doing it.

"I have my pills at home—they might be enough to do the job, but I don't feel like I'd take them," she says. There's a special irony for a psychiatrist when a patient overdoses with the pills you yourself have given her. It's as if you've handed her the bullets to the gun. It is a very personal betrayal by the patient. I react to Karen's comment about the pills by giving her a brand-new antidepressant, Prozac, and something to help her sleep better. The Prozac won't kill her if she overdoses on it.

"Are you doing anything else to prepare for killing yourself?" I ask.

"Well, I'm staying away from my family. They don't really need me anymore." She curls up into the chair.

"How can we keep you safe?" I ask.

"I don't want to go back into the hospital," she says quickly. She looks at me and sets her jaw.

I'm very worried she might make a suicide attempt, but I don't want to force her into the hospital. I don't believe a brief hospitalization will do any good, except to keep her temporarily safe, and she'd be discharged in the same shape she is now. It may yet come to that, but I'd like to be able to keep her safe outside the hospital.

"This is Wednesday," I say. "We should meet again on Friday. You need to throw your old antidepressant pills down the toilet, and call me if you feel worse or think you might hurt yourself." I look right at her, searching for any dissembling. "Do you agree?"

"Okay." She says quietly, and she turns her head away.

"You promise?" I challenge.

She looks at me again, then down at her hands. "I promise."

I often go home at night knowing I have two or three patients at as much risk as Karen. Handling suicidal patients—making judgments on whom to hospitalize and whom to handle with phone calls or extra sessions—is the most difficult thing a psychiatrist does. Every psychiatrist has had patients commit suicide. It's not always preventable; I've had three patients take their lives, and each loss was devastating. Deep down, I expect my ability to keep everyone safe to be infallible, but sometimes reality intervenes, and I lose somebody under circumstances I can't control.

Since I'm a solo practitioner, I'm always on call for my patients 24/7, unless I'm on vacation and I ask a colleague to cover for me while I'm away. When the phone rings or my pager goes off, I wonder whether something has happened and to whom. I'm glad when a patient calls simply seeking support and contact, because at least I know they're not dead. During these months in early 1990 I receive frequent calls from Karen, sometimes two or three times a week, seeking support so she doesn't kill herself. I worry she's only a step away.

It's February 1990, and Karen tells me about the history of the scar on her forehead. She had an aneurysm or angioma (a benign tumor formed from a tangle of blood vessels) removed from her forehead when she was nineteen months old. She says that as a child, her scars were prominent and the other kids made fun of her, calling her Frankenstein. Her father couldn't deal with her medical problems, and blamed her for the costly hospital bills. He'd yell, *If it weren't for you and your hospital bills, what we'd have!* She was a good scapegoat for his failures, I think.

While Karen was in the hospital for her surgery, her father stole some restraints, which he later used to tie her to the bed at home. If she cried, he'd bind her and beat her to *give her something to cry about!* Karen says she was mute at times; that is, she'd refuse to speak. When she was ten, she convinced everyone she'd gone deaf. She was in the hospital for weeks for this; she says she'd just "stopped listening."

She grew up wishing her parents would die. Her father wished her dead, too, she says. Once, when she was very ill with pneumonia, her father refused to take her to the emergency room. At last, her mother and uncle took her. She says she had a respiratory arrest when she got there. If they'd waited any longer, she says, she would have died.

The more Karen reveals, the more I'm amazed at what she's suffered—but I'm skeptical it's all true. In addition to her physical hardships, the emerging pattern of sadistic emotional abuse is striking. It's hard to know how accurate these childhood memories are, but she calls them up with such conviction, clarity, and wrenching sincerity. She says our sessions exhaust her.

. . .

During the next several sessions, I feel I'm just along for the ride. Karen proffers a dizzying array of physical symptoms and terrible memories, but at the same time is overall less depressed and more animated.

"Once, when I was a little girl, I was making clothes for my dolls," she says with no particular emotion. "I asked my father if I could have an old red tie of his to use for a skirt. He said okay, but first I had to put it on myself and tie it properly. After I was finished, I turned to him and he grabbed the tie, picked me up by it, choking me. He was laughing, telling me I shouldn't trust anybody." She tells me this with no dramatic flair, but morosely, as if the memory weighs her down and is part of her burden. At the end she adds, "All the relationships I've had with men end up somehow hurting me."

Alarms are going off in my head at this. A therapist should always listen to what a patient says with an ear to what it might mean in terms of that patient's relationship to the therapist. It seems self-centered on the therapist's part, but it's absolutely true that practically everything a patient talks about has a latent meaning for the doctor-patient relationship. Karen has recently made her first real progress in therapy by revealing some terrible things about her past. Yet at the same time, she intimates, by referring to *all her relationships with men,* that I, too, will be like all the other men who've abused her. On the one hand, she's found a place with me where she can begin to speak about the abused life she's led, but on the other, deep down, she's convinced I'll be like all the others, that it will blow up in her face.

This is a critical point in therapy, where it can either deepen or burst apart. I'm about to get the chance to say something important to Karen, really for the first time: to help her fully understand the deep mistrust she has of people, even those of us who may be trustworthy.

I've already said many things to Karen, but none were truly insightful; they were merely exploratory, supportive, or motivational. The reason we've gotten this far is because I've learned to listen better. That, and Karen has a crushing need to be listened to.

"Karen, I've been thinking about what you said, and I think

During the next several sessions, I feel I'm just along for the ride. Karen proffers a dizzying array of physical symptoms and terrible memories, but at the same time is overall less depressed and more animated.

"Once, when I was a little girl, I was making clothes for my dolls," she says with no particular emotion. "I asked my father if I could have an old red tie of his to use for a skirt. He said okay, but first I had to put it on myself and tie it properly. After I was finished, I turned to him and he grabbed the tie, picked me up by it, choking me. He was laughing, telling me I shouldn't trust anybody." She tells me this with no dramatic flair, but morosely, as if the memory weighs her down and is part of her burden. At the end she adds, "All the relationships I've had with men end up somehow hurting me."

Alarms are going off in my head at this. A therapist should always listen to what a patient says with an ear to what it might mean in terms of that patient's relationship to the therapist. It seems self-centered on the therapist's part, but it's absolutely true that practically everything a patient talks about has a latent meaning for the doctor-patient relationship. Karen has recently made her first real progress in therapy by revealing some terrible things about her past. Yet at the same time, she intimates, by referring to *all her relationships with men*, that I, too, will be like all the other men who've abused her. On the one hand, she's found a place with me where she can begin to speak about the abused life she's led, but on the other, deep down, she's convinced I'll be like all the others, that it will blow up in her face.

This is a critical point in therapy, where it can either deepen or burst apart. I'm about to get the chance to say something important to Karen, really for the first time: to help her fully understand the deep mistrust she has of people, even those of us who may be trustworthy.

I've already said many things to Karen, but none were truly insightful; they were merely exploratory, supportive, or motivational. The reason we've gotten this far is because I've learned to listen better. That, and Karen has a crushing need to be listened to.

"Karen, I've been thinking about what you said, and I think

Since I'm a solo practitioner, I'm always on call for my patients 24/7, unless I'm on vacation and I ask a colleague to cover for me while I'm away. When the phone rings or my pager goes off, I wonder whether something has happened and to whom. I'm glad when a patient calls simply seeking support and contact, because at least I know they're not dead. During these months in early 1990 I receive frequent calls from Karen, sometimes two or three times a week, seeking support so she doesn't kill herself. I worry she's only a step away.

It's February 1990, and Karen tells me about the history of the scar on her forehead. She had an aneurysm or angioma (a benign tumor formed from a tangle of blood vessels) removed from her forehead when she was nineteen months old. She says that as a child, her scars were prominent and the other kids made fun of her, calling her Frankenstein. Her father couldn't deal with her medical problems, and blamed her for the costly hospital bills. He'd yell, *If it weren't for you and your hospital bills, what we'd have!* She was a good scapegoat for his failures, I think.

While Karen was in the hospital for her surgery, her father stole some restraints, which he later used to tie her to the bed at home. If she cried, he'd bind her and beat her to *give her something to cry about!* Karen says she was mute at times; that is, she'd refuse to speak. When she was ten, she convinced everyone she'd gone deaf. She was in the hospital for weeks for this; she says she'd just "stopped listening."

She grew up wishing her parents would die. Her father wished her dead, too, she says. Once, when she was very ill with pneumonia, her father refused to take her to the emergency room. At last, her mother and uncle took her. She says she had a respiratory arrest when she got there. If they'd waited any longer, she says, she would have died.

The more Karen reveals, the more I'm amazed at what she's suffered—but I'm skeptical it's all true. In addition to her physical hardships, the emerging pattern of sadistic emotional abuse is striking. It's hard to know how accurate these childhood memories are, but she calls them up with such conviction, clarity, and wrenching sincerity. She says our sessions exhaust her.

your fear is that if you get close to me, I'll abuse you just like every other man you've known. You want to get closer, but you're afraid." Karen looks at me and nods slowly; her eyes moisten and her face turns crimson at the edges. She's heard me, but the words will have to sit with her for a while for her to believe that perhaps I could be different. If I've hit the mark, she'll feel understood, safer, and be able to move to the next level. Later that day she writes:

Dear Dr. Baer,

After leaving your office today, I thought about what we talked about, and I need to let you know that I am really glad that I'm in therapy. There is so much I need to tell you, but when I get to your office, I get confused. I'm glad that you are patient with me, and I hope you don't feel as though I'm wasting your time. What will happen to me when I'm able to really talk to you? Will I be able to handle it? What if I can't? I feel like I'm on a roller coaster that doesn't stop. I know that you can help me help myself.

Karen

She seems to know exactly what's facing her. She's on a roller-coaster ride, plummeting down into an abyss. I'm on her roller coaster, too, aware that I've barely scratched the surface, and that deep secrets remain to be unearthed. Thinking about it, I feel a certain dread. One week her mood is up, the next it's down. She wants to work on her problems, but can both of us handle it? The roller coaster goes up; the roller coaster goes down.

A lot of the time a therapist spends in psychotherapy involves just waiting to see what unfolds. On this particular roller coaster, I feel I'm blindfolded, unable to see what's ahead. I've found that all patients have an unerring, unconscious sense of the best way to tell their story, if you just let them. They do it one layer at a time. One of the better pieces of advice I got in my psychiatry training was that my job as a therapist is simply to try to understand the patient. Not tell them what to do, not make them change, not tell them about myself. My job is to understand them. Once I come to that understanding, I can share it with them. It's a perspective that will help a therapist remain patient and stay out of a lot of trouble.

I want to understand more about Karen's unconscious feelings, about the secrets she doesn't yet have the courage to verbalize, so I tell her it might be helpful if she can write down some of her dreams. If interpreted carefully, dreams can pinpoint the current state of a patient's unconscious conflicts and the source of current symptoms. Karen takes up the task, and at her next visit she strides in clutching a piece of paper with these words:

I'm falling very fast from a tall building. I can't stop myself. I have no control. I'm getting closer to the ground. I see cars and people below. I don't want to die this way. Who pushed me out the window? Did I jump myself? I can't seem to remember how I started falling. I think I'm downtown falling from an office building. I'm trying to control myself, but I can't. Just before I hit the ground, I wake up shaking. My heart is beating very fast. I'm sweating. I'm in a panic. I have to hold on to the bed because I am still falling.

In therapy one can consider dreams to have three components: elements of the past, the present (also called the day residue), and the therapy relationship. The most important is the relationship with the therapist. That's where the strongest opportunity for change resides. The other two elements serve to illuminate the third. This is what I focus on with Karen.

"I think this dream represents your panic about increasing the frequency of the therapy sessions and feeling closer to me," I say. "You're falling from an office building, like mine, and you're feeling out of control as you open up to me more and more." It's another metaphor for the roller coaster. The next dream takes her fears a step further:

I'm in an operating room just about to have surgery. The doctors are strapping me down to the table. I don't know what kind of surgery. The doctors are wearing masks. I can't see their faces. They're laughing. The surgeon starts with an incision on my abdomen and I feel the pain like a hot iron. They're all still laughing. Their laughter is humiliating. The surgeon then looks at my foot and says, "She doesn't need this," and cuts it off. He throws it over his shoulder. Then he cuts out my heart and says, "You have no heart, no feeling." He continues to laugh. I'm dying; every-one wants a piece of me. I try to get away, but I can't break the straps. No one is helping me. I wake up in panic.

My ears always perk up when a patient has a dream with a doctor in it. The doctor always represents, in part, me. It's one way to know how a patient really feels about you.

"I think this dream represents more of your fears about me," I say. "You worry that if you submit to the therapy and let me 'operate' on you, you'll only suffer and feel helpless." Her cesarean section was like this dream, and only pain and depression followed.

At the next session, Karen gives me some memories she's written down. She says she isn't sure why she's remembering them now. Before we begin, I read some of them.

I am lying on a table in a dark room. I am scared of the dark. There are hands touching me all over. I'm crying. Please don't touch me! The hands don't stop. I hear laughter, a man's voice. Please leave me alone!

My father forced me to sit and watch a porno flick of a woman having oral sex with a man. He wanted me to learn the right way to please a man. He said he was teaching me.

I'm on the porch of my grandfather's house. I am playing with my Barbie dolls. I am 8 years old or younger. My grandfather calls me into the bedroom. He touches me. I do not respond. He threatens to throw out my Barbie dolls. I can't really hear him. I am really not there. I can't feel anything. He fondles me and then starts to _____.

I note the blank at the end of Karen's last entry. I don't know what it represents, but I decide to allow her to leave it blank for now. The first question that occurs to me is: Did these things really happen? I'm careful never to ask Karen for such stories or to suggest that such things might have happened to her, and yet these tales are offered up in such a detailed and consistent way that I find them compelling and believable.

As a practical matter for therapy, however, it matters less what actually happened—how much of these memories are real. These are the images in Karen's mind, and they, and the feelings associated with them, are *real to her.* Memories from childhood can be distorted, combined, substituted, and altered in a number of different ways. Although I have no reason to doubt Karen, and I know that children are sexually abused all the time, it still seems incredible to be sitting with someone who's survived all this. But I don't have to decide exactly what happened; I just need to understand what Karen thinks and feels. That's enough for now.

3

LOSING TIME

For the first time, in July 1990, Karen discusses in detail having periods of time for which she can't account. She describes a trip to Las Vegas the previous New Year's. She found herself at different parts of the casino and didn't know how she got there. Sometimes she had more money, sometimes less. When her husband and friends finally caught up with her, she had $2,500 in her purse. She'd started with $25, and had to make excuses about where she'd been and why she wasn't in her room lying down because of the headache she'd complained about.

She's told me before that she's forgetful, or that something had happened that she couldn't recall, and I'd noted that she had said she's had periods of time for which she couldn't account, but at the time I sensed she wasn't ready to be confronted about them. This is the first time she's told me about losing time—discreet periods when she "wasn't there."

During the next few weeks, Karen begins to tell me more about these episodes:

"One day, I left the house to go grocery shopping, but then I 'awoke' at the mall. I don't remember the decision not to go grocery shopping." Karen looks confused and apologetic at the craziness of her story. "Instead, I'm at Carson's buying my son a hat, but I don't really remember making the purchase or know how I got there. This kind of thing has happened a number of times before." She pauses a moment. "Another day, after attending a depression support group at the hospital, I went to dinner, but I don't remember dinner. The next thing I remember is waking in the morning with a headache."

Clearly, Karen has been having dissociative episodes, that is, periods of time where her consciousness is split. Part of her experiences reality, and part of her is cut off from it. I've suspected this for some time now, but exactly what type of episodes she's been having, I don't know. She'd already told me she was afraid to narrow in on one problem, so I decide to let her tell me about these episodes in her own time. I'm wary of encouraging these stories—I'm not sure I'd be able to tell if she were making them up just to please me.

The next session she tells me she was in a fight with her husband. She'd left her daughter at her mother's house overnight, and her husband got angry about it. She started punching him in the face, but she doesn't feel it was her doing it; he hit her back, and she ended up going to the hospital, but she doesn't remember the hospital. Her husband was all bruised. She says her periods of losing time are getting worse.

She got a call from a man who said he met her last Friday night. She doesn't remember meeting him. She went to a movie, but she can't remember parts of it. She says she doesn't really remember ages six through ten. Once, a nun in Catholic school said she was possessed and poured holy water on her head.

Karen is describing dissociative episodes that seem to have occurred off and on for most of her life. She asked me why she loses time. I suggest it could be a way to cope with being in pain. I have my own suspicions, but don't really have a better answer to give her now.

In August 1990, Karen is beginning to lose time more regularly, or at least she's telling me more about it now. On Thursday night, she found a knife under her pillow. She doesn't know how it got there. She lost three to four hours on Friday night. She wrote me the following note:

It's 2:00 a.m. and I don't know where I am or how I got here. I don't know what city I'm in. There are no homes; it seems deserted. I don't know what to do. Should I ask for help or just keep driving until something seems familiar? I can't call my husband. He wouldn't understand. I am alone and scared. I'm at a gas station and there's a lady inside. I'll ask her.

The lady was very helpful. She told me I am in Tinley Park. I know where I am. We will get home okay.

Interesting use of the word "we," I think. She was alone, but "We will get home." She says she "came to" instantaneously, and realized she was lost. It started during a shopping trip for groceries. She left home at 8:30 p.m. and "woke" at 2:00 a.m. She had no groceries, and there was $15 missing from her purse. She was thankful when she found out she was actually not far from home.

She's given me enough history now to know she has dissociative identity disorder (DID). I wonder if she has actual multiple personality disorder (MPD), which I feel is a better name for the disorder where a person has multiple autonomous discreet personalities. Most psychiatrists have never seen a case of MPD, and I think a true multiple personality is quite rare, although many have been "suggested" into being by overzealous therapists who want to say they've treated one. If Karen has MPD, our first problem is that the part of her that comes to see me doesn't realize it. Knowing she has dissociative identity disorder is the easy part; knowing how to approach it with Karen isn't so clear. I'm not ready to confront her with this; I'm afraid of her reaction. She's barely hanging on as it is. I don't want to give her another big thing to want to die over and push her over the edge. I'll talk to her about this possibility when she herself brings it more clearly into the therapy. For now, I'll focus on strengthening our bond and managing her crises.

Karen, who's told me often of her urge to punish herself because she's "bad," claims the last time she hurt herself was about three months ago. She can't live with the fact of her father's having touched and hurt her. She doesn't think she ever wants to be touched again. She says she has thoughts of cutting out her genitals. I look at her while she says this and she's too calm. That's how people are when they're serious about it. This talk of cutting off parts of herself is getting frightening. I need to try to undermine her thoughts about cutting.

"By talking about the abuse you've suffered and sharing it with me, you're losing some of your familiar pain, and you feel the urge to replace it," I say. I'm trying to tell her that hurting herself might make some kind of sense. Two days later, on October 30, 1990, I receive this letter:

Dear Dr. Baer,

I need to let you know that I lied to you about the last time I hurt myself. I told you that it was three months ago, but it's been less than a week. I'm sorry. I was just caught off guard and was afraid of what you would think of me. I didn't mean to lie. I couldn't tell you the whole truth at that time. I'm really scared there is something terribly wrong with me. I need your help. I don't understand why I want to do this. I hurt myself like this during high school but stopped when I was 19 years old. It started again last October and has increased during the time we've talked about the sexual abuse. I don't know how to stop.

The urge to hurt herself came back about a year ago, she tells me. When she hurts herself, she says she sticks a wire hanger up inside her vagina. She thinks she hurts herself there so as to not be able to be sexually active. Her injuries need to be kept fresh. She writes me in some detail about it.

The next session, Karen is on time as always, but as I open the door for her, she gives me a wider berth than usual. There are lines down her forehead and at the corners of her eyes. She won't quite look at me as she sits down.

"I've read what you have written," I say, and the look of pain on her face increases.

"Do you still want to see me," she asks, "or am I too disgusting for you to talk to?" She can't look at me.

"I'm glad you are finally able to tell me this secret, and I am very interested to help you understand why you have these feelings."

"I didn't want to tell you about it; I was getting too close to you, but I've already told you so much, now I'm afraid of making you mad and losing you." I'm glad to see she herself appreciates the bind she's in.

"It sounds like you can't live with me or without me," I say, supporting her interpretation. She agrees and says it's getting to be more of a problem, especially since her thoughts of wanting to hurt herself have been getting worse, and she's been afraid to tell me about it.

Sometimes there's nothing I can say that will soothe the pain she bares to me. I try to say something that shows I understand her, and moreover, that I feel some of what she's feeling. I can't exactly say I know how she feels. How can I imagine what she has gone through? But through Karen, I'm learning to be a better listener.

Shortly after Christmas 1990, I leave for vacation. It's hard for me not to feel guilty about it. Not just for Karen, but for other patients as well who are in different stages of crisis or degrees of need, and will suffer and regress while I'm gone. But Karen seems to suffer the worst. I want to talk more with her about her experience of losing time, but each time we approach it, some new crisis or suicidal risk rips us away from it.

I suggest she write down her thoughts and dreams while I'm away, so we can look at them together when I get back, to help bridge the gap. I wonder what I'll come home to.

4.

CHOOSING DEATH

Saturday–12/29/90

    I tried to convince myself today that I hated you. I was so sad; I felt you had abandoned me. I knew in reality you were on vacation, but I still felt terrible. I think the person I really hate for needing you is me. I decided to stop taking my medication. I don't need it. I don't need anything.

Friday–1/4/91

    Something is terribly wrong. Lost time for about 2 hours. During that time I attacked my husband. He said I kicked him, punched him, and scratched him badly. I can see the cuts, but I don't remember hurting him. I also cut myself again. I don't understand why I'm doing this.

Thursday–1/10/91

    I recall more memories and I feel sick. I can't write them down. I don't know if I can talk about them. I want to forget, but I can't. I can't block the words or the pain.

When I get back from vacation, I find an envelope in the mail with Karen's writing waiting for me. I read a few of the entries before I see her. She walks in slowly and doesn't look so good. Her shoulders slump and her head is bowed.

"My husband seems to enjoy hurting me," she says at last, "but I don't see how I can afford to leave."

"I know, but what more might you do now? How might you better protect yourself from him?" I ask.

Karen shrugs and shakes her head. "He corners me," she says, resignation in her voice. "I have fantasies about killing him, just like the fantasies I've had about killing my father." I look at her for some sign she'll actually do it, but her eyes show hopelessness and there's no will in her body.

"What do you do about these fantasies?" I ask.

"When they get really bad, I hurt myself."

"How does that help?"

"It puts the fantasies out of my mind."

"This hurting yourself—could you be protecting your husband and father from your anger by turning it on yourself . . . pointing it in another direction?"

Karen looks at me and doesn't answer, but I can see she's intrigued by this.

"And could that explain why your urge to hurt yourself increased while I was on vacation?" I add. Karen looks at me, uncomprehending. There are a couple of steps that I left out, hoping Karen will make the connection between her anger at me for abandoning her during my vacation and her increased hurting of herself. She needs to know I know she's secretly enraged at me for abandoning her during my vacation, but that her rage will not destroy our relationship.

That night, Karen has a prophetic dream.

I dreamt I came to visit you and you were in the kitchen stirring something in a large white pot. I sat down on a stool and suddenly there were different people coming out of me. Some were children and some were adults. It seemed like all these people wanted to meet you. These people were all translucent. One child looked into the pot while another hid behind me. One adult seemed very rude, while another seemed afraid. You could not see them but I felt them all around me. As we talked they started to disappear, one by one. Then suddenly everything seemed to fast forward and we were still talking, but it seemed like years later. Only you were still stirring something in the same white pot. All of the people were gone.

Once in a while, early in therapy, patients may have a sort of summary dream, where they encapsulate, in an almost clairvoyant way, the path they will follow through their entire years of therapy. I think this is just such a dream. My role in the dream stays the same. I am the cook, but all I do is keep the pot stirring. What happens to her in the dream amazes me. These shadow people, adults and children, emerge from her, and while we are still talking and I am continuing to stir the pot, they gradually disappear. This dream is more evidence that Karen has multiple personality disorder, with separate adult and children personalities, and that our path together leads toward trying to make them disappear.

Of course, Karen has trouble sustaining her relationship with me long enough for that to happen. In other words, she's panicked by the heat and often wants to run from the kitchen. Once a person has been abused as Karen has, the most difficult thing to do is to trust another person not to do the same. Karen wrote to me in her journal:

I know what's bothering me. I just don't know how to deal with it. I feel as though I have gotten myself into this mess and I have to get myself out. While you were on vacation, I came to realize that the relationship I'm building with you is too dangerous for me. I know that eventually I will be hurt. I can't allow that to happen. I've become too dependent on you. I couldn't handle you being gone. I fell apart. I don't remember ever feeling this way before. You've become the most important person in my life, and it scares me.

At a later session, Karen walks into my office and goes straight to her chair without greeting me, which is unusual. She walks slowly but with purpose. She settles in her chair, her face grim.

"I feel suicide is my solution," she says, without emotion. "I've been biding my time, but now's the right time." She then looks me straight in the eye. "I feel comfortable about this."

"Why is now the right time?" I ask. I know that every time she feels closer to me, she reacts by getting more suicidal. I'm glad it's early in the session so we can deal with this before my next patient.

"My mother is making a trip to Hungary, where she's from." Karen has already described to me a lifelong pattern of being criticized and humiliated by her mother.

"Does that make it the right time?" I ask.

"No, I don't have any feelings about that." Hmmm, I think, then why was that your answer to my question? It doesn't make sense that she should have such a reaction to her mother's departure. It must symbolize something else.

"You make me feel guilty about these thoughts of suicide," she says, looking down. After a pause she continues, "You're the only one who's tried to help."

"Did you think about how I might feel about your suicide?" I ask.

She looks up suddenly. "Well, yes, I wrote you a letter about it, but I didn't send it." She reaches into her purse, leans forward, and, looking away, hands me the letter. I take it, put it aside, and continue to focus on what she's saying.

"I always knew suicide was inevitable . . . now's a good time." She is far away for a moment. "I just don't want to live."

I let her comment hang in the air, thinking about the deep hole she's maneuvered herself into.

"You're going through a kind of transition here with me in the therapy," I say finally. "After years of trying not to see the extent of the abuse you've suffered, you've come to see it, here, with me, and you're overwhelmed by it." I look for a sign that I am in tune with the question of "Why now?" She stirs a bit, but shows no real signs of shifting her feelings. I've missed and will need to try again.

"I worried this might happen," I continue. "This would be a hard time for anyone who's been hurt the way you have. And hard for anyone, who's been hurt like you have, to trust someone to help them." She cries a little harder, a good sign.

"Your mother is leaving, you feel all alone, with only me to help you, and you wonder, can you trust me?" Karen starts to weep with her face buried in her hands. The weeping is a cleansing, too. "Your feelings for me have grown; they're getting stronger, but more dangerous, too. Should you let yourself trust me, or should you die?" Karen breaks down and sobs, her chest heaving. I stay silent, waiting for her to recover.

"I don't want you to commit suicide," I say, leaning toward her. "How can we prevent it?" I look at her, waiting for an answer. I need a partner in this. She manages a shrug of the shoulders.

"One thing we could do would be to put you in the hospital," I say. "That would keep you safe." I know this is the professionally necessary thing to propose, but it's a lousy option. She's run out of insurance for days in a psychiatric unit, and once she goes to the emergency room, she'll be transferred, under civil commitment, to the state mental hospital. They'll discharge her quickly when she lies and says she isn't suicidal, she'll be no better, and I'll lose contact with her. I've worked in those institutions, and I know the drill. I want to find an alternative.

"I don't want to go to the hospital," Karen says firmly. "That would make things even worse."

"Nothing would be worse than losing you," I say with directness and conviction. She's paying attention now. We sit for a moment as my declaration of interest in her settles in.

"Perhaps if we understood more about why you have these strong feelings now," I say, "we could do something to help." Now is the time for me to shut up. When you put an important question to a patient, whatever comes out next is the answer. The difficult but important thing for me to do is to be able to tolerate the ensuing silence longer than she can, and wait for it.

I watch Karen think, wondering where her associations are going. Her face betrays only sadness. After about a minute and a half, she shifts in her seat and says, "I always knew my mother didn't love me, but I never fully realized it." She pauses. "I thought if I could give her enough, she would love me, but I just can't do it." I think what she also means is she's afraid that like her mother, I don't love her either, so why would I stick with her and help her. If her mother doesn't love her, how could she expect me to care about her?

"And why now?" I ask.

"It just seems like the right time," she says, with a sigh of despair.

"I think you're afraid of how close you've become to me, and you're looking for an escape." I look at her. My statement is a challenge and a seduction. She looks away. It is another time for me to shut up. She is either in or out; she has to decide. She pauses and shifts in her chair uncomfortably.

"I don't know . . . I'm afraid to hope." Karen looks confused, but she's sitting more upright in her chair. Maybe she's in.

"I have a plan," I say. I need to enhance her hope by binding her closer to me. "I understand now how hard it has been for you to realize your mother's failure to love you, and therefore you despair that I could be trusted to stay by you, better than your mother could, through all you may need to go through in therapy. At the same time, with all your father's abuse of you, you fear if you get close to me, I'll do the same." I wait for Karen to absorb that big dose of understanding.

"But it's important that no harm come to you," I continue. "Today's Wednesday. I'm going to call you tonight, and tomorrow night, and I'll see you on Friday at one p.m. Will you promise to keep yourself safe until I call tonight?" I look at her and hold her gaze, waiting for her promise.

"Okay," she says.

"And will you keep yourself safe until I call tomorrow night?" Again I wait.

"I'll try," she says, with less assurance. I hold her gaze and after a moment, she nods.

"That will have to do for now," I say. "If I can't reach you or you don't show up on Friday, I will call the police and have them look for you." I want her to know I mean business and the lengths I will go to ensure her safety.

"Okay." Karen manages a smile of thanks and I secretly sigh with relief as she leaves the office. The issue of trust is so hard for Karen. We have been meeting for two and a half years and she's just now fully grappling with it. I hope she is turning the corner. At least she's leaving in better shape than when she came in.

Here is the letter Karen handed me at the beginning of the session:

June 13, 1991

Dear Dr. Baer,

Thank you so much for all the help you have given me. I feel very thankful having you as my doctor. If it weren't for you, I feel as though I wouldn't have lived this long. I just want you to know that whatever happens to me, it will be my own fault. I just can't go on any longer, so I've planned an escape. This has nothing to do with depression. I just don't want to live. The only way to escape is to end it. I'll try to explain my thoughts the best way I know how.

I choose to die. It's better than living. I'll be free of nightmares that constantly haunt me. I will never have to face my father or grandfather again. I will not have to deal with my mother. I will be happy and at peace. I feel no guilt in leaving. I will never feel dirty or unclean again. I will not hurt myself anymore. I will not have to deal with the feelings I have for you. The empty feeling I have inside will no longer be a burden to carry. I feel that this is the right time.

Every piece falls into place. I made reservations at a motel near my house. I decided to try to take the pills I have. If that doesn't work, I have a gun. I really feel all alone. I would have liked to share this with you, but I know you would have had to try to talk me out of it, and I couldn't let that happen. Please understand that I just can't go on. I'm so sad. I'm glad I met you and I hope you don't hate me for this.

I wish you the very best in the future. You are an excellent doctor and deserve only the best. Take care of yourself and your family.

Love,
Karen Overhill

I call her that same evening at 5:20 p.m., but there's no answer. I know how desperate she is, but I hope her bond to me will make her decide against killing herself. This is one of those difficult times as a psychiatrist when, with someone as damaged as Karen, you have to simply wait and see if they want to live or not. If she chooses life, it means she chooses life in part because of me. And if she chooses not to live, it means she chooses death despite me.

I call again and she answers, and I talk to her on the phone at length that evening and the next. She comes back to see me two days later. She looks better, although the signs are subtle—more spring in her step, quicker movements, better posture, more eye contact. She always dresses approximately the same, and there's very little change in her grooming. She says she felt a little bit better each day. Although she thought it would no longer matter if she weren't around, she's now ambivalent about wanting to commit suicide; part of her wants to change her mind and live. Last night, for the first time, she was frightened of her suicidal thoughts. Somehow she hadn't realized that if she commits suicide, everything would *really* be gone: her children, her husband, and me.

"I wonder if part of wanting to die is because I don't want to be intimate with my husband again," she says, asking the question to herself. "It's funny, I don't remember ever having sex with him." I look at her quizzically. "I know I have," she continues, "but I must have blocked it all out."

Blocked it out?

She sits for a while and is quiet and seems lost in thought. "Somehow, deep inside me," she says, "I know I don't want to live. I bought some bullets for my husband's gun," she confesses.

I'm really interested in the "blocking out," but first I need to reel her back in, fortify her against the appeal of bullets and death.

"Do you feel you could have a relationship with me where we really trust each other?" I ask. "Where you can really trust me to hear and understand everything you have to say?" She looks puzzled at first, then seems to gnaw on what I've said. She doesn't answer, but I hope I've reinforced the possibility for her.

As she walks out the door, she turns and says, "I used to want you to give up on me." I watch her broad, slumped back disappear as the door closes behind her.

I think about the plans she's made to commit suicide. I know she could easily take them up again, so we need to dismantle them altogether. The next time I see her, I ask about the bullets. She admits they provide her with comfort—since as long as she has them, she knows she can kill herself.

"Why is such a thought a comfort?" I ask. She stops for a

moment, surprised by my question, because she hasn't considered that such a feeling might be peculiar.

"I've had a suicide plan for most of my life," she says. "When I was nine or ten years old, I had a plan where I'd lie down on the train tracks and wait for the train to come." She speaks of these things with a calm voice and a dead look in her eyes that sends a chill up my spine. "It seemed the only solution to my life."

Yesterday Karen got a call from her aunt who said her grandfather is sick and in the hospital. She wants Karen to visit, but Karen is afraid to see him. That thought triggered a memory from when she was eight or nine years old and the family went to the beach.

Karen sits in the backseat of her grandfather's Buick between her two younger brothers. The boys reach over Karen to poke at each other; they're six and eight, Karen is nine. As the boys' play escalates, they jostle and push Karen.

"Stop it!" she complains.

"Karen! Settle down!" Her mother turns around from between Karen's grandfather, who is driving, and her father. "If there's any more trouble, you'll stay in the car." All three in the backseat become quiet as the grandfather parks the car at North Avenue beach.

Karen follows her mother out onto the beach; the sun is shining, it's hot, and the beach is already crowded. Her mother lays out a blanket and her grandfather opens a lawn chair and a beer. Her father follows the boys to the water; they run on ahead and their father begins to straggle through the sunbathers, staring at a group of young women. Karen wanders toward the water and goes in up to her knees, but the water is cold and she turns back. Halfway toward her mother, she plops down in the sand and begins to build a sand castle. She makes several trips to carry handfuls of water to make the sand moist so it will stick together.

When it's time to leave, her grandfather comes over and puts his hand out to fetch Karen. Sadly, Karen leaves the little city she's built and follows him back to her mother and the car. Karen climbs into the middle of the backseat and her two brothers scram-

ble in afterward. When they arrive home, Karen slides out of the backseat, her legs and swimsuit still full of sand. When her grandfather sees the sand on Karen and the sand in the backseat, his face grows red.

"Karen! You've made a mess! The car is all full of sand!" Karen freezes. She looks at her mother, who turns away and takes the boys in the house. Karen begins to follow the boys. "Stop!" says her grandfather. "I don't want you to track sand through the house." He grabs her hand and strides toward the backyard. Dragged along, she struggles to keep on her feet; he's cussing and yanking her arm, and takes her through the backyard and into the shed; they called it the shandy. He opens the door and pushes Karen into the dark.

"Stay here." She stands back in the shandy, confused, looking out through the open doorway. Her grandfather goes to the back porch and picks up the hose, turns on the faucet, and lurches back to Karen, his lips moving in a stream of profanity. He hands the hose to Karen and stands back.

"Here, rinse yourself off!" She takes the outstretched hose with trembling hands and moves the water quickly over her feet and ankles. "You're not doing it right!" He grabs the hose and puts his thumb over the end, making a stronger spray. "Turn around!" He sprays her back and legs, and watches her while she stiffens and shivers from the cold water. "Lay down. I have to wash all the sand away."

Karen lies down on the gray concrete floor of the shandy, trembling and shivering, as her grandfather looms over her with the hose in his hand. He brings the water up her thighs and splashes some water across her belly. She squeals because it is cold, but her grandfather, with a look that makes her freeze, tells her to be quiet. He lays the hose on the concrete floor, and with his hands, spreads her legs apart. He brings the end of the hose to her crotch and directs the water there.

"Hold still," he barks. He takes his finger and pulls aside the fabric of the swimsuit. "I have to wash all the sand away," he says again. Karen shuts her eyes tight. He puts the metal of the end of the hose against her vulva, and lets the cold water pour into her. Karen feels pain and a cold-hot pressure inside of her. Her throat *fills up with a scream, but she can make no sound. Grandfather takes the hose away, replaces the fabric of her swimsuit, and gets up. "There," he said, "all clean. Let's get some ice cream."*

Karen staggers up and walks toward the car. Her grandfather takes her hand and walks beside her. They go to the Tastee-Freez at 51st and Damen, and on the way home, she sits in the front seat, taking small licks from her vanilla cone.

At the stoplight, he looks down at her. "Don't drop your ice cream," he says and pokes her in the ribs. Karen holds on to her cone; he pokes her again, this time from both sides. "Don't drop it." Karen squirms and fumbles with the cone and the ice cream tumbles onto her lap.

"Look at what you've done now." Karen feels the cold ice cream begin to melt on her legs, and looks at him, waiting for him to hit her. He takes his right hand and starts to smear the ice cream over Karen's legs and belly and between her thighs. Karen feels relief and nausea. When they arrive home, grandfather takes her by the hand and leads her to the back of the house.

"We have to clean you up again." He goes to fetch the hose.

As Karen finishes her story, she hangs her head and begins to weep. I wait a few moments.

"What is it?" I ask.

"You must think I'm disgusting," she says.

"What do you mean?"

"I feel so dirty," she says.

"I understand how that must have made you feel," I say. Karen continues to weep. I don't really understand; how can I? Oftentimes, the best thing to do, when you don't know what to say, is just to empathize the best you can with the feeling.

"I see our time is up. We can pick up where we left off next time."

Karen enters the office, dripping wet, with her purse under her arm like a halfback with a football. It's the end of June 1991 and the windows looking out at the park are streaming with rain. She nods at me quickly as she barrels toward her chair.

"For the last two weeks, I've brought the bullets with me," she says, clutching her purse in her lap. "Each time I thought I'd give them to you, but I didn't. I'm not sure I'm going to today."

"It sounds like a part of you wants to give them to me, since you bring them and tell me about them," I say. I have to be careful about directly asking for them. I need her giving them to me to be her idea.

Karen sits in indecision, her eyes gazing off to the side, and I wait. She finally looks down, reaches into her purse, and takes out a square plastic container that holds about two hundred .22-caliber bullets. She looks at it for several moments, and then holds it out to me. I take the container and put it down on the table next to me.

"Is there anything else you'd like to give me?" I ask. Her head jerks up and her eyes are wide. She then looks down for several moments, reaches into her purse, pauses, and takes out a small folding knife with a razor blade in it. She holds it in her hand a moment as if reminiscing, then reaches out and gives it to me. It's as if she's just put her life in my hands.

"Anything else?" I ask. She shakes her head quickly twice without looking up. "It's important not to have things around that can hurt you," I say.

"But everything can hurt me," she says.

"What do you mean?" Now I'm the one who's surprised.

"Everything can hurt me," she says again, as if I hadn't heard her the first time.

"I don't understand," I say—she clearly has something on her mind. Karen looks down and speaks in a soft voice.

"My father used to hurt me with all sorts of things," she says. "He liked to stick things inside of me, like spoons and knives . . . screwdrivers . . . and hangers. Lots of things."

"I see." Karen doesn't say any more than that. I don't press for details. She's just beginning to tell me some of the horrors she's experienced. I need to be the best listener I can be, and not interfere with what she has to say. I need to make sure she feels she's acceptable to me and that what she tells me won't destroy our relationship.

FATHER'S ARREST

Karen is feeling closer to me, but it terrifies her. The more she trusts me, the more all she's been keeping inside begins to spill out—sometimes faster than either of us can manage. A series of her writings to me, composed between sessions, shows how she's becoming consumed by her resurrected memories.

July 24, 1991

I feel sad. I was thinking of my friend, Jane, and about a new friend, Tammy. I feel jealous of both of them, not because they had good relationships with their doctors, but because their doctors hugged them. I don't understand why this upsets me, because I never thought I would want to be touched by anyone. I always fantasize that you're hugging me.

August 1, 1991

Last night I dreamt I was drowning in a pool. A man's hand was holding my head below water. The man's hand was his left hand with a gold ring on it. I've had this dream many times but it's the first time I remember seeing a ring.

August 3, 1991

> *Last night I kept having flashbacks from my childhood. I remember where I hid my bloody underpants after my grandfather abused me. My grandmother found them. I was about eight years old. They were in the rag box and she asked me why I put them there. She thought I was ashamed of starting my period. Only this happened about three years before I really did. The underpants were thrown away and the subject was never brought up again.*

When Karen comes in on August 5 we talk about the writings she's given me from July 24 to August 3. There's so much in them, it's difficult to know where to begin. But since our relationship is the glue that holds the therapy together, I'll start there.

"Does my not hugging you make you feel that I don't care about you?" She nods, and says that's how she feels. I tell her I can understand how she could feel that way, and that most people would feel the same way in her situation. These statements may seem condescending, but I'm trying to establish, by making them, that although I recognize she feels I don't *want* to hug her, maybe the possibility exists that I *would* want to hug her, but for some other reason can't. I can't intellectually rationalize to her why hugging is a bad idea, is nontherapeutic, a breach of boundaries, etc.; she'd only think I'm making excuses.

Sometimes I ask myself, What harm would there be in giving Karen, who's in such elemental human distress, a hug—a bit of ordinary human comforting? Unfortunately, although she claims she's longing for a hug the way a young child does, I can't be sure that's really how she'd experience it. Because of the chance that a hug could be experienced by part of her as abusive touching, I decide I can't risk doing it.

"I'm curious about your grandmother finding the bloodstain on your panties," I push on. "I'm surprised your grandmother didn't investigate this further. It seems to be a remarkable and unconscionable lapse on her part." I tell her this because I want to distinguish myself from those in her past who conspired to cover up her abuse.

We also talk about the dream in which the man's hand pushes her head under the water. Although I suspect that the hand with the wedding ring is mine, I'm curious to know what she thinks about it.

"Whose hand do you think it is pushing your head under the water?" I ask. She looks at my left hand and shifts uncomfortably.

"I don't know," she says, turning away.

"What did it feel like to be under the water?"

"Choking. Desperate."

All psychotherapists need the temperament of both a masochistic woman and an arrogant man. On one hand, a therapist needs to sit passively and be endlessly selfless and empathic. On the other, he needs to seduce the patient into the therapeutic process and insist on becoming the emotional center of the patient's life. During my career, I started out good at the former but timid at the latter. I could sit with patients all day long, day after day, staying attuned to every flicker of their lambent emotional flame. Well, okay, I wasn't that good, but I was really fascinated to learn how people operated mentally, and I worked hard at it.

It's 1991, I've been in practice almost ten years, and I find my capabilities are reversing, and I'm growing restless sitting all day and seeing patients. Although each patient's story is unique, how they came by their stories is the same. Not everyone is as riveting as Karen. Like I felt that day looking at the traffic on 95th Street, I fear being stuck in my chair, listening to patients' stories, until I am too feeble to get up.

When Karen comes in on November 4, 1991, she tells me that her grandfather has died. She went to the wake, but doesn't remember it; she lost time for six hours. She says she has mixed feelings about her grandfather, because he was nice to her sometimes. Following the wake, the thoughts of hurting herself increased. She acted on them, in a horrible fashion, and is now filled with self-loathing.

After listening to her specify the nature of her self-mutilation I ask, "Do you think these feelings are in response to your grandfather's death?"

"I'm not sure," she says. "It may be that." She doesn't seem too enthusiastic about my suggestion.

"Can you think what else it might be?" Karen looks out the window; it's unclear she really heard me.

"Dr. Baer, I want to apologize to you for asking you to hold me." She doesn't look at me while she's speaking; it's more as if she's speaking to herself. "I had no right to ask you. I feel the need to be held. I think about how you don't want to hug me. It seems like it's the only thing on my mind. I feel wrong for wanting touch, but I feel like a child that needs a hug—a safe touch that is not harmful: just a nonsexual, nurturing touch. You are the only safe person I know. This is the first time in my life I actually want to be touched. I never meant any harm by it. Maybe I need reassurance that you'll be there."

I'm surprised at this. Not because she wants a hug and apologized to me for wanting it from me; that in itself is touching and very poignant. Rather, I'm surprised by *when* she apologized to me. Usually when an association follows a question, the way her apology for wanting a hug sprang from her talking about why she hurt herself, there's an underlying emotional connection. Are these feelings of wanting to hurt herself not so much a reaction to her grandfather's death, but really a reaction to my unwillingness to hold her? Are both involved? How do they relate to each other? Karen looks pained and uncomfortable. Maybe I haven't fully appreciated her dilemma. She wants me to touch her, but hates herself for wanting that touch. If she hurts herself for wanting me to touch her, what would she do to herself if I actually did?

It's the end of January 1992, late in the afternoon, and the city lights make the snow glisten as it falls over the park. I'm waiting for Karen. I haven't seen her for a couple of weeks while I was on vacation. I have some dread about what crisis she'll bring in today.

"My sister-in-law has made a police report accusing my father of molesting my niece, Nina, and also my daughter, Sara," Karen says, bolting through the door, her coat flying. She looks anxious despite what I would think would be satisfaction that her father may finally be punished for his monstrous behavior.

"What's worrying you?" I ask.

"He has a court date coming up soon, and my mother keeps calling me. She keeps asking if my father molested me." Karen looks frightened. "If I tell the truth, I feel like someone will cut my throat."

"Cut your throat?"

"It's what my father always told me. He said if I ever told anyone, he'd cut my throat. He'd hold a knife to my neck and go 'pffffttt, just like that' and make like he'd done it." She's wide-eyed.

"You thought he'd really do it?"

"Of course."

At the end of February, Karen announces that the police are scheduled to arrest her father the next day.

"My husband says it's my fault if anything happened to Sara," Karen says. "I never left her alone with my father because I knew what he might do." Karen looks pained and hopeless. "But maybe twice I left Sara with both of my parents together. Maybe it happened then." Karen sinks deeper into her feelings.

I sit and wait for her to continue. I've often wondered why years ago she didn't run as far from her parents as she could get. She never has an answer for this—she only shrugs. Karen begins to break down, tears forming at the corners of her eyes.

"My husband's right," she cries. "It is my fault. I should never have left her there, ever." Karen is sunk so deeply in a pit of despair, I don't know if I can reach her to help her out.

"You did make sure you never left her alone with your father," I say, trying to be encouraging. "You believed if your mother was there, your father wouldn't hurt Sara."

"Yes," Karen says, unrelieved.

"What does Sara say?" I ask. Karen sits up a little.

"She says he never did anything."

"Do you believe her?" I ask.

"That's what I would have said when I was her age." Karen smiles weakly.

"But all that happened to you has not happened to Sara, has it?"

"No," she says.

"Do you think Sara could be telling you the truth?"

Karen hesitates, and I think she's starting to climb out of the pit. "I don't know," she says, shifting uneasily.

"I asked her if he threatened her, and she said no, and she didn't looked scared."

"She didn't seem to feel the way you felt when you were threatened with having your throat cut if you told anyone," I say.

"No, she didn't."

"So there's a good chance Sara wasn't harmed by your father like you were and Nina was." Karen nods, still feeling bad, but better. She's still severely depressed, but no longer aching to die. That will have to do for now, as our session is just up.

In early March 1992, after Karen's father has been arrested and jailed, Karen's mother and aunt start pressuring Karen to testify that her father never molested her daughter. Karen has no real evidence either way, so she's reluctant to say anything. Karen describes to me in detail a recent conversation she had with Katrina, her mother:

"Your father would never do such a thing!" Katrina screamed. "He'd never hurt any little girl!"

"Oh, yes, he would," Karen said quietly.

"What are you talking about?" Katrina yelled. Her tone was more accusatory than surprised. "I suppose you think he molested you, had sex with you!" Karen looked down and didn't respond. "It's all in your imagination!" Katrina had a way of thrusting her opinion that made argument seem dangerous. "You probably abused yourself! You must have asked for it! It's all your imagination!" Katrina was relentless. Karen felt sick. It was at these times that she began to doubt what happened to her. But then Karen recalled the electrical cords her father used to bind her wrists and feet to his bed, and it was all real to her again.

The police ask that Sara be examined for signs of sexual abuse. Karen consents, but none are found. However, signs of sexual trauma are found on Nina. Katrina as well as Karen's aunt say they don't believe her father abused anyone and they want Karen to bail him out of jail. Katrina, in particular, is anxious to get her husband out of jail because while he is there, there is no paycheck. Katrina repeatedly begs, threatens, and degrades Karen in an attempt to get her to post the $1,000 bond required.

While in jail, her father calls Karen, collect, several times every night. Karen refuses the charges. With her father's constant calls, her headaches are getting so bad she's vomiting. One of the police detectives, Detective Flaherty, tells her she should notify him if her father continues to harass her. She's reluctant to do this, because she's afraid of her father's retaliation, and of receiving even more of her mother's wrath.

In early April 1992, Karen's aunt bails the father out of jail. He's been there about six weeks. As soon as he gets out, he calls Karen throughout the night, trying to get her to testify on his behalf. She finally calls Detective Flaherty, who warns the father not to contact Karen, or he'll go back to jail.

"My mother wants me to testify in my father's trial," says Karen, with her voice trailing off, "and my husband blames me for everything." She sighs heavily and collapses into her chair. She looks at me with hopelessness in her eyes. "I don't want to deal with life anymore."

Mother, father, husband, suicide: quick—I need to think what to tackle first.

"Your mother wants you to testify?" I ask.

"Yes, she wants me to say my father never abused me."

"What do you want to do?" I ask.

"I want to die! I have dreams of these big hands choking me; I can't breathe. I wake up gasping, and when I go back to sleep, I have the same dream again and again." Karen is breathing hard with her hands at her throat, as if she's living her dream.

"The big hands sound like how a man's hands are experienced by a child," I say.

"I told you, my father always said if I ever told anyone he hurt me, he'd kill me. He wasn't kidding. Once he showed me by choking me until I couldn't breathe. Before I passed out, he stopped, but he said he could have just as well kept going if he wanted to."

"Have either of the lawyers asked you to testify?" I ask. She shakes her head. "Then let's not worry right now about testifying.

We'll assume you won't have to unless you're subpoenaed by the court. I don't think you will be. If your mother asks you again, simply tell her if you're put on the witness stand, you won't lie. We'll leave it to her to know what that means. Okay?" Karen nods her head, looking at me intently. This isn't exactly therapy, but Karen needs direction. I use the pause to move on.

"We've talked before about the idea of your leaving your husband because of how he treats you. What are your thoughts about that now?" I'm trying to tackle the topics that seem responsible for her not wanting to live. If I can provide some support and better reality processing, she may not be so hopeless. I need to plumb her more about her situation at home.

"I'm not ready to deal with the problem of my marriage," she says, sighing again. I watch her sitting there, immobile, slumped, and I'm trying to resist the contagiousness of her depression. I want to help her move ahead, but it's hard to push a depressed person. "My son doesn't respect me either," she continues. "He follows his father's example. I'm afraid to spank him, because if I do, I'm afraid I won't stop, like my father. My husband spoils all my attempts at discipline anyway; if I ground my son, he lets him go, so he can be the good guy." She falls quiet for a moment, and then says, "I'd rather die than go through a divorce and try to live alone."

Okay, this is not getting any easier, I think. I wonder if she and I can begin to chip away at this and at least make baby-step progress.

"If you could pick one thing," I say, "what would you change that would help your situation?" Okay, maybe that's a stupid question, but I have to start somewhere in getting her to think about making changes instead of blaming herself and feeling hopeless.

"Josh's drinking," she says. "He starts as soon as he gets home and doesn't stop until he passes out."

"Tell me again, what is he like when he drinks?"

"After a few beers he gets quiet, then after more, he's vicious." She looks away from me. "That's when he hits me. After his rage, he falls asleep." This is hard, I think. We can't do anything about Josh's drinking. Only he can modify his behavior. Perhaps, though, we can do something to protect her from it.

"When he starts drinking and becomes quiet, what do you do?" I ask.

"I try to keep the kids quiet and stay out of his way," she says, "and wait."

"Like with your father," I say. She looks at me and I can see her turn this over in her mind, as she compares her father's abuse and her husband's, and sees the similarities.

"When you were an abused child," I say, "you had no options but to cope within the house as best you could. Although you're in a similar abusive situation now, you're an adult and your options are wider. If you feel you can't get divorced, you can leave for those periods of time when you're most vulnerable. When he starts drinking, get yourself and the kids ready to go out, and when he falls quiet, leave for an hour or more. Get ice cream or go to the movies. Come back when he's asleep, and avoid that abusive time." Karen is attentive and nods.

"What else about your husband would you change, if you could?" I ask.

"He fights with me about coming to see you," she says. I nod for her to continue. "We argued about it last Saturday, and he beat me, punched me, here." She points to the lower-left portion of her abdomen. "I've had pain, constant pain in my side, since then."

"Did you go see the doctor?" I ask. I look at her and try to imagine what internal organs could be responsible for her persistent pain.

"No," Karen says, in a small voice.

"How come?" I ask, a little frantic.

Karen's eyes start to tear, and she has trouble speaking. "I hoped I might die," she says, turning from me in shame. I wait again for her to continue.

"I don't know what to do," she says. "He constantly screams at me. He says it's just a matter of time before I molest my children because I'm no different from my father. He tells me over and over again I should kill myself. He says I should stop seeing you, that it's a waste of time and money. He takes the insurance checks I'm supposed to pay you with and cashes them and keeps the money for beer and cigarettes."

"There are places women who are abused can turn to—" Karen raises her hand to stop me.

"I know," she says. "I've already gotten that information."

"Why haven't you taken some action?"

Karen wears her ashamed look again. "I didn't think it would be worth it; I didn't think I'd live that long. Part of me thinks it's a weakness not to have killed myself yet. If I were stronger, I would have done it."

"The first thing," I say to her directly so she knows this is an instruction, "is to get your pain evaluated. You need to go to the emergency room when you leave here. It may only be a bruise, but your husband's punching may have caused some internal bleeding."

"How do I know I didn't do it to myself?" she asks. I look a little confused, and she sees this. "Sometimes I hurt myself, too." This is all too much to try to make right.

"Whatever the cause," I say, with some exasperation creeping into my voice, "you need to go to the doctor to make sure your insides are all right." Karen shrugs and turns sadly to leave. "And phone me tomorrow," I call after her. She makes no sign as she closes the door behind her.

At 10:30 p.m. one evening in October 1992, I receive a phone call from Karen. Her voice is a whisper and diminishing.

"I want to hurt myself."

"What happened?"

"My husband beat me up," she says, weeping into the phone. I wait for her to continue. ". . . with a baseball bat . . . I don't want to live anymore."

"Where are you hurt?"

"My legs, back, I don't know."

We talk about all the actions she might take: call the police, go to a women's shelter, take her and the children to a friend's house, et cetera. She doesn't want to do any of these. Her husband has passed out now and won't wake again tonight, she tells me. I tell her to take some of the tranquilizer I'd given her, so that she might sleep, and I tell her I should call Detective Flaherty. She reluctantly agrees and gives me his number. When I call, he's not there, but I talk to a woman, Sergeant Jameson, who understands my concern after I tell her of Karen's husband's abuse; she says she'll relay the message to Flaherty and he'll call me in the morning. I call Karen back and tell her of my conversation with the police department. She seems relieved I've taken the action and she agrees not to hurt herself. We confirm our next appointment. I call Jameson back, relay the gist of my last conversation with Karen, including that Karen has promised not to hurt herself (to cover my own butt), confirm that Flaherty will call me in the morning, and that if he calls tonight, he should call me at home. When I hang up, it's only 11:00 p.m., but it seems as if I've been on the phone for hours. This is all so stressful for me, but curiously, I never think how to get rid of Karen. It's as if I've spotted a child who's fallen into a river and can't swim. How can I not jump in to save her? I've been thrashing in the river a long time now, struggling to get to her, but she keeps being torn from my grasp. I feel a little as if I'm drowning myself, but I always seem to come up to the surface and I keep extending my hand. I wonder if we'll ever get to shore.

It is the end of November 1992. Karen tells me her father telephones her relentlessly. His trial is in a week. He wants her to help him. She hangs up on him, but he calls again and again. The thoughts of hurting herself keep coming back.

She says in the past she used to keep a razor blade to hold on to, the one she gave to me, and that would comfort her, but now she wants something else, something from me. She, too, is reaching for me in the turbulent river. I tell her I'll find something to give her when next I see her. She leaves happier than I'd ever seen her before, and turns and flashes me a smile as she goes out the door. I need to think what I can give her.

At our next meeting, Karen walks in briskly, smiling at me with a little embarrassment, carrying a shoe box. She sits down with it resting on her lap. She looks at me as if waiting for permission, and I nod, indicating the box with my eyes. From inside she pulls out a handkerchief of her grandmother's, a pin from her best friend from high school, a lock of her brother's hair, a swatch from one of her husband's suits, and several small items from men she's dated.

These items represent the same phenomenon that toddlers exhibit when they carry around a favorite blanket or stuffed animal they can't be separated from, and from which they get comfort. It is thought that for these children, the object, whether a blanket or doll, represents the mother. It enables the young child to suffer being separated from its mother while still experiencing the tangible comfort it receives from the mother's presence through the blanket. The blanket is called a transitional object, an object that helps the child transition from dependence on the mother's presence to being independent from the mother, and although not present in every child, it's a part of normal childhood development.

Karen has used such items for a long time to keep connected with people when they're absent. Since this is a reliable and familiar device for her, I'll try to use it to keep her better connected to me, and less connected to her internal images of pain and abuse.

"I said I'd give you something that will help you think of me," I say, reaching down to the side of my chair, out of her sight. "This might be something that will work." I show her a ceramic bear, about five inches tall. I found it in the gift shop downstairs. It's seated, rotund, smiling, wearing a casual vest and a bow tie and appearing very happy and content. Karen's eyes get big as I hand it to her and she cradles it in both her hands, as if it were priceless. Perhaps to her it is. She looks at me with gratitude and sheepishness that says she knows this is a childish thing, but she appreciates that I understand it's necessary.

Karen continues to resist the pleas of her father and mother to intercede on her father's behalf during his trial. In January 1993, Karen's father stands trial and is convicted on nineteen counts of sexual abuse of Karen's niece, Nina. Karen does not attend the trial at all.

Over the next several sessions, Karen describes the events following her father's trial. Shortly after the sentencing, her father suffers what her mother describes as a heart attack. He actually had an anxiety attack, but is hospitalized for a couple of days.

"It's your fault your father is in the hospital!" her mother says to Karen. "If you would have testified for your father, he wouldn't have gotten sick!" Karen suspects her mother's motivation for wanting her to get involved with her father's trial goes beyond trying to help her husband. Karen thinks her mother wants to distance herself from her husband following the guilty verdict, and wants Karen to support the pretense that no abuse occurred to her, and if it did, that her mother had no knowledge of it.

While Karen's father is hospitalized and receives a diagnostic workup for cardiac disease, his doctors find other abnormalities. Karen says it came as a surprise to everyone when colon cancer, which had spread to the liver, was discovered. At first, she says, her mother and father deny the seriousness of the diagnosis. But as his illness progresses, her mother looks to Karen to help take care of her father. Karen has been refusing to have anything to do with him; she did not go to court during his trial and did not visit him in jail, but her mother is determined to get Karen reinvolved and under the control of her father once again.

One Sunday morning, while her father is back in the hospital for treatment (his sentencing for the child molestation conviction was delayed until he completes his cancer treatment), Karen's mother calls and asks Karen to take her to the hospital to pick up his car. Karen at first refuses, saying she does not want to see her father, but her mother insists, claiming they're just going to pick up the car. When they get to the hospital, her father is waiting on a bench with his suitcase. Karen becomes nauseous at the sight of him but automatically pulls over to pick him up. Her mother acts as if nothing has happened and gets out to help with the suitcase. Once in the car, her mother talks about her upcoming trip to Hungary.

"While I'm gone, you'll need to check in on your father every day," she tells Karen. Karen doesn't answer. "Did you hear me?" her mother says, louder.

"I can't," Karen says quietly.

"You got no gratitude!" says her father from the backseat.

"You owe it to your father for what he did for you," her mother says. "How many times did we take you to the hospital when you were sick, when you had that tumor on your face? We could have just let you die. But we took care of you. We could have had a home and a new car if we didn't pay your hospital bills . . . if we didn't pay for your Catholic-school tuition. Now it's your turn to pay us back. You owe us; you have to pay us back for what we did for you . . ."

Karen says she doesn't remember the rest of the car ride. With my support, she never does participate in the subsequent care of her father.

6.

MOTHER AND FATHER

Karen's mother, Katrina, was born in Hungary, one of eight siblings, and her family lived in near poverty next to where American soldiers were being housed during World War II. The soldiers gave Katrina and her sisters food and chocolate. She longed to see America and always said she was going to marry an American soldier.

The daughter of bakers, Katrina became an accomplished cook while still young. She attended Catholic church regularly and never dated until she met Karen's father. When she met Martin, she thought he looked like Elvis Presley, with clear blue eyes and a cruel mouth. She grew up in ignorance of men, and became, in effect, a prisoner of her own naïveté.

When Karen was eight years old, her mother, to escape her husband's brutality, began working the evening shift at a local factory, leaving Karen to warm up dinner for her two younger brothers, help them with their homework, and get them ready for bed. Once the brothers were asleep, with her mother at work, it was time for Martin to come for Karen. Katrina ignored the signs of Karen's abuse that most mothers would have seen. Karen felt her mother, to spare herself, sacrificed her so her father would turn his perversions toward his daughter instead. In her mother's fantasies, Karen says, the children were never abused and they lived a wonderful life. Her mother denies all that happened to them.

Karen's father, Martin, was born in 1933, and was the first of two siblings. His sister, Karen's aunt Deborah, followed two years later. Martin's father, Martin Sr., constantly degraded his son during his childhood, and Martin was never good enough in his father's eyes. By contrast, his sister, Deborah, could do no wrong and was showered with affection and gifts. His mother, Judith, apparently tried to show her son affection when her husband wasn't around, but she was a weak and illiterate woman who was dominated by her husband and was only sporadically successful at nurturing Martin.

As a young boy, Martin was annoying, loud, and stubborn and always had to have the last word. By high school, these traits had transformed into his being a smooth talker, able to lie at any moment without guilt or expression. He managed to cajole a few girls into dating him, but when he demanded sex and they refused, he'd get angry, mistreat the girl, and lose her. Her aunt told Karen that Martin often bruised his dates by gripping their upper arms when they tried to pull away, and that he'd then try to make up through apologies, false promises, and begging for another chance. He managed to appear caring and sorrowful until the next time he was frustrated, and the cycle started all over again.

During the Korean War, Martin was drafted and stationed in Hungary, where one day he spied Katrina walking down the street with her sisters. She was sixteen. Although she spoke no English and he no Hungarian, he called on her and managed to win her family's approval. He asked Katrina's father for her hand and sent for her once he was discharged. When she arrived in Chicago, seventeen, with no English and still a virgin, she lived with Martin Sr. and Judith until she and Martin could be married. Martin Sr. wanted Katrina and repeatedly tried to force himself on her. He and Martin argued violently about it. Martin Sr. said if he didn't get what he wanted, he'd turn them all out on the street. Karen doesn't know if her grandfather was ever successful.

Karen's mother told her that one day when she was sent up to tell Martin it was time for dinner, he threw her down on the bed and raped her. She cried and wanted to go back to Hungary, but Martin wouldn't let her. He begged forgiveness and gave her gifts; the cycle had begun. She said the grandfather taught Martin how to control and dominate his wife, and Martin did whatever his father told him, including raping and beating Katrina.

After Katrina and Martin were married, Martin forced himself on her continuously. She became pregnant immediately and Karen was born. Her grandmother told her stories of how Martin raped Katrina repeatedly during her pregnancy, and he resumed forcing himself on her as soon as she came home from the hospital. Karen's brother, named after the father, was born ten months later.

Throughout their childhood, Karen and her brothers repeatedly heard their father forcing himself on their mother. Martin always flirted inappropriately with all women and had many affairs. He was fired from one job for sexual harassment. To him, all women were sexual objects.

Karen brings me a tape recording of a conversation between her mother and father, made by her mother while her father was awaiting sentencing. I'm very interested to hear it. Karen's mother planted the tape recorder where it would record her conversation with Karen's father. She did this, Karen and I surmise, to try to exonerate herself from the guilt of the father's molestations of Karen's niece, and by extension, of Karen herself. Karen had listened to some of it, but it disgusted her. She says she's heard this kind of talk all her life, and doesn't want to hear any more.

At the end of the day, before I go home, I turn on the tape recorder. The tape starts with the conversation in progress:

FATHER: Lay over here.

MOTHER: No, I'm not laying down.

FATHER: Just lay down here for a few minutes, okay? I didn't ask you to fuck me or something like that. There's nothing wrong with it, but I didn't ask you to.

MOTHER: Shut up! Don't talk dirty to me. You talked dirty all my life to me.

FATHER: Maybe you're tired. But you always did it. All a sudden it's a sin for you to suck on my dick . . .

MOTHER: Aw, shut up!

FATHER: Or kiss it.

MOTHER: No, I didn't always do it! You're filthy . . .

FATHER: There's nothing wrong with it!

MOTHER: It's the way you say it! You are rude!

FATHER: Well, your fucking husband—I'm going to die, and I'm going to jail!

MOTHER: If you're dying, it's about time! I'm looking out for myself!

FATHER: You should say, "My husband's dying, so I'm not going to let go of his pink dick." And you should love this pink dick, because I'm dying. You couldn't give me a little love?

MOTHER: No, I'm leaving!

FATHER: Okay, but you're not going this minute. You could lay by my side and talk to me. I don't want to talk to your backside. Be human. If I tell you to fuck me, suck me, kiss my dick, well . . . there's nothing wrong with it. It's okay. Come kiss it for a few minutes . . . you don't even want to do it for a second? Why? It's not ugly. Why not just go down on me?

MOTHER: Is that all you ever talk about?

FATHER: Okay, yeah, but, Trina . . .

MOTHER: No one can take it!

FATHER: (softly) You don't talk nice to me.

MOTHER: (shouting) You don't talk nice to me!

FATHER: Trina, shhh, do you talk nice to me?

MOTHER: You even abused me.

FATHER: No, no, no, no, man, you're a liar! A fucking liar!

MOTHER: I am a fucking liar?

FATHER: A dirty, fucking liar. You don't talk nice to me. You've got no respect for me. Because I've got no money. I've got no money.

MOTHER: (shouting) Because I can't stand you anymore! Your mouth . . .

FATHER: Nah, that isn't it.

MOTHER: All you have . . .

FATHER: Trina . . .

MOTHER: . . . is sex in your head!

FATHER: Go fuck yourself! Go ahead, be an ignorant bitch! But, Trina, you're going to suffer. You're going to suffer because you're hurting me. We're part of each other. Go ahead, have your fun. You won't even touch me. I didn't expect you to do something like fuck me.

MOTHER: Aw, filthy dog!

FATHER: There's nothing dirty, nothing wrong with that! I'm talking to my wife; I'm not talking to a stranger. I'm talking to my wife, to come here, to give me some company.

I listen, half disgusted, half fascinated, as Martin continues to wheedle Katrina to submit to what he considers to be her wifely duties, calling her an ignorant bitch when she refuses. Martin is alternatively overbearing and cajoling, and Katrina is strident and nasty. The more she resists, the more he pursues.

FATHER: (softly murmuring again) It's not dirty to try to make love, it's okay. It's okay to fuck. Let me touch you between your legs . . . you're frigid, Trina, you're frigid. C'mon, be a wife and let me touch between your legs, kiss your body . . . why do you make it so ugly and dirty and filthy . . . c'mon, take off your clothes. Be comfortable. You can't be comfortable with your clothes on like that. . . . Don't feel cheap because I ask you to touch me. Don't feel cheap because I ask you to make love to me. Don't feel cheap; do it from your heart. I don't get a hard-on watching movies of naked girls. I get a hard-on when I see you. When I touch you . . . I don't think I'm asking for too much.

MOTHER: I don't want to do any sex with you. It's all you think of.

I sit in morbid fascination at the relentless sexual preoccupation of the father, and the feigned, I think, outrage of the mother. She knew the tape was running, and wanted to demonstrate this sexual obsession in her husband, and her own victimization, after he was convicted. This is the kind of conversation Karen heard, and was the object of, all her life.

DEEPENING COMMITMENT

In late February, Karen visits my office with more reluctance than usual. As I wait for her to begin, she shifts uncomfortably in the chair and finally says, "I have some questions . . . there are some things I'd like to know."

"What are they?" I ask. Karen reaches down to her purse and pulls out a piece of paper.

"I wrote them down," she says as she hands it to me. I look at the paper and read the questions aloud:

1. *When is your birthday?*
2. *What are your parents like?*
3. *Any brothers, sisters?*
4. *What nationality are you?*
5. *Were you abused?*
6. *Were you ever in therapy?*
7. *Did you ever feel suicidal?*
8. *Do you have any medical problems?*
9. *Why did you choose to become a psychiatrist?*
10. *Is it true that you've learned not to have feelings for your patients?*

11. What does it feel like to be loved?

12. Do you believe in euthanasia?

These are interesting questions. I can understand why Karen wants to know these things; all patients get curious about the private lives of their therapists. Like Karen's, my parents were the product of the postwar 1950s. They married in the late '40s and my sister was born in 1950. I followed in 1952, and my younger brother in 1957. After my father's roofing company went bankrupt, he worked as a salesman for a kitchen-cabinet company and traveled a lot. He started spending more and more time away from home, and not alone; my parents divorced when I was eight. The next three years were tough on my mother; the stress of raising three small children (while every week my father's $50 child support checks arrived late and then bounced) was more than she could manage. While I was in fifth and sixth grades, my mother worked days as a secretary at a small manufacturing plant and evenings in the coat department at a large department store. More than once we had our electricity turned off and I remember looking in the bottom of her purses and in the pockets of her winter coats to find enough change to buy bread for sandwiches for school. During the three years after the divorce, my mother developed hypertension, an ulcer, and Graves disease—a hyperthyroid condition—all from the stress.

An energetic young boy, I was tested and placed in an afternoon program for gifted children. There were about twelve of us from all the grade schools in the district, and it was a blessed afternoon respite from the tedium of my morning classes. The special curriculum was mostly independent study on topics that interested us; we'd present reports on our studies in class. My mother was very proud of me, especially since there was no other part of her life that was successful, and I was fiercely loyal to her.

My mother remarried the summer before I started seventh grade, and although none of us children formed a close relationship with my mother's new husband, we moved, and life for us slid toward normal. Our financial crisis ceased, but in three or four years, my mother's second marriage began to fail. I continued to be an overachiever and she continued to be proud. On through junior high, high school, college, and medical school, I crafted my own version of manhood without a father at hand to model myself after.

My younger brother, whom I left behind when I went off to college, struggled in high school. He'd hardly known my father at all. And although we visited my father, who lived in Pennsylvania, once or twice a year, my brother was craving a stable fathering relationship, one I tried to give him, but couldn't. He went to live with my father at the beginning of his sophomore year. He was happy there, but one night, six months after he'd arrived, with new driver's license in hand, he drove into a utility pole and was killed instantly. My mother never recovered; she didn't want him to go to live with my father in the first place, and over the next several years, my sweet, loving, fragile mother descended into alcoholism. An army of caretakers was unable to save her.

But of course I didn't tell Karen any of this. I'm used to deflecting these types of questions as they come up during the course of therapy. It's important to understand that Karen's questions show that she's turned her attention toward me and is invested in the treatment. But such questions also indicate the patient is trying to steer the relationship into a bond that will be directly gratifying, as in a friendship. Directly gratifying a patient, as in a real relationship, nearly always sabotages the effectiveness of the therapeutic relationship. If you gratify her, she'll stop talking and exploring, and will focus instead on obtaining the gratification. The trick is to deal with the questions in a way that satisfies the patient's reason for asking without revealing too much personal information.

"I'm glad you brought these questions in, Karen," I begin. "But before I answer some, I'd like to talk to you a little about what prompted your bringing them in. Have you had these questions for a while?"

"Yes, some," Karen says. I can see she's embarrassed to have been so bold as to ask these things directly. She looks at me, but I look back at her and wait.

"I've always wondered about these things," she continues. "I wanted to know about your life outside the office. What your family is like, why you do this . . ." Her voice trails off.

"If you've had these questions for a long time, why do you think it's important to ask them now?" Time to sit back and wait again. With questions like these, whatever comes out of Karen's mouth, even if it seems unrelated, is the answer. The important thing for me to do is shut up. If a patient is silent, the worst thing you can do is bail her out by offering a suggestion or asking another question. The reason this question is so important is because I think the real answer is: because I'm beginning to get really serious and invested in the treatment and I want to make sure you're the right one to accompany me on this terrifying journey. I am curious to see how Karen will find her answer.

"I was just wondering," she asks, tentatively, "what if this takes a long time?" She looks to me for reassurance.

"Do you mean, will I stick it out with you?" I ask.

"Yes, will you be there . . . even if . . ." Her voice trails off again.

"If . . . ?"

"Well, I don't know, if . . ." She's struggling, but I can't step in to help. "If you don't like what I say," she says finally.

"Are you afraid you could tell me something that would hurt me or make me go away?"

"Yes," she says quietly, revealing in that "yes" the possibility that she has terrible secrets to tell. Given that admission, I feel I can give her some help.

"You can talk about anything you want in here. Talking is what we do. We don't take actions in here, we *talk*. Talking is safe. There's nothing you can say to me that will cause me harm. Actions can cause harm. You can talk to me about wanting to die; that's okay. But taking actions around wanting to die is *not* all right." Karen takes this in and nods slowly.

"Your list of questions is very interesting," I say, perusing the list. "There are some ordinary questions, like my birthday, brothers and sisters, but this one, was I abused? I wonder if you're curious whether I have experiences that would help me hear and understand what you've begun to tell me has happened to you." This question relates, I think, to Karen's fear of saying something that could drive me away.

"I *am* interested," I continue, "in hearing all that you need to tell me about how you've been hurt." Karen looks at me, again nodding slowly. I go down the list. "Was I ever in therapy? Yes, I was in psychoanalysis for about nine years with a wonderful man who taught me a lot. He was on the faculty of the psychoanalytic institute where I trained." Karen's eyes get big. I give her this information for two reasons. First, so she'll know that my training includes being in therapy myself, and second, so she'll know I'm comfortable with intensive long-term treatment, which she may be intuiting she herself needs.

"Let's see," I say, "do I have any medical problems? No. Nothing I know of." That's another question relating to "will I stick it out with her," that is, will I live long enough. I look down the list again.

"Why did I choose to become a psychiatrist? Because it was the most interesting thing I studied when becoming a doctor. There's nothing more interesting than understanding the emotions of another person and helping them." It's true, actually, and I tell Karen this to let her know why I can be invested in *her* treatment.

"Is it true that I've learned not to have feelings for my patients?" I look at Karen; I know this is very important to her. It isn't enough that I'm interested in understanding her; she wants to know if I can care about her. How to answer?

"No, it's not true that I've learned not to have feelings for my patients," I say. "It would be impossible not to have feelings." Karen relaxes a little. "But I've learned to try to understand those feelings, so they can't interfere too much in doing what is best for my patients."

I look at the rest of the list and say, "These others are important questions, too, but I think the primary thing for us to understand is that this list indicates you're growing more invested and deeply involved in our work together here, and the more of yourself you put into this, the more you need to know I'll be there with you, wanting to help you."

Karen looks away and chews on her lower lip. "I have one more question," she says.

"Yes?"

She takes a dramatic pause. "What's wrong with me?" She looks at me for a moment, then leans back into her chair. She's been observing well, I think. Now *she* is going to sit and wait.

I ponder for a second how I'll answer her. I don't want to frighten her.

"It's clear to me you're troubled by depression," I begin, "and that this depression was triggered by the pain following Sara's birth, but is chiefly caused by the hurtful relationships you've suffered, and continue to suffer, throughout your life." This is the easy part. The diagnosis of depression is something we've been talking about openly all along.

"You also suffer from what's called a personality disorder," I continue, "that is, damage to your overall personality structure, such as losing time during periods of stress, due to the painful early relationships you had with your mother and father, and to a lesser extent, your grandfather."

This is vague, I know, but I say it as if I know exactly what I'm talking about. What sort of damage I leave out. I don't altogether know what sort of damage, not exactly. But she seems to accept my explanation.

Why don't I just tell her she has dissociative identity disorder? Because I'm chicken. I don't know how she'd react, and I fear she'd react badly: that it might be just the blow that would make her take that final suicidal step. I'm confident she'll bring it into sharper focus when she is ready.

The next session is remarkable for the fact that for the first time in more than three years, Karen fixes her hair in anticipation of coming to see me. It may seem like a small thing, but this is an outstanding event. She's a little more animated, and tells me she's taken a job as a night cashier at the drugstore near her house. She says she hopes to gain some financial independence from her husband. She also reports a dream from the previous night.

"I dreamt I was in a hospital," she says, "and I was in a coma. I'd just had my legs amputated and I was dying. I was hooked up to life support systems. The doctor was saying I wasn't going to come out; I was going to die. Then you came to visit and asked everyone to leave the room. You start talking to me, telling me the reasons to live. I heard you, but I couldn't talk, couldn't move. I knew I wasn't really in a coma; I just shut down. I didn't want to live. You then took my hand and told me to try to squeeze your hand if I heard you. I did."

"You squeezed my hand?" I ask.

"Yes, I did," she answers.

Karen sits back, distracted by her subsequent thoughts.

"What occurs to you in relation to the dream?" I ask.

"When I was eleven," she begins, "I had pneumonia, and the doctors said I wouldn't survive, but I always thought I would. I was in a coma for two or three weeks." Her voice trails off. I can't be certain that Karen was actually in a coma for two to three weeks when she was twelve; perhaps it was a dissociative episode, but it doesn't really matter right now. This is how she remembers it.

"What else?" I ask.

Karen thinks a second, and then continues, "I've been having pains in my legs recently, just where my legs were amputated in the dream. I don't know what's causing the pain; I don't think there's anything wrong with my legs."

"You were in a coma, yet you were aware of other people in the room?" I ask.

"Yes," she says, "I was unconscious, but I could hear what was going on."

"It sounds to me your coma is a little bit like losing time," I suggest.

"Yeah," she says, "I could hear, but I wasn't really there."

"So after I cleared the room of all the people who saw you as dead and hopeless, I talked to you of living, and despite your 'coma,' you heard me, and squeezed my hand."

"Yeah."

I want to end the session on the idea of her squeezing my hand, which is the image most powerfully representing her connection to me in the service of wanting her to live. The fabric of the therapy with Karen is so fragile at this point, I want to continually try to multiply the wisps of positive emotional threads between us, weave them together into something stronger, in order to resist having them be blown apart by the destructive people in Karen's life, or from violent forces from within Karen, herself.

CHILDHOOD HORRORS

"I don't think I can do this, Dr. Baer," Karen says as she sinks into her chair, defeated, deflated, and immobile.

"Tell me about it," I say. Karen is always despairing. This is my standard response. Karen agonizes. I wait.

". . . I'm no good," she says at last.

I pause to see if she'll continue. "What makes you say so?" I finally ask. Throughout the sessions, I continue to try to ferret out each notion, belief, or memory that contributes to this "I want to die" mantra, so we can get past this obstacle and begin other work. Karen shakes her head, but goes on.

"There's been too much." She pauses. "I'm so ashamed."

"About what?" I prompt.

"I should be punished."

"For what?" I prompt again.

Karen, looking even more distressed, says, "for stealing." I'm surprised; Karen is so afraid of disapproval, she never acts dishonestly.

"Stealing?" I ask. Karen nods. Her nod is not enough answer, so I fall silent and wait.

"My father made us steal." I give her the slightest nod, to

indicate I am ready to hear what she has to say but am not going to actively participate. The floor is hers.

"My father was always stealing things, small items, pocket-sized." She pauses. "He'd always say he got a 'five-finger discount.' " She pauses again. I can see the disgust rise in her throat and her swallowing it down again. "Some of the things included candy, breath mints, or food," she continued. "He'd say 'the police can't arrest us if we're caught with stuff under ten dollars.' " Her brow draws into itself and strains. "He also stole women's panties and bras." She looks at me, but I don't respond; I just let her struggle on. She continues, "A few years ago, I remember going out with the family for pizza. My son was about ten months old. My father offered to carry him for me and handed me my son's diaper bag, which he'd been holding. When we got to the car, I mentioned I needed to lighten the things I was carrying, and he started laughing. Inside the diaper bag, my father had put stolen items: a wine carafe, two wineglasses, and four silverware settings. He claimed he paid for them when he left the tip. My father always stole something when we went out to eat. Salt and pepper shakers, glasses, silverware—we had whole drawers full of the stuff at home. It was as if he couldn't go into a restaurant without taking something. He used us—my brothers and me—by slipping things into our pockets or telling us to take things. I didn't want to, but I was afraid he'd hurt me if I didn't, so I did." Karen falls silent, suffused with the shame of revealing the petty thievery that was an ordinary part of her family life.

"Do you feel like a criminal, just like your father was?" I use a strong word because that's how Karen seems to feel. She nods, her lips turning down in a frown and tears escaping the corners of her eyes.

"By being made to participate in your father's stealing, you seem to feel that you're a thief, too." Karen nods again.

"But if you didn't go along with him, he'd hurt you," I ask rhetorically. Karen nods once more, a little more vigorously, and more tears stream down her cheeks. "What were you to do?" Karen needs to process this situation from an adult's point of view. Karen shrugs, crying harder. I let her sit with this for a few minutes. I can see she's trying to unburden herself of these memories.

"You're having trouble seeing yourself as different from your father, and that's one reason why you want to die." Karen doesn't nod, but she cries harder.

It's March 1993, and Karen tells me her mother has been calling her to ask for money. She had given her mother a little money the previous week, hoping she'd stop calling, but encouraged by Karen's weakness, her mother has been calling even more. After dialing for her messages, Karen hands me her cell phone and I listen. Each message is more strident than the last.

Karen, call your mother. I need to talk to you. (Beep)

Call me! I need something. After all I've done for you, you owe me! Call me! Don't be so fucking rude, bitch! (Beep)

This is your mother! Call me! What the fuck! The least you can do is call me. You owe me the money I spent on you your whole life! Call me or you're dead to me! (Beep)

You're nothing but a fat-assed slob! Don't ever ask me for a fucking dime. If you can't help me, you can kiss my bloody ass! (Beep)

I'm calling your precious Dr. Baer and telling him you're a no-good piece of shit. I wish you would've died at birth! Screw yourself and rotate! (Beep)

I look at Karen; she looks back at me with what now has become such familiar humiliation. *Screw yourself and rotate,* I think—my God.

"I used to give her money all the time, hoping she'd like me," Karen says, "but then she'd just start asking for more. She always says she'll pay me back, but she never does. *Everybody* asks me for money, all my family and friends. I don't have it to give, but I can't say no."

"Have you been saying no to your mother?" I ask.

"Yes, that's why she's angry."

"If you give her some money," I continue, "will she stop asking?" Reality processing time again.

"No," Karen says right away, "she'll just stop for a couple days."

"If you give her some money," I press, "will she like you?" Karen pauses at this.

"Maybe . . . ," she says, but she knows it is not true. The admission is painful. "No," she says. I wait a moment.

"When you give her money, and she doesn't like you any better, how does it make you feel?" I ask.

"I want to hurt myself," she says softly.

"So what must you do?" She looks at me uncertainly.

"There's nothing I can do."

"That's what you've always thought," I say. "You can say no."

"She won't give up," Karen is resigned.

"She'll have to."

"She won't."

"You're an adult now," I say. Karen is unconvinced; this has gone on for so long. We'll need to let this go for now; you can bring a patient to reality, but you can't make her believe. Karen will have to mull this over.

Karen has fallen behind in paying my bill. I know what effect it will have on Karen when I bring it up. Mother and I, asking her for money. This is my bind. If I'd asked her all along to keep up with the bill, before it got out of hand, I'd be seen as constantly asking for money, just like her mother. If I don't ask, and her balance gets large, at some point I'll have to bring it up, and then I'll be asking for more than she can give, just like her mother. There are good, technical, psychotherapeutic ways to handle these situations; I've just never been very good at them. So, somewhere in between being a nag and letting it go too long, a few sessions after Karen complains about her mother, I finally bring it up to her.

"I see you've fallen somewhat behind in the bill," I say as I hand her the bill for the past three months. Karen's face blanches, and she begins to cry.

"I gave the money to my mother. I always have to pay for my friends," she says. "My mother always says I owe her; now I owe you, too."

"It's interesting what getting behind in the bill sets up," I say, trying to keep my voice even and not betray my irritation that she's given my money away. "It makes you feel like I'm no different than your mother." Karen thinks a moment. I continue, "It also makes me feel like *you*—your mother has your money and your mother has my money; we both don't like it, but we both feel helpless about it." Karen looks at me and almost smiles. It seems better to her that she and I are in the same boat, rather than viewing it as me being no better than her mother. She falls sad again.

"This is just a job for you," she says, "that's all it is." Meaning, of course, that I don't care about her, only the money.

"It's not *just* a job," I say, "it's a very special job." I don't know if she believes me. She thinks about it a moment, but doesn't seem much appeased. We continue to struggle with the money issue.

It's important that Karen start to protect herself from those who abuse her, even if she won't physically leave them. Although at times she feels like a beaten prizefighter with no referee to stop the fight, she begins to find small ways to defend herself. With her mother, she begins screening her calls, and when her mother leaves a message that sounds vicious, Karen will delete it at the beginning, before she hears the entire tirade. She begins making excuses, such as saying she needs to be at her children's school, when her mother wants to be driven somewhere. With her husband, she plans activities with the children outside the house between the time her husband comes home from work and starts drinking and the time he passes out.

These maneuvers are fledgling attempts that aren't always successful. So often she is still in her child's frame of mind when facing her abusers: Submit or die. If the abuse becomes intolerable, and she can no longer submit, she longs to kill herself. She has very few adult ways of dealing with an abusive parent or husband, which involve self-assertion, limit setting, or leaving. These options are not real for Karen; she regards these adult actions as beyond her. It's my job to try to make them real. Despite the forces that beat up on Karen, she's getting stronger. As she feels increasingly trustful of me, she reveals more.

It's September 1993, and Karen walks in, clearly shaken, with the first fall chill still on her.

"I don't know what happened to me last night," Karen says. I can see she's reluctant to talk.

"What can you tell me about it?" I ask.

"I went to the doctor's office yesterday; at least I think I did. I don't remember the exam, but I found some medication—vaginal suppositories. I was trying to follow the instructions in the package, and my hands began to shake; I felt panicky and nauseous. I put one of the suppositories inside me and I threw up when I was done. I don't know why I had such a reaction."

"What thoughts does it bring to mind?" I ask.

"It made me feel like I was being hurt at my parents' parties . . . I want to tell you, but I can't talk about it." She falls silent and retreats inside herself.

"Do you think you could talk into your tape recorder?" I want to find a way for Karen to tell me what she needs to tell me; we just don't have enough time to wait for her to do so in the office.

"I think so."

The next week, Karen brings me a microcassette. I take it home, and after dinner, I go upstairs to listen. On it, told in pieces, is the following story.

Karen's father, Martin, a foreman in a small machine shop, walks over to the press where Harry is working. "Who the fuck told you to run that job?" Martin yells over the noise of the machines. "We don't need that fucking job until next week! Shit, Harry, you're making me sorry I hired you!"

"I'm sorry, Martin. Stan set this job up. He told me to run it," Harry says. Martin knew this; it was discussed in the morning meeting.

"Fuck, you should have known better. Well, since you've started, I guess you should go ahead and finish."

"I'm sorry, Martin. Please, I need this job. I won't do it again."

"Well, Harry, you know no one else would have you, a fucking rummy with a dishonorable discharge. If it wasn't for me, you'd be a bum. Now you've got a good job. You owe me. You owe me big."

Harry looks down. "I'm sorry, Martin. Please don't be mad at me."

"Aw, what the fuck, you're not so bad. Why don't you come to my house tonight? We're having a party. We always have a good time."

"Okay . . . geez, thanks, Martin. Then you're not mad?"

"Nah, come over at eight; bring some beer."

When Harry arrives at eight thirty, he hears laughing and a woman's squeal as he walks into the living room. The lights are down, and there is the whir and flicker of a projector. On the screen, a woman is being entered from the rear while giving oral sex to another man facing her. Harry sees Martin sitting watching the movie. There are two other couples there. One woman has her breasts out, and two men are playing with them.

"Harry, c'mon in! Sit over here." With a beer in one hand, Martin points with his free hand to the empty spot next to him. Harry's eyes are large as he takes in the scene in front of him. He sits down next to Martin, but his eyes are still darting around the room. He fixes on the exposed woman.

"You want some?" Martin asks. Harry looks at Martin with surprise and uncertainty. "I've got something special for you, Harry, but it will cost you." Martin knows since it's Friday, Harry will have cashed his check after work.

Harry pops open a beer and watches the movie, but his eyes keep straying to the woman being played with by the two men across the room. There's another woman sitting to the side of one of the men, looking bored and angry. The man next to her, who now has one hand down the pants of the woman with the exposed breasts, puts his hand on her leg.

"Don't touch me!" she says. The man continues to knead the flesh on her thigh. The woman continues to sulk, but allows the man to touch her. She takes another drink from her beer can. Martin watches Harry look hungrily at the two couples across the room.

"Give me fifty bucks, Harry, and I'll get you laid," Martin says in Harry's ear.

"Oh, I don't know . . ."

"Don't be a fucking faggot, Harry. You don't like girls? You a faggot?"

"Okay, Martin." Harry looks over at the woman being worked over by the two men as he reaches for his wallet. He thinks it would be okay to play with her, too.

"Follow me." Martin heads down the hallway. Harry follows him, looking back at the woman, who now is rubbing one of the men's penis through his pants. Martin takes Harry to his bedroom.

"Wait here," says Martin. Harry sits on the bed and waits for the woman from the living room to be separated from the two men.

Karen is sleeping in a double bed with her two younger brothers. She is eleven years old. Martin opens the vinyl accordion door to the small bedroom where the children sleep, and touches Karen on the shoulder. Karen startles awake.

"Get up!" Martin yanks Karen up by the arm and drags her into his bedroom. Harry looks up, surprised to see the young girl. He looks at Martin, and from the look on his face, realizes that he's just paid to have sex with Martin's daughter.

"Take off your clothes," Martin says to Karen, who looks terrified. Karen quickly sheds her pajamas.

"Now, Martin, I don't think . . . ," Harry starts.

"You paid for it," Martin says. "I don't want no faggots working for me."

Harry, afraid of Martin, looks at Karen.

"Touch her; she likes it," Martin says. Harry is trembling and confused, but reaches out timidly and strokes Karen's thigh. . . .

I listen for two more minutes then turn off the tape and sit back, my heart beating fast. I feel a little nauseous, too. This story is told in pieces, in a collage of images, thoughts, and remembered sensations. It is hard to imagine these events being played out in real life. What damage must have occurred to Karen having these people as parents, as role models? How must she regard herself, having been an involuntary participant in her parents' sordid lives? No wonder she wants to die. It's amazing she hangs on at all.

My wife is putting the children to bed. I want to go help her, live my normal life, see the smiling faces of my children as they squeal and splash in the bath, and separate myself from these stories of horror. I should put the tape recorder down and listen to the rest of Karen's story another day; but another part of me is compelled to press on. That part wins.

It's summer, and Karen, age twelve, dressed in shorts and T-shirt, walks from the living room to the kitchen on her way out to play. Her mother and father are sitting at the kitchen table, arguing.

"I don't get no respect around here. I don't get the respect a husband deserves from a wife!" Martin glares at Katrina, and then looks at Karen as she enters the kitchen.

Katrina persists, "I was only saying we should look for a new apartment—"

"Where you going?" Martin shouts at Karen, and his hand shoots out and grasps Karen's left nipple and pulls her towards him. Katrina looks away. Karen's face screws up in pain, but she doesn't make a sound.

"Where you going? You deaf?" Martin holds her there like that.

"To Donna's," Karen says, and her father releases her. Karen's hand comes up to her breast, but her father slaps it away.

"Look at these titties!" Martin says, his gaze fixed on Karen's chest. "How big are they? This big?" He holds up both hands in the shape of small cups. "Let's see." He places his large hands over Karen's small breasts and squeezes her, hard. "Are they more than a mouthful? Anything more than a mouthful is wasteful." He laughs at his own joke.

Karen walks slowly down the gangway between her house and the neighbor's, still rubbing her nipple where her father had pinched and held her. She walks the half block to the back of Pankratz & Sons Funeral Home, where her friend Donna lives. Donna is nine, three years younger than Karen. The garage is open and Donna is playing with her dolls inside. The garage is large; it has room for three vehicles, but only one hearse is there. Karen goes inside to where Donna is sitting on the steps leading down into the room where the embalming is done. Donna has two dolls, one large and one small.

"Hi," says Karen, sitting next to Donna.

"Hi," says Donna, as she tends to her dolls. Donna has arranged the dolls so the smaller one is cradled by the larger. "Betty is sad," says Donna, referring to the smaller doll. Karen sits looking at Donna stroke the head of the smaller doll using the hand of the larger doll.

"Let's pretend they're eating tea and cookies," Karen says.

Donna looks around. "I think my tea set is inside."

Just then, a large gray hearse pulls up, and backs partway into the garage. Karen and Donna watch three men get out: Donna's father, Mr. Pankratz, who is a friend of Karen's father, and two other men who help him when he goes to pick up bodies. The men go around and open the back of the hearse and pull the stretcher out that holds a corpse. Donna's father looks at the other two men, grins and winks, and then unzips the bag. The bag falls open and reveals the body of a withered old man who has, in death, an erect penis. Karen gasps and Donna screams. The three men laugh and Donna's father walks over to them, standing between them and the still-open garage door.

"C'mon, girls, want to see a really stiff dick, a frozen Popsicle? Want to take off your clothes and see how good it feels to sit on it ice cold?" Donna's father starts to move toward the girls, pushing them toward the back of the hearse. The other two men are snickering, and Donna's father continues urging the girls toward the dead Mr. Stankowski. Simultaneously, Karen and Donna bolt past either side of Donna's father and out of the garage. Once outside, Donna stops, sits down, and begins to cry. Karen sits next to her and strokes her hair. They sit like that for a few minutes.

Karen hears the door of the hearse slam, and one of the men comes toward them with a shoe box in his hands. Donna doesn't look up, but Karen regards the man warily. He comes over and crouches down and shows the girls the inside of the box. Curled up on one side is a white pigeon, breathing heavily. The man picks up the bird and holds it out to Donna, who reaches for it and cradles it in her arms. The pigeon's breathing calms down a bit, but it makes no effort to move.

"We found it on the side of the parking lot at the hospital," he says. "It doesn't want to move, so maybe it got hurt." He takes the bird back from Donna and holds it out to Karen, who pets it, feeling its soft feathers and the quick but delicate breathing.

"Maybe we could nurse it," says Karen, looking up into the face of the man holding the pigeon. She sees a mixture of mirth and wickedness. The man stands up and looks over at Donna's father and the other man, who are now sitting on the front of the hearse, snickering, watching the scene with the bird.

"Sure, we could nurse it," he says, smiling, as he walks back towards the garage. "Here, maybe it can fly!" The man throws the bird up in the air, between himself and Karen. Karen lurches.

"No!" she cries, and leaps up towards the pigeon, but it hits the cement driveway before Karen can reach it.

"I'm sorry, I'm sorry," she cries, "I'm sorry I didn't catch you."

As I listen to this scene, I'm struck by the anguish in Karen's voice at not being able to save the pigeon, as if she could have. It's also hard to believe that grown men could be so immature and sadistic as to torture a bird in order to torment little girls. I don't know why that should surprise me; I know there are people like this, but all these episodes depict such an astounding degree of immature sadism, it's still surprising. I turn the tape on again.

At 1:30 a.m. the telephone rings. Martin is still up, waiting for the call. He talks briefly, nodding in agreement, and hangs up. Katrina has gone to bed and is sleeping. Martin goes into Karen's bedroom, where she sleeps with her two brothers, and sits her up.

"Get your shoes on, we're going out," he whispers, as he helps her on with her coat. Karen is not quite awake, but she offers no resistance to her father's instructions. She's been awakened like this many times before. She walks, automatonlike, through the kitchen, in her shoes, pajamas, and winter coat, slightly ahead of and urged on by her father. She feels the cold wind on her cheek as she walks absently down the familiar back steps. They walk down the alley and go through the open garage door of Pankratz's funeral home. Karen hears the door closing as she reaches the inner door. She stumbles up the two steps to go inside. She tries not to open her eyes as she's being led. They turn and begin to go downstairs. The smell of formaldehyde grows stronger as she descends, as does the sound of voices. The room is dimly lit by several candles, and there are five or six men already there. Empty beer bottles litter the stainless-steel counters; among the plastic bottles are steel knives and hoses. In the center of the room are two stainless-steel tables, used for cleaning, draining, embalming, and dressing bodies. Martin leads Karen to the nearer table and takes off her coat.

"Take off your pants, Karen," her father says, "we're going to make you feel good." He smiles at her in an odd and cold way, and he tosses her coat into the corner. Karen pulls down her pajama bottoms quickly and steps out of them. She's naked from the waist down. A few of the men come closer and stare at Karen as she stands by the side of the table. She looks at the men briefly, and seeing no kindness, looks straight ahead of her. Karen seems far away or absent to the men, who have attended these gatherings before.

"Jump up, Karen," her father says, and Karen climbs up and sits in the middle of the embalming table. Her father turns to her and unbuttons her pajama top, eases it off her shoulders, and tosses it over by her coat.

"Do you want us to love you?" her father asks, running his hand over Karen's chest and shoulders. Karen sits mute and motionless, but wide-eyed with fear. "You have a black heart and soul," her father continues, "you're damaged goods; everyone knows you're evil."

Martin leaves the table and the other men approach Karen and begin stroking her. She is confused between the affectionate, pleasurable touching by the men, and her fear about being touched. Martin comes back with six white pearl–tipped needles in his hand. Karen doesn't see them; her eyes are closed, lost in the fear and sensations the touching has elicited.

While Karen is being stroked by the men, Martin sticks one of the needles quickly into Karen's abdomen and pulls it out. Karen lets out a yelp, tenses, and then falls back motionless, trying to stifle her fear and pain. Martin sticks Karen's abdomen a second and third time. Karen tries to keep still, but recoils at each pinprick.

"To be loved, you have to be hurt," Martin says. "You need to feel pain to experience love. You can't know love if you don't know pain." Karen, poised in a tense motionlessness, keeps her eyes shut. "Maybe we should bring your little brothers here and help you know love by seeing their pain?" Karen opens her eyes wide. She recalls the last time her brothers were beaten by her father. He'd said their beating was her fault, that they were being punished for her sins. It was terrible. She promised herself she'd never again let them be hurt because she was bad. She'd be perfect, so she could protect them. She'd be their shield of armor.

"You need to thank us for loving you," Martin says, moving toward her again with the pins.

Karen talks about these events on the tape in a halting, tired, and reluctant tone. She seems repulsed by these memories—I hear the utter distress in her voice—but she tells them anyway. It amazes me to think this behavior could have gone on in this near west-side city neighborhood. Who were these people? It seems unlikely Karen could have generated these images as childhood fantasies. They're too sadistic and manipulative to be of her authorship.

There's more tape left, about fifteen minutes more. My children are surely asleep now, with visions of loving parents and a safe
warm bed couching their dreams. I'm so blessed to have my children spared from any knowledge of this kind of hurt. My mind is
swimming with images, reactions, disbelief, horror, and trepidation.
I am unnerved thinking about trying to help this woman who's suffered so much. This kind of abuse has been termed "soul murder,"
to describe how it kills the will to live. Is Karen beyond redemp-
tion? I put my headphones back on and press the Play button.

Karen looks at the clock. Her mother left for work about an hour
ago, and her father will be home in a few minutes. She checks the living
room and kitchen to make sure everything is picked up and put in
place. She goes to her bedroom for a last-minute check to make sure
her brothers have not made a mess of the room since she straightened
it half an hour ago. Her brothers are playing on the floor with their
green plastic soldiers. Karen picks up the few extra toys they've taken
out and goes to the kitchen table to work on her homework. As she sits
down, she hears the front-room door open, and the heavy footsteps of
her father come down the hall.

"There you are!" he says, looking hard at Karen, who sits at the table
with her schoolbook. "The house is a fucking mess! What good are you?
I don't know why we keep you. You just cost us money." Karen tries to
look small behind the table. Martin turns to the refrigerator and opens
the door. He pulls out a carton of milk.

"This milk is old!" he says, and throws the carton into the sink. He
pulls out a beer and a slice of leftover pizza. Then he goes to the cabi-
net to find a plate for the pizza. He pulls out one plate, then another.

"These plates are dirty!" he shouts, turning toward Karen. "Get over
here and wash these plates. I don't want to see no spots on them!" She
goes quickly to the sink and Martin turns on the hot water. She begins
to wash the first plate as her father stands next to her, watching, and
the water begins to steam. He grabs her by the wrists. "You need hot
water to get these plates clean!" He puts her hands under the scalding
water. "Go on, wash them!" Karen winces as she quickly washes the
plate and tries desperately not to drop it as the burning becomes worse.
"I have to teach you everything." She tries to fight back the tears and
hold herself together, knowing if she complains, her fate will be worse.
Martin turns off the water after she's washed the second plate. The
backs of her hands are bright red. Martin looks down at Karen, who
puts her hands behind her back.

"Why are you wearing that brown belt? Didn't I tell you brown was
a nigger's color? Are you a nigger lover? Do you want to fuck niggers?"

His face is close to Karen's, who stands in front of him, speechless and immobile. "You're bad and you need to be punished. Go to your room and go to bed. I want you asleep!"

At 2:00 a.m. that same night, after her mother has come home from work and gone to bed, Karen's father and grandfather come into Karen's room and sit her up. Her father has her coat.

"C'mon, Karen, we're going for ice cream," her father says as he threads her arm into her coat. Karen sits up, groggy, not wanting to wake up, but letting her arms be put into the coat over her pajamas. The two men walk Karen down the back stairs and into her grandfather's car. It's a ten-minute ride to the chemical factory where her grandfather is a supervisor during the day. There's no one working there at this hour of the night. Karen keeps her eyes closed for most of the ride. She's taken this route several times before. They park the car near the back entrance, where several other cars are already parked. Karen's grandfather uses his key to open the door. The lights are dim, but there's enough illumination to see their way to the freight elevator. They walk along the old wooden plank floor. They pass large vats, some open and some closed, with a foul-smelling purple taint splashed on the sides. They come to a large metal door to the elevator that opens horizontally from the middle, with a heavy black canvas strap protruding from the center, like a tongue sticking out.

Karen's grandfather pushes the Call button and Karen hears the machinery shift into place as the elevator rises from the basement. Her grandfather grabs the canvas strap and pulls the doors apart. They creak loudly as they open. Behind them is a heavy metal mesh door that opens from the bottom. Martin bends down and picks up its canvas strap and pulls up. The three of them go into the large, dark elevator car. Martin holds Karen by the arm while her grandfather closes both doors with successive bangs that echo throughout the factory.

As the elevator descends, Martin takes off Karen's coat and hands it to her grandfather. Karen stands passively. He unbuttons her pajama top and slides it off her shoulders. He pulls her bottoms down, and takes them off her feet in turn. Her grandfather puts her coat back around her shoulders and holds it closed in front of her. When they reach the bottom, Martin opens the doors and her grandfather pushes the Emergency Stop button, preventing the elevator from being called back up.

The two men walk into the large basement room, guiding Karen forward between them. The room is lit by a dozen candles. There are about ten people already in the room. Three or four are women, and two of the women are naked. There's laughter and loud voices, and a squeal as one of the naked women is grabbed by a man. As Karen is positioned in the center of the room, the voices quiet, and everyone turns toward her. The faces of the people are indistinct and flickering in the light, but Karen recognizes most. Karen's grandfather opens her coat and throws it aside. Karen stands naked between the two men, facing the group, who are partially hidden, partially illuminated by the candlelight.

"Here she is, the evil bitch," her grandfather bellows. "It's time to punish her, to remove the blackness from her soul! She must be taught a lesson. She must be punished. It's time!" Her grandfather walks Karen into the middle of the room and steps back, leaving Karen alone at the center of everyone's gaze.

"God's words brought us together!" He continues, "The world's a mess. People are starving, acting like fools, with sicknesses like plague and VD, because of evil children like this one. To feel the pain of those who are hungry, you must be starved. To feel the pain of the innocent, you must suffer. Bring me the knife!"

A man comes forward from the group with a small kitchen paring knife. "Hold out your hand!" her grandfather says to Karen. With eyes still half closed, she holds out her hand. The man places the blade in her palm and closes her fingers around it. He encircles her small hand holding the blade with his own. He slowly begins to squeeze his hand over hers. She winces and starts to cry, and then suddenly goes still, as drops of blood seep over the knife handle. "Mother Mary did the same things to baby Jesus as we done to you," Karen's grandfather continues. "It was needed to be done before the wise men came and told her he'd be punished in later life. He died for your sins." The grandfather nods to the man, who loosens his grip on Karen and removes the knife from her hand. Karen drops her hand to her side, blood dripping from her fingers.

Her grandfather continues, "We say you must be punished, and you must forever punish yourself while here on earth. This is God's word. If you tell any outsiders of God's word, you must kill yourself, after killing the person you told. You must do this, or evil will always be with you. You must kill anyone who dares befriend you. If you betray us, you will be doomed to hell on earth and after death." Her grandfather looks at Martin and then over at the long table next to the wall. Martin goes to the table, a large rectangular table with folding legs, and begins to drag it to the center of the room. Karen is led to the table and the two men pick her up by the arms and sit her on the table. She sits there, naked, with her eyes closed. Through her closed eyes she sees a bright light and hears the whirring of an 8-mm home movie camera.

"Everything is about God," her grandfather says, his voice becoming a monotone patter. "We can do whatever we want because God tells us so." Karen is laid down on the table. She is bathed in the light of the movie camera. Her father and several others move in. Karen remains motionless, her eyes closed. "Evil does not exist, only mistakes like this one . . ." her grandfather continues. Karen feels numb from her neck to her stomach, like she's empty. Her chest tightens up; a big . . . huge presence begins to push its way into her. Then she feels her consciousness slip away.

"Good morning, Karen," her mother says as Karen walks into the kitchen, dressed for school. She rubs her head as she sits down at the table. "Can't you say good morning?" her mother asks, with a bite in her tone. Karen sits, rubbing the side of her head. "What's the matter?" her mother asks.

"I have a headache," Karen says, looking sad and in pain.

"Again?" her mother asks. "Did you have another nasty dream? You dream all kinds of evil things. You mustn't tell anyone about your bad thoughts!" Her mother turns away and attends to the stove. Karen eats her cereal. Her mother notices the cut on her hand.

"What did you do to yourself now?" her mother asks crossly. Karen shrinks into herself and slides out of her chair. She grabs her books and leaves. Her hand hurts, her head hurts, and her insides hurt as she walks the six blocks to school. She doesn't talk to anyone.

This portion of the tape makes me realize even more the depth of the damage done to Karen. Karen describes these events in bits and pieces, as if she's recalling random memory fragments, and she describes them with such matter-of-fact tiredness. I assume the feelings from these events have been walled off from the telling of the memories, but the situations she's describing are so extreme, terrible, and damaging, I don't know what to believe.

She describes a consistent, at least loosely organized, small group of people, including some women, who regularly sadistically tortured and psychologically tormented children for their own entertainment. And what is all that quasireligious mumbo jumbo about? I wonder.

The question of how much of this is "true" always comes up as I listen to Karen's horrific stories. But she always tells her stories in a way that is utterly convincing: with pain, depression, and wretchedness. She's never glad to tell these stories, but does so always at the risk, she feels, that each will be too much for me and will be the one to make me break off treatment. I know children get abused all the time, but it's always been outside my personal experience to witness someone who's survived such a childhood.

Could she be trying to deceive me or manipulate me to obtain something from me? After working with her for four years, this doesn't seem to make sense; at least I can't imagine what purpose such a deception could serve. I suppose it could be a test, to see if my willingness to stick with her can weather what she sees as off-putting information—damage that suggests she's too sick for me to treat. But if so, why now, after four years of therapy, would she need such an abrupt and striking demonstration of trust, especially using deception, a trait so out of character for her and a tactic that threatens to destroy the trust we've formed?

About this time, in November 1993, she gives me a cartoon that shows a psychiatrist pulling a lever that slides the patient off the couch and down through a trapdoor. The caption reads, *Next patient please; you're too screwed up!*

"What is this about?" I ask, holding the cartoon. Karen squirms uneasily and I see the regret in her face. She's been bold enough to give me the cartoon, but one would think, by this time, she'd know that I'll ask her to talk about it.

"I'm afraid at some point you'll have had enough and say 'Forget it,' " Karen says. "Part of me thinks you wouldn't do that, but the other part is really scared. These memories scare me, and telling them scares me. My family told me even my closest friends would betray and humiliate me." Karen sobs and collects herself. "You're the only one I've ever trusted. I'm so confused; I don't know what to do about it. If anything were to happen, and you did . . . couldn't treat me anymore, I'd understand. I really would. But I don't know what I'd do if I didn't have you. I'm just afraid of losing you." What a trial, and what an opportunity for Karen, I think, to feel trust for the first time. No wonder she's terrified.

As it happens, there *are* possible changes for our relationship looming. I've been interviewing for the chairmanship at departments of psychiatry at three of the teaching hospitals in the city and suburbs. Taking one of these positions would still allow me to see Karen, but I don't know in what part of the city I'd end up, and I worry about the upheaval for her. I don't know if anything will come of these interviews, and I'll wait until I have definite plans to tell her anything.

With all the history of lost time and her abusive childhood, I'm working under the hypothesis that Karen suffers from multiple personality disorder (although the part that comes to see me doesn't know it). I wonder if the other children she sometimes mentions being tortured could be other parts of herself that she remembers as separate children, each with their own individual experiences. Or could these memories have been some type of childhood sadistic/masochistic fantasy that she's recalling as actual events—fantasies that have the force of hallucinations? Although I understand the possibility of her making up these stories (though why she'd conjure up such perversity is beyond me), I'm swayed by the utterly convincing way in which she narrates these events on tape. She's trying to describe as best she can, despite a lot of discomfort, the events as she remembers them.

I tell Karen I've listened to the tape and understand the seriousness of what's been done to her. I don't ask her to elaborate on any particular aspect, because I don't want to be seen by her as selectively interested in one form of abuse over another and prompting her into supplying me with details on those particular things. The last thing I want to do with this kind of material is lead her in one direction or another. I always want her to take the lead.

Unfortunately, after giving me this tape, she's continually suicidal. We spend all our time on our every-other-day telephone calls and weekly therapy sessions assessing her suicide risk and managing it.

At some point a thought occurs to me: If what was on the tape actually happened, then she may be thinking of killing not only herself but also me, as the recipient of information she's been warned never to divulge.

"Have you had thoughts of needing to kill me?" I ask Karen during one of our sessions. She looks startled, as if she's been caught.

"I was told I'd have to kill anyone I ever talked to about this. I remember them trying to teach me that," she says, shaking and fearful. "It makes me afraid trying to talk about all of it." She pauses, then continues, "I'd never really. I mean, I'd never really kill anyone. I always thought that if it came to that, I'd kill myself, since I was meant to die anyway."

"You're an adult now," I remind her, "and although these feelings seem fresh, they come from things that happened many years ago. They told you you'd have to kill me and yourself only because they didn't want to be found out, so they could keep their terrible deeds secret. But it's safe to tell me about them, and for us to share them together." Karen leans over, bows her head, and sobs into her hands, relieved to have acknowledged the unmentionable.

THE ALTERS

PART TWO

CLAIRE'S LETTER

It's early October 1993, and the clouds have been thick and overcast, obscuring the view of the traffic on Lake Shore Drive and the remaining few boats bobbing in Monroe Harbor. Karen comes in reluctantly. She moves to her chair and doesn't look at me directly. I can tell something's up, and she takes several minutes before she speaks. It's one of those times when I need to wait particularly long for her to begin. Helping her at this point would only derail what she's struggling with. She looks as if she's about to tell me something. She starts to speak, then falls silent and looks out the window. Finally, she begins:

"I keep having these . . . spells. . . . I call it switching." She's lost in thought, still gazing out the window. After a moment she continues. "There are periods, different lengths of time, from minutes to months, that I don't remember." She pauses again. "For example . . . I have no memory of ever having sex with my husband." She pauses, blushing but baffled. "I know I must have, since I have two children, but I have no knowledge of how it happened." Karen looks at me finally. "I don't really have any sexual feelings at all."

"What happens when you switch?" I'm excited she's brought this up at last, but I need to let her tell it at her own pace, and in her own way.

"Well, I lose time. I remember feeling weak for a second, and then I simply don't remember for a while. When I come out of it, I feel tired and drained, then that goes away, and I feel okay. That's about all."

Karen is "disassociating" or "undergoing a fugue state," I think. These are different terms for going into a trance state, similar to a hypnotic trance, during which time she can't recall what happens to her. The question is what does she do during these times she can't remember? I'm amazed she hasn't talked about this experience more before now, since it must distress and bewilder her. But I think she needed to reach a certain level of trust in me first. Karen herself seems to have little knowledge of the switching, at least no more knowledge than she's already shared. However, she's able to tell me more than she knows in other special ways.

By November, Karen indirectly begins to reveal the secrets of her inner life. In a letter dated November 7, 1993, she reports a dream.

I'm talking to you on the phone and we decide to bring my mother to one of our sessions. As we enter the elevator, I start to hear other people talking. These people come into your office with me. You open the door to invite my mother and me in. I can't understand why you let all these people in the room and don't talk to them. You then start talking to my mother. I don't remember a single word you say because I'm too busy watching the others in the room. There's a boy standing next to you sticking his tongue out at my mother. There's a girl sitting on your lap starting to go to sleep. There are two teenagers arguing about who you're going to talk to first. There is a baby crawling around your desk. There's a lady calling my mother a bitch. There's another lady sitting at your desk mocking everything my mother is saying, and another woman cleaning and organizing your office. The session seems so hectic. As I listen to all these people, I feel I already know them. I'm amazed how calm you are and that none of the noise bothers you. I cannot remember how this dream ends, but as I wake up, I feel peaceful and I giggle.

"What occurs to you," I ask, "as you think about the dream?"

Karen shrugs her shoulders and says she doesn't know, but she thinks the people were funny, and they seemed kind of familiar.

"I think the people in the room represent different sides of yourself, and the different feelings you have about me and your mother." I've suspected that when Karen loses time, or switches, she switches to another personality. I'm reluctant to tell Karen what I really think, that is, that the people in the dream represent her alternate personalities, and that I believe her diagnosis is multiple personality disorder. But I feel we're getting close, because Karen is bringing these images and associations into the sessions. She's pushing us forward.

The next day I receive a letter in the mail. It is postmarked November 5, 1993, two days before Karen's dream. I receive it on the seventh. The envelope has Karen's return address and the letter is written in pencil on three-ring notebook paper.

> Dear Doctor Bear,
>
>   My name is Claire. I am 7 years old. I live inside Karen I listin to you all the time. I want to talk to you, but I dont now how. I play games with James and Sara, and I sing to. I dont want to die. Can you help me tie my shoes
>
>   Claire

I don't call and discuss the note immediately with Karen. I wait a few days as I try to think exactly how I'll approach her with it. I worry: Will it be too much? She is dangerously suicidal every day as it is. Will this tip the scales—be more than she can live with? How many others are there besides Claire? I have lots of questions, but my questions will have to wait. I need to concentrate on Karen: her reaction, her questions, her actions, and her safety.

I've been collecting material on multiple personality disorder for some time now: articles, monographs, textbooks, and meeting abstracts. I've devoted a whole bookshelf to the subject. One of the most often cited books is *Diagnosis and Treatment of Multiple Personality Disorder,* by Frank W. Putnam, M.D. (Guilford Press: New York, 1989). In it he describes childhood sexual abuse as the most common cause of MPD, especially abuse accompanied by extreme sadism, assaults with objects, bondage, burning and cutting, and participating in "Black Masses." That would fit Karen.

Suicide risk and self-cutting are also described as common in MPD, as are headache, fainting, and hysterical symptoms such as numbness, deafness, and in Karen's case pain from where her legs were bound and whipped. There's general consensus among all the authors on the causes and symptomatology of MPD. Putnam also reports that MPD patients don't readily reveal their symptoms because they fear being labeled as "crazy," but that an alter may come forward through, among other means, a letter to the therapist. He also mentions that it's important not to get into the position of keeping secrets from one alter at the request of another. Claire's letter is such a secret.

When Karen next comes in, I have the letter ready to show her. I decide to introduce the letter in the beginning of the session, so we'll have as much time as possible to deal with it.

"I've been thinking about the other day when you told me you hear voices in your head," I start, "especially at night before you go to sleep. I've also been thinking about the dream you shared with me, where all those other people accompanied you to my office. I've been wondering if there isn't more going on inside you than we've really been aware of." I'm trying to approach this as gingerly as I can, but Karen is beginning to realize something is up. She seems uncomfortable and apprehensive, but I plow on.

"I received a letter I'd like to show you." Karen stiffens and looks alarmed. "I think it's something we should talk about," I say, gently handing her the letter and the envelope. Karen reads the letter, sees the return address. She becomes pale and a wave of nausea passes over her face. She looks as if she might faint.

"This letter may be a clue for us to what's been troubling you all this time." I'm trying to support the idea that understanding this letter is something I want to collaborate with her on. "I've been thinking for some time that you have what's called multiple personality disorder," I say. Now that I've said it, she needs to hear it plainly and unequivocally.

"With all of your experiences losing time, and since, by the expression on your face, you don't remember writing the letter, I think it's the only explanation." Okay, time for me to shut up and let Karen react.

Karen is trembling; she looks at the door and seems ready to bolt. Her face is white. I see her go through a number of emotions, from confusion to terror to resignation. Gradually she relaxes and her feelings of panic and disgust roll into sadness and acceptance.

"I wasn't prepared for this," she says at last, quietly.

"I didn't really know how to prepare you," I say. "I thought the letter was a real sign that some part of you wanted this out in the open."

"I understand," says Karen. I sit back again and wait.

"I used to think about the voices as imaginary friends." She pauses and says more quietly, "Sometimes I think I'm not very important to me."

I'm not sure what she means by that.

"Have you ever heard of this disorder before? Did you see the movie *Sybil?*"

"No. I've heard the term, but I always stayed away from those movies; I'm not sure why."

Karen looks as if she feels cut open and exposed. She turns away from me so I can't see her face. She stares out the window for a long while and looks back at me, distressed and depressed.

"Can you help me," Karen asks at last, "or am I beyond help?"

"I'm very interested in trying to help you," I say as clearly and forthrightly as I can manage. Karen closes her eyes and lets out a big breath. "We all have different sides to our personality. But for you, there are separations to the different parts of you, and they're not fully aware of one another." Karen ponders this for a moment and then turns to me.

"I've always wondered why I don't feel very much."

"We may have come upon something to explain that kind of

thing; it's something we can explore together," I say. I want to use the words "we," "us," and "together" as much as possible to reinforce to Karen that she has in me a partner and resource of steadfast help.

"I'm glad we're talking about these things now," she says, softly. Our time is up, yet I worry about the impact our conversation has had on her.

"Will you be okay going home?"

"I think so."

I ask her to call me in the evening. I'm concerned—even more than I usually am—she may hurt herself. She leaves shaken and dazed. It went as well as it could, I think.

After the revelation of Claire's letter, Karen seems to have more awareness of the other parts inside her, especially in the evening and during the night. She says she occasionally experiences different parts of her functioning for her in different ways. She can feel her mind switch, and she can now sometimes sit back and watch herself function. She says it's not really scary, except for the part inside her that wants her to hurt herself. Last night she heard, or felt, a man's voice tell her not to talk to me, or she would be hurt. When she gets mad, which is rare, she'll hear that same voice telling her *how* to get mad. At night, she hears different voices discussing the events of the day, events she may not even remember; it seems to be a way for all of them to catch up.

"I feel like when I go to sleep," she tries to explain, "other parts come out to function. Even routine things during the day, such as cooking dinner, housecleaning, or driving the kids, seem unfamiliar, because they're carried out by other parts of me. I know I've done them a thousand times, but I feel I've never really done them at all."

Karen is speaking quickly, leaning forward in her chair, animated; she seems relieved to share this with me.

"What else happens to you?"

"I can read, watch TV, and listen to music all at the same time, with different parts attending to the different things." She pauses and her face grows sad. "Sometimes I feel the abuse I've been telling you about didn't happen to *me*. I can tell you about these memories, but the feelings connected to them belong to some other part of me." Karen looks out the window and loses herself in thought.

"How are you feeling lately?"

She turns back to me and says, "I've had a lot of pain in my legs recently, but I don't think there's really anything wrong with them." She pauses and tilts her head as if she's listening. "The baby's voice crying inside my head has subsided."

"The baby's voice? How many voices do you hear?"

"I think about six."

"Why didn't you tell me about all this before?" I said, trying unsuccessfully to mask my exasperation.

"I was afraid you'd think I was too crazy and give up." She shrugs her shoulders in apology and smiles sheepishly.

Six voices. Whose, I wonder? I've known about multiple personality patients since early in my training. They are rare, and Karen is the first I've had myself. I'm aware of how excited I am to have a patient like this, but I need to keep my feelings under control and focus on continuing to treat her correctly, or I could muck up this whole process. I'm not going to do anything differently at this point. Just because she has multiple personality doesn't mean I should stray from standard psychotherapeutic technique. What do the voices say? Six of them! Only six?

One day, Karen asks me what would happen if she lost time during our sessions, so I could see and talk to the other sides of her. She's hesitant about this, but the prospect intrigues me, although I'm not sure how to go about it. Frankly, I'm a little scared by the possibility, because I wouldn't really know what to expect. I've read about MPD and taken courses in hypnosis, but I haven't applied hypnotic technique to a case like this. Karen is meek, polite, conscientious, and apologetic. I don't think the other parts will necessarily be so quiet and manageable. So far, all during the time I've been treating her, I've been following a standard technique called psychoanalytically informed psychotherapy. This is a technique that places me in the position of being receptive to whatever Karen brings up, but not directing her associations in any way. That way, everything she brings up comes from within her, and I get closer to the true unconscious thought processes that are at the heart of her pain. Left to their own devices, patients always unconsciously plot the best course to their own healing. I feel this is why we've been successful thus far. Talking to other "parts" within Karen, under hypnosis, takes me into a whole new realm.

At the next session, Karen gives me a list of the parts she's been able to identify within herself. She's not quite sure how she knows this, but this is what she wrote down. These descriptions were neatly written on three sheets of lined yellow paper—very organized:

Clair—Age 7—Female
   Likes to play games. Has trouble tying shoes. Likes chocolate milk. Needs to be held. Scared of the dark. Holdon sometimes comforts.

Holdon—Age 34—Male
   The protector. The comforter. Helps keep the Angry One hidden. Decision maker. Strong. Tall. Masculine. Left-handed. Drives. Bowls sometimes.

Katherine—Age 34—Female
   Businesslike, handles all transactions. Likes to read. Loves classical music. Opera. Plays clarinet. Makes and keeps appointments for Karen 3.

Karen Boo—Age 21 months—Female
   Cries. Cannot speak English, speaks very little Hungarian. In a lot of pain. Drowsy, sad, cannot walk.

Julie—Age 13—Female
   Always in pain, especially in legs. Afraid of men, the sight of blood. Can't breathe when people smoke. Can't walk.

The Angry One—Age Unknown—Male?
   Hates everyone. Cuts, bruises, stabs. Hates being in a woman's body. Hurts Karen 3 when she wears makeup, nice clothes. The Punisher. Punishes Karen 3 when she tells of ritual abuse.

Sidney—Age 5—Male

Likes to have fun. Likes to steal. Plays tricks on people. Lies. Cries. Likes to get Karen 2 and Karen 3 in trouble with the husband. Abused.

Sandy—Age 18—Female

Compulsive eater. Eats junk food. Blurred vision. Stares out windows. Seems to be in shock. Suicidal. Spends money she doesn't have. Gets Karen 3 in trouble. Quiet. Sad.

Karen 1—Age 10—Female

Very sensitive. Shy. Went to St. Christopher Catholic School. Abused. Wants to stay small. Severe headaches. Hates father. Hates mother. Lonely. Afraid of noises. Hates clowns, polka dots, and coconut. Always hides her chest.

Karen 2—Age 21—Female

Went to college. Worked as secretary. Married Josh. Had two children: James and Sara. No pain, no headaches. Happy. Loves people. Wife, mother.

Karen 3—Age 30—Female

In therapy with Dr. Baer. Depressed. Suicidal. Has headaches. Dormant before Sara's birth.

So Karen 3 is the one who comes to see me! So much is clarified with this little document. I now know there are at least eleven distinct alternate personalities, or "alters" as they are sometimes called, within Karen; they have names, ages, unique and separate personality traits, and their own individual histories. Also, since Claire's letter, Karen is becoming more aware of and familiar with her split-up internal system and I can now talk to her about it. For the past four years, indeed for Karen's whole life, all this has been going on outside of her awareness, and therefore, outside mine. I knew she was disassociating, and I knew the phenomenon was likely due to multiple personality disorder, but we lacked access to the richness of detail that's now being supplied. She's becoming aware of the separate parts within her. This is intensely interesting to me, yet it's important I not show any excitement, lest she be alarmed or think she has to do more of this to please me. I need to keep steady and open and accepting of whatever she brings to me. But it's a real psychiatric adventure.

It's December 1993 and Karen tells me she's beginning to observe the other parts more. She starts describing what's happening inside.

"You mean you can see them?" I ask.

"Sort of." Karen points to the space in front of her. "I can't see them, but I can see what they're doing and hear what they're saying."

"What have you observed?"

"Well, 'Claire' has been crying for several days," says Karen. "Another part, 'Holdon,' takes care of her. When he's occupied with Claire, he isn't available to drive, and a more disabled part takes over and we can't get anywhere." She thinks a moment, her eyes turned up to her left. "We were switching all day Monday and we couldn't function at all. I ran into a woman who I didn't recognize, but who talked to me easily and has apparently known me for many years. I can only assume she must have had a friendship with another part of me. We went to a store and 'Sidney' stole a Christmas ornament; 'Katherine' later paid for it. It's exhausting." I notice she's using the pronoun "we" a lot, as if she sees herself now more as a collective. "All the children inside want love and attention—they want to be touched and held in a nonabusive way."

I hear this last statement as a request for me to "touch and hold" her, but I can't let myself be led down that path.

"Can you get this experience through touching and hugging your children?" I ask.

"Claire doesn't feel anything when I hug my children," says Karen. She's not letting me slip away so easily, I think.

"What have you felt when you've gotten physically close to your husband?"

"I feel my husband married another part of me. We haven't been physically close for years."

We'll have to leave the hugging issue for now, I think, but I want to encourage her to continue to observe the activities of the other parts.

"I think it will be helpful if you learn more about the other parts and observe them when they're out," I say.

"I don't really know much about them yet," she says, "but I feel some parts are quite familiar with all the other parts. Maybe I'm not the part you should be talking to. Sometimes I feel like a passenger in my own life."

Although she feels there are other parts inside her that are more capable of talking to me, I regard Karen 3 as the person I'm talking to and treating. But I really have no basis for regarding her as any more dominant or primary than any other part in her system. Karen 3 is simply the one I know.

During our final session in 1993, before my vacation, Karen gives me a letter from Holdon. The handwriting is round, upright, and shaky. I recall that Holdon is left-handed, so I assume Karen has written this with her left hand.

Dear Dr. Baer,
Please help me with the children.

Even though you may not realize it, since you broke into our system, the children need you more than they need me. Is it possible to explain to them what you're doing over the holidays? It's a mess inside. Claire is crying, Sid is stealing little things, Karen 2 is writing checks with no money in the account, and Julie and Karen 1 are suicidal. The Angry One is trying to convince Karen 3 to kill all of us. The baby is sleeping. Katherine and Karen 2 are trying to stay out and keep control. Karen 2 did all the Christmas decorating and wrapped all the presents that Karen 1 and Karen 3 bought. I come out to make some decisions, to drive, and to try to keep all of us out of trouble. Can you help?

Holdon

I'm not sure how to respond. What do I do? How do I communicate my answer? How can I help?

I still don't have any direct access to the various parts within Karen, and it seems I would need that to give Holdon the help he's requesting. I review again the several books and articles I've gathered on multiple personality disorder and they confirm that I need to make contact with and deal directly with Karen's alternate personalities. I'm uncertain how to go about this. I know how to do it in theory, but theory is not practice.

I'm overwhelmed by what we've uncovered already, and the only course seems to be to continue to uncover more and find a way to talk to Holdon.

In early January 1994, Karen comes to a session looking haggard and worn. She's shivering from the cold and walks quickly to her chair. Her coat is thin and she can't fasten it in the front. I look at her expectantly and she understands her cue to start.

"I've been losing a lot of time," she says. "I'm able to be out with some of the other parts, especially Katherine, Sandy, and Holdon. When relatives came over at Christmas, I watched Katherine organize the entertaining. At night, I'm having dreams about the events that happen during the day when I lose time."

This may be progress, I think, but I point to the cuts on her arm.

"I don't remember how I got them," Karen tells me. "The Angry One had a deadline for New Year's Eve for everyone to die. I think that might have something to do with it."

One day Karen shows me her father's medical report. Although her father was convicted of molesting Karen's niece, I recall his sentencing was delayed because of his illness. The record describes his treatment for liver cancer, not colon cancer, and doesn't give him a good prognosis. It suggests he'll die of his tumor, and fairly soon. Karen still hopes he'll say he is sorry for what he's done.

Meanwhile, since Martin's illness, Karen's mother has been seeking out old acquaintances, some of whom participated in the ring responsible for Karen's abuse, and Karen has been getting strange calls. She's afraid they'll come after her because of what she's told me.

"Someone called last night and asked for me by my maiden

name, laughed, and hung up. I've gotten other calls, too. They frighten me. Someone threatened to hurt me if I continued seeing you. I'm scared. I'm afraid they're going to abuse my kids." Karen shifts uneasily in her chair. I wonder if the people who abused Karen are really still around. I thought most of them were dead.

"You should discuss these harassing calls with Detective Flaherty," I suggest.

"Okay."

I shake my head as she leaves my office. That's all we need— another reason for her to be afraid to come here.

*On April 20, 1994, I begin my first day as Associate Med*ical Director for the Medicare Program. This is a big step for me. I've been thinking about moving into administrative medicine for a few years. I'd thought to become a department chair in psychiatry at some hospital, but through my work as president of the Illinois Psychiatric Society, I met the Medicare Medical Director, a physician who's about ten years older than myself and who has been in administration practically his whole career, and he asked me to apply for the job as his associate. For me, this is like going back to medical school; this job is not in psychiatry, but covers all of medicine.

When the Medical Director first suggested I apply, I said no. I hated Medicare; all I knew about it was they didn't pay doctors enough money. But he talked to me and we got along well. I thought about it overnight, and realized it was an even better position than a department chair, so I signed up.

In my position with Medicare, instead of taking care of individual patients, I take care of a system of medical care. The number of patients under my care has jumped from about a hundred to 2.3 million. I'll never see any of the 2.3 million, but everything I do affects them. Instead of providing care, I developed rules for providing care. It's to be the next phase in my career.

With the Medicare position, I'm able to keep seeing patients a half day a week, and Karen of course is one of the patients I keep. The others I have to refer away, which is hard. Some I've seen for years, and it isn't really fair to sever our relationship, even with the long notice I've given them to prepare. It's sad for all of us.

I'll miss my patients. Once or twice a day in my practice, there'd be a moment, a poignant and moving connection with a patient that touched us both deeply. Usually it involved an insight into some sensitive struggle, some maladaptive feeling or action, that turned out to have been taught to them long ago, learned of necessity, and finally understood and forgivable. In contrast, my compensation for going into the Medicare program will be the constant learning. I'll need to keep up on all the new medical technologies to decide what Medicare will cover locally, and I'll review cases of all types of medical practice. I hope the new position will be continually stimulating.

*Karen continues to lose time unpredictably, although it usu-*ally seems to serve her well when she does. Because she's distressed about the gaps in her life, I want to find a way to communicate with the other parts of her that have remained hidden. The standard technique for this is to use hypnosis and communicate with alternate personalities while the patient is in a hypnotic trance.

It's difficult to define exactly what happens in hypnosis. Although hypnotic trance states have been described for centuries, and studied in medicine for more than a hundred years, there's no way to measure them, no diagnostic test where you can say, yup, she's in a trance. Magnetic resonance imaging (MRI) and positron-emission tomography (PET) scans show little difference between hypnosis and just closing your eyes and using your imagination. But research shows people under hypnosis do act differently from those who aren't. Although the word "hypnosis," coined in 1820 by a French physician, comes from the Greek for "sleep," hypnosis is not sleep or sleep related. Electroencephalogram studies show that individuals in a trance are awake, that they're experiencing a relaxed wakefulness. Their attention may be focused on the words of the hypnotist to the exclusion of all else, or their attention may be focused internally, deep inside themselves, to areas that are more unconscious and not normally accessible to them.

Hypnotizability may be rated by a number of psychological measures, and patients with MPD are notoriously capable of and adept at being hypnotized. But I still was anxious about doing it with Karen, if for no other reason than fear of the unknown. And perhaps fear of my capability to be expert enough at it. For the patient, hypnosis is a talent; for the therapist, it's an art.

Hypnosis also turns upside down the position I've been trying to maintain with Karen all this time. I've always tried to let Karen take the lead in our sessions so as to not influence what may emerge spontaneously from her. But in hypnosis, I take the lead and guide her through the trance experience, fostering a focused attention on what I say or suggest. I can try to keep my suggestions to a minimum, but still it's a significant change from how we've been operating.

Having thought about this, I think it's time to try. I know Karen is ready; I'm more concerned about me. Am I ready?

I suggest to Karen that we start with some relaxation exercises to get her used to relaxing and regressing, that is, going deeper inside herself and getting in touch more with her unconscious self. A technique to induce a hypnotic trance that is sometimes used is to have the patient picture a place that has safe, comfortable associations, and then place herself in it. The place Karen chooses she remembers from childhood: a crawl space behind a plasterboard panel at the back of the front-hall closet. Her grandfather opened this area underneath the stairs when he repaired a pipe. No one ever found her when she hid there. She'd stocked it with dolls and toys that she treasured. This will be the place that I'll have her visualize she's going to when I hypnotize her.

"You'll do just fine," I say on April 21, 1994, the day we begin. "Don't worry; it may take a couple tries to get this to work." Because I know how hypnotizable multiple personality patients are reputed to be, I don't doubt that I can hypnotize Karen. I'm just uncertain what will happen when I do.

"Find a comfortable position in your chair," I start, "and close your eyes." Karen settles in a little and begins to relax. I'm not sure which of us is more nervous; I think it's me.

"Take deep slow breaths . . . feel the tension leave your feet and hands . . . and now your legs and arms . . . all the tension is flowing out through your fingers and toes . . . your shoulders and neck are relaxing, and your body is feeling light." I watch Karen's body language to make sure she's with me, and I'm not getting ahead of her ability to relax with my directions. As I repeat these instructions to her in a slow, soothing patter, I watch her melt into her chair.

"Feel yourself falling deep inside of yourself . . . deeper and deeper . . . more and more relaxed . . . and find yourself in your safe little room . . . where all the items in the room are vivid . . . you can see the colors and textures, and they bring you comfort. Nothing can hurt you in your safe place." I pause a few moments. "Are you there?"

Karen nods her head slowly. "I'm here," she says, drawing out the words, mumbling, as if from sleep.

"What do you see?" I ask.

"I see my two dolls, Raggedy Ann and Raggedy Andy . . ."

"What else?" I ask.

"My blanket and my books." I let her rest there a moment.

"You may not have noticed it before," I say, setting up a structure for this and our succeeding hypnosis interviews, "but there's another door to your safe place. Through this door we may meet some of the other parts within you. Do you see the door?"

"Yes," Karen says slowly.

"Can you describe it to me?" I ask.

"It's small, and it has lots of locks on it," she says. Locks—that's interesting.

"Do you think you could unlock the locks if you wanted to?"

Karen pauses; she has a look of uncertainty about her. "I think so," she says, finally.

"When you feel comfortable enough, go ahead and unlock the locks and peer out the door. Tell me what you see." I'm making all this up as we go, but I need for Karen to have a mechanism to meet her other selves. I sit back and wait for Karen to do whatever she needs to do to accomplish this task, if she's willing to do it at all. My heart is beating faster, waiting for her to open the door, but my voice must remain calm and positive. It seems I wait a long time.

"I'm looking out," Karen says, and pauses.

"And what do you see?"

"I see figures."

"Can you describe them?"

". . . Different . . . different sizes . . . some are tall, some are short . . . children?"

"How many?"

Karen pauses. Is she counting?

"Eleven," she says.

"What else?"

"Some are telling me their names. There's a man, he's tall, he says his name is Holdon. There's little Claire with Katherine. Katherine is thin and older. There's a boy called the Angry One, and a girl-child in boy's clothes. Holdon has his hand over the mouth of the Angry One."

I'm fascinated by what is happening to Karen, but I see she starts to squirm a little in her chair, as if she is becoming uncomfortable or growing fatigued.

"Would you like to return to your little room now?" I ask.

Karen nods her head.

"Why don't you wave good-bye, and let them know you'll return again soon."

I can see in Karen's face she's carrying out these instructions within her trance.

"Why don't you go ahead and close the door and lock it up, and relax again in your little room." Karen relaxes in her chair. I give her a moment. "You can come back to the office here with me as I count backwards from five to one. Five . . . four . . . three . . . two . . . one." Karen slowly opens her eyes as if she has been asleep for hours. She looks distracted and squints to adjust to the light in the room. She also looks a little embarrassed. I smile at her.

"What happened?" Karen asks shyly.

"Do you remember anything?" I ask.

"I'm not sure. I remember looking at something, but I don't remember at what."

"I think it went very well," I say. "You were able to see some of the other parts inside of you, and you told me about them. Overall, they seem pretty friendly."

I am really pleased, relieved really, at how well behaved everybody was, and that Holdon had control of the Angry One. Karen smiles wearily. The whole hypnosis session took only fifteen minutes, but it seemed much longer.

"I think we've made a good start," I say.

A few minutes later Karen makes her way to the door, still a little dazed. I plop back into my chair, dazed, too.

INTRODUCTIONS

The next session, we try hypnosis again, but it doesn't go well. Karen shifts in her chair and can't get comfortable. Her brow is furrowed with worry lines. She can't get very deep in her trance; perhaps I rushed her. She says Claire wants to talk, but she won't come out. I think maybe I'm the nervous one and she's picking it up from me. I reassure her that Claire can come out whenever she likes, and if she's afraid today, there will be lots of other opportunities for her to talk to me. We end the hypnosis part of the session after only a few minutes. I need to make sure I give Karen a safe, calm, and reliable environment in which to experience her hypnotic trance. I vow to do better next time.

The following session, Karen is ten minutes late and tearful. She rushes to her chair, looks about as if unsure of the surroundings, and says she couldn't find the office. She's very agitated, but can't understand why. I suggest we might find out what's troubling her if we can talk to the other parts inside her. She agrees, glad to be bailed out of her present distress. I go through the same relaxation procedure as before, asking her to go deep down inside herself. Once she's fully within her hypnotic trance, her face moves quickly from one frame to the next, and it sounds as if there are several voices speaking in turn.

"Pain!"
"We have to die when he dies."
"The others came about and were born."
"The pain only goes away when you die."
"He said God said so."
"She wanted him dead all her life; that's why she has to kill herself first."

Karen is having a conversation with herself, or there are parts of her all talking to me. She alternately shrieks, grumbles, warns, and prophesies.

I'm really spooked by all this. I suggest to Karen, who is still under hypnosis, and to whoever else might be listening, that she does not have to die. I point out that she can just let her father die and go on living without him. It will give her freedom, and she shouldn't be afraid. She gives no response, but I can see her relax, and when I bring her out of her trance, she's lost all of her initial agitation. I'm not sure which part of her initially came to the session. I want to continue working on the hypnosis, but other events intervene. Her father dies the next week.

With her father's death, Karen starts writing me letters. I say Karen, but I suspect it's a group effort. The first letter she gives me, in a round cursive adult script, is dated May 14, 1994.

Dear Dr. Baer,

On the day of my father's funeral I woke up late and felt disoriented. I lost time in and out of sleep; some of us were restless. At the church, I felt faint and couldn't concentrate on the service. Then I drove myself to the cemetery and I lost time during the memorial service. During this time, all of us kept going in and out, making comments and taking notice. I distanced myself and watched as this was happening. The service lasted about 15 minutes, and this is what I heard the others say.

Karen Boo, "Szeretlek!" [I love you!]

Claire (to Holdon), "Are you sure he's in there? Is this one of his games? It must be dark inside. Are you sure we aren't going to get hurt? I'm still scared."

Holdon, "He can't hurt us anymore. He's dead, gone forever. Remember what Dr. Baer said, 'there are no ghosts.' "

Angry One, "I hope he rots in hell. Let's open his coffin to make sure he's in there."

Sidney, "Can I take the cross? Is that Holy water protecting him?"

Karen 1, "I know he can still hurt me. He never said he was sorry. How come he didn't apologize? Maybe God didn't tell him to do things. Maybe I'm wrong."

Sandy, "It's so sad. Sad, sad, sad: I feel depressed. He always loved me. Without him, I can't live."

Julie, "I'm still in pain. I can't feel my legs. I can't breathe. I want to die."

Karen 2, "Dying is part of life. We must move on. We can have a great future if we try."

Katherine, "It's sad that he had to die this way. Not admitting to himself and others his mistakes. He was in total denial. I don't think anyone really loved him. I won't miss him. I'll have to handle the details. Not much time. Must go. Must notify."

Karen 3, "Why don't I feel anything? Why are they crying? Aren't they relieved? There are less than 20 people here. Nobody really cared."

This letter seems to represent a summary of Karen's reaction, the reaction of all of her, to her father's death. I'm intrigued to note that the different parts of Karen seem to operate autonomously, yet their concerns mirror what Karen has said to me on different occasions.

Karen sends me a thank-you card two days later, with appreciation for my support at her father's death. She ends it by saying, "I feel as though a burden has been lifted off my shoulders, but at the same time I'm so scared. I really don't know how to live. Please, never give up on me."

The Karen who comes to see me isn't the only one calling for help. Mailed and postmarked two days prior to the letter above is another letter.

> Dear Doctor Bear,
>
> Miles says not to talk to you because you will hurt us, says you will lauf at me. I want to tell you about me. I was born on October 29, 1967 on Karen's Communion day. Karen was being hurt. Karen died that day and I was born. Sara is going to be hurt the same way because God said it must be done if you want to go to heaven. Can you stop that man.
>
> Claire

Miles? Who is Miles? And Claire is still stuck in the past when the hurtful men will come to her at any moment.

As a consequence of her father's death, several parts within Karen begin to unravel. Karen begins to have unexplained symptoms. She has rashes that appear and disappear, weakness, swelling, and pain in her legs that apparently belongs to Julie and comes and goes within minutes. She has constant headaches, and her doctor orders an MRI to see what could be the cause. Sandy says she has "swelling of the brain."

There are parts of Karen, especially Julie and Sandy, who have been very close to her parents, and are devastated by their father's death and their mother's vacation in Hungary. Their reaction is a desire to re-create the pain and humiliation that had been the tie that bound them to their parents. Because of this, Karen reports she's been intentionally aggravating her husband so he'll yell at her and hit her. She was always told she should suffer, she says. That was how she achieved closeness with her mother and father: through her suffering. Now that they're gone, her father dead, and her mother in Hungary, parts of her are trying to suffer even more to symbolically reunite with them.

I receive another letter on June 14, this one from Katherine. The handwriting is again different. It's a woman's handwriting, with little loops beginning most capital letters that don't occur with Karen's writing, and *r*'s made in an old-fashioned way.

Dearest Dr. Bear, June 11, 1994

My name is Katherine. I'm part of a system. I take responsibility

for all of the children in this system. It is my job to keep Karen functioning. Painful things have happened to me which I handle as well as I can. Obstacles were put in my path and I don't know why. These problems are not unfair accidents of fate. I was chosen for this. I was born when Karen was 1 year old. It was I that made her leave her parent's home when she was 17. It was I that took over her secretary's job. The year was 1977. Our system has several children (Claire 7, Miles 8, Sidney 5, Karen Boo 2, Julie 13, and Karen 1). Holdon and I keep these children pretty much under control. Each of these children has been severely trauma-tized. I would like to explain to the best of my knowledge their reason for being.

Claire–7 years old–Even though Claire is 7 her age never changed. Claire was born on Karen's Communion Day when Karen's father inserted a cross inside her vagina while pray-ing to God and sprinkling holy water over her to rid her of the demon inside her. Karen couldn't handle the pain so Claire was created. Claire needs warmth and affection.

Miles–8 years old–Miles can't trust anyone, but has developed some feelings for you, Dr. Bear. Miles was created to hold all of the anger. He doesn't want anyone to know about the sys-tem. He is in constant pain. Miles would very much like to kill all of us. Miles was born in 1967; he was 6 years old at birth, aged until 1969 and then stopped and was stuck at 8 years old when the ritual abuse started. Miles was born male and hates being in a female body. Given the chance, he can hurt you, especially if you hurt him first.

Sidney–5 years old–Sidney needs attention. He steals to make others happy. He lies to protect Karen from harm. Sidney has played tricks on others. He likes to have fun when no one is looking. Sidney was born in 1962 when Karen was 3 years old. Karen's father scared her and she had a bowel movement in her underwear. Her father took that bowel movement and made her eat it. Sidney was born to cover up for her father and pretend he doesn't do anything to her.

Karen Boo–2 years old–was born in 1960; she was 2 years old at birth. Karen Boo doesn't understand English, only Hungarian. Karen Boo suffers from severe pain in the head and legs. She took the pain away from Karen during her tumor surgery when she heard her parents wanted to give her up for adoption. Karen pretended not to understand English and Karen Boo was born. Karen Boo took the pain away when Father choked her and bound her legs, arms, and mouth with duct tape hoping she would die. Karen Boo was also thrown against the wall after surgery. Karen Boo was ugly, she had the tumor, nobody loved her, and everyone made fun of her. No one would hug her.

Julie–13 years old–Julie was born 13 years old in 1970 when Karen's father lent her out to his friends for sex. Karen was 11 years old. Julie can't move her legs because of the weight of all the men on top of her. Julie is afraid of men, is afraid of the dark, and gets nauseous at the sight of blood. Julie has asthma and cannot breathe very well. Julie cannot walk. Julie's reason for being is to erase these memories from Karen. Julie's pain is so severe, she is now dying.

Karen 1–10 years old–Karen 1 was born in 1969 when Karen was 10 years old. Karen was raped and sadistically tortured by her grandmother's brother, Constantine. Karen 1 took on this burden. Karen 1 is very sensitive and shy; she wants to stay small and never grow up. She suffers from severe headaches. She is very lonely, and doesn't think anyone likes her, including you. She bound Karen's chest tightly in gauze, *causing pain in her newly developed breasts. She is extremely scared of noises and gets startled quite often. She despises her father and her father's father. This grandfather used clown masks to scare and abuse Karen. Karen 1 hates clowns and polka dots.*

I hope some of this information will help you in treating Karen. Although I would totally understand and trust how you would use this information, I feel Karen is not ready for it. Somehow, someday, I hope we can talk. Although I hear everything being told to Karen, she doesn't have any idea of what my thoughts or actions are.

Sincerely,
Katherine

I take Katherine's advice and don't show Karen the letter at this time. It contains the very kind of information that Karen was being protected from, and I'm not certain when she'll be able to bear it. The information about Miles is disconcerting. He sounds dangerous and unpredictable. And there are several parts, most notably Julie and Karen Boo, who seem to be repositories of pain. What will it be like getting to know them? What I'm learning about Karen is both engrossing and scary.

It is July 1994 and Karen is disassociating multiple times throughout the day. Perhaps she always has, but she's more aware of it now. She's having trouble holding herself together, almost as if she is being torn apart by the switching and turmoil. At the end of July, she ends a session with an uncontrollable crying spell; she's in pain, has a headache, and is frustrated and exhausted with what she's going through. A letter arrives two days later in Katherine's handwriting.

Dearest Dr. Baer,
I'm truly sorry I haven't written sooner but I've been quite busy. You see, there have been many problems within, and I hope

with your help they can be resolved. Karen is in desperate need of help and I thank God you are on the outside helping us. The drug store job is not for her. I've decided not to help out, so Miles and Sidney are working there. They are not capable of doing this type of work; Miles can't organize and Sidney steals. It must stop.

The following is happening within. Miles is quite active these days; he's been out more than usual. He was trying very hard to eliminate your therapy with Karen. Miles is realizing he can't compete and is for the first time calming down. I believe he's starting to like you. Keep up the good work.

Holdon and I are trying to keep up with all activities and appointments, but we are having great difficulty.

Sincerely,
Katherine

It's nice to have Katherine as an ally on the inside. So Miles likes me. That's good. He's been pretty scary. It will be important to form an alliance with him to decrease Karen's self-harm.

I've begun receiving letters from several other parts within Karen. The correspondence is a big help. Often the notes are mailed, but Karen will sometimes deliver them without opening them. She'll find the letters left out by her car keys and she'll know to bring them to me. A disturbing letter from Claire explains Karen's hasty retreat from the last session.

Dear Doctor Bear,

I am sorry I cried and ran out of your office. I did not know I was supposed to pay you to talk to me. I feel sad. I think you don't want to talk to me. I think I want to die now. Those other men pay to hurt me. Do you want to hurt me too?

Claire

Two days later, another letter arrives with Karen's return address, but written in pencil in a small, compact, and regular script. I must admit, I await each letter with both trepidation and excitement. This one reads:

Dear Dr. Baer,

My name is Miles and I am 8 years old. I have black hair and blue eyes. I am mean, I can say the

meanest things you could imagine. I am hard and cold and dark. The only time you can hear me is when we talk about cult things. Most of the time other voices do all the talking for me, mostly Holdon and Sidney. Holdon says it's not socially acceptable for me to talk. I have to be silent so other people will like us. I am in pain all the time. They said I was bad and belonged with bad people. They told me if I told anyone they would come back and kill my loved ones and me. I went to the rituals so Karen wouldn't feel the pain. I am made of three different parts. Myself and Elise, she keeps cult and non-cult things separate for me. Karl handles day to day things. I am tired now.

Miles

I look back at the letter Karen gave me describing her eleven personalities. Miles makes twelve, and now Karl and Elise make fourteen. I wonder if there are more, and how many there might be altogether. It seems for the time being, the other personalities are revealing themselves gradually, and their best mode of communication with me is through these letters. They all seem to be trying to help me—even Miles. The chief benefit to adhering to standard psychotherapeutic technique—that is, not directing, pressuring, or touching Karen—is that I've developed a trusting relationship with all the parts individually, as they observed my treatment of Karen.

A few days later, I receive an envelope with two letters in it: one from Katherine and one from Holdon. Each continues to try to educate me on the architecture of Karen's inner world, of which they're a part. I'm beginning to be able to recognize their respective handwriting. Katherine's letter starts:

> *Dearest Dr. Baer,*
>
> *I hope you received the package of information I sent you. I hope that it was of some use. As I promised I'd like to expand on some of the others within:*
>
> *Juliann is 15 years old, she is the newest*

part of our family. She has a lot of energy and is needed to help with the children within. The only problem is Juliann isn't very organized . . .

. . . Miles is slowly getting used to you. Karl is 10 years old and talks inside to Karen #1. Elise is 8 years old and is very shy. She is very nervous about the fact that Miles told you about her. She wants to be left alone.

Holdon's letter begins:

> *Dear Dr. Baer,*
>
> *Just to let you know everyone was present at our last session, including Ann who hasn't been out in 19 years. The meeting*

has given us some hope. I was worried you wouldn't understand our system. I would like to give you an update.

Claire needs the most immediate attention since she is remembering the abuse. She is feeling guilty because she had to give her pain to Miles. Miles likes pain . . .

. . . The following are still present (name and age):

Claire–7, Karen 2–21, Miles–8, Karl–10, Elise–8, Sidney–5, Juliann–15, Karen Boo–2, Karen 1–10, Katherine–34, Karen 3–30, Holdon (myself)–34, Ann–16.

I'm still making sure Karen gets to your office. Helping her get well isn't easy and we are all happy you are here for us.

Holdon

Is that everybody? After reading the letter, I take a count—thirteen distinct alternate personalities, or alters, so far. I look back at the note Karen gave me some months ago and there were eleven, including one called the Angry One, and Julie and Sandy, which Holdon doesn't mention. That would make potentially sixteen. Are more alters forming, recombining, or simply being revealed? At this point I have two main tasks: to take care of the Karen who comes to see me, whichever part that might be, and to learn about her inner world from its inhabitants. The letters are certainly helpful; Karen's parts seem eager to let me get to know them.

It's August 17, 1994, and we again incorporate hypnosis into our therapy sessions. Once Karen is deep in her trance, I ask if there's anyone who'd like to come and talk with me.

Karen's shoulders go up and she curls her leg to the side and looks at me from the corners of her eyes; it's a small, girlish posture. She says her name is Claire. She begins to tell me the story of what happened to her at the funeral home. She was taken there and tied to one of the stainless-steel tables. She was terrified. There were three men there and they had a metal stick. Then Claire lost time. . . . She asks me to keep the bad men away from her.

Two days later I receive the following letter from Miles, which continues Claire's story.

Dear Dr. Baer,

It's me again and you probably don't want to hear from me. I wanted to tell you about the story Claire couldn't finish. After Claire was tied to the table 3 men put this electric rod inside *her she told them to stop and they shocked her. I got mad and came out and started to scream so they put the gray tape on my mouth. They kept saying that I like it. If I shook my head no, they shocked me, and if I nod yes it feels good, they left me alone for one minute only. After they shocked us Karl came out. These men put Karl into a coffin and closed the lid. I don't know how long we were in there but after a while we heard talking and I came out to hear it. People were looking for us. I pounded on the coffin lid. The mother lady opened the coffin and I let Karen come out. The mother lady, surprised, said "you are alive, you are reborn. I am so happy to see you, why were you hiding in the coffin. You were supposed to be helping Grandpa paint the parlor."*

Do you hate us because of this?

Miles

At the end of one session Karen hands me three letters. One is from Miles. After Karen leaves, I open it. He describes a ceremony called the Midnight Host.

Dear Dr. Baer,

Last night we were to go to the Midnight Host, that is where a girl gets something cut off like her nipple or a piece

of her ear or vagina. Holdon would not take us; he said these people aren't there anymore. I don't believe Holdon, because they are still there in the factory. They were calling us. I hear there voices. The others can't hear them. How can I stop them, they will come and get me and kill us. I can fight, but what about the others? Do you think they will come and get me? I am scared but don't tell the others because they think I am not a scared of anything. If I am scared no one will like me anymore.

Miles

What do I do with this information? He refers to something horrific, but what do I make of it? Is it true? Is it a fantasy? Miles believes it, and so it has to be dealt with. I decide not to ask about it and to wait and see if this comes up during a session.

The next time I see Karen, I mention the letters and suggest hypnosis to see if there's more information that the other parts of her want to offer. The first alter to speak is Sidney. Karen closes her eyes and her facial expression disappears for a moment. Then she opens her eyes and sits back in the chair with her head cocked up at an angle, looking at me askance. Then she quickly surveys the room, as if for the first time.

"I like our job at the drugstore," she says. Karen, as Sidney, speaks fast, and her eyes dart about the room. "I take things I never had before—toys and things, although Katherine usually brings them back. I stole a bunch of Superballs. I put them in Karen's purse. James and Sara really liked them. I know I shouldn't take things, but the father makes me do it. After I take them, I have to be punished, so sometimes I'll also take something to cut myself with, like a fingernail file. The drugstore is great."

As I listen to Sidney, I hear an impulse-ridden little boy without any self-control. I don't want to comment too much, so I just say, "Stealing requires cutting as punishment?" He confirms this, but I put a seed of doubt in his mind, since my question, while not disparaging, does show him that I don't regard his actions as necessary and obvious. It will make him think. I thank Sidney for coming to talk and ask him to step back so we can see if anyone else would like to talk. Karen closes her eyes and Sidney vanishes from her expression. It amazes me how clearly Karen transforms herself when a different part of her appears. She becomes completely that alter. There's no bleeding of one alter's mannerisms into another. Miles comes forward next. Karen sits up a little straighter; she keeps her eyes closed, her brows knit together, and her voice becomes gruff.

"I like work, too," Miles says. "At work I get to be the boss."

"You're in charge," I confirm.

"Yeah, I like to talk to people, and if they get out of line, I tell them."

It's clear Miles likes to get the chance to feel important. This is something I need to foster. I want to build an alliance with each of Karen's parts, and Miles is a very important one, as he, and to a lesser extent Sidney, seem to be the parts responsible for harming Karen. If I can be seen by them as a trusted and powerful person, I might be able to influence their self-destructive actions.

After we speak for a few minutes, I thank Miles and ask him to step back. I then ask if there's anyone else who'd like to talk to me. Karen relaxes a little, closes her eyes, and goes blank again for a moment. Then, in an instant, she melts and becomes small and childlike. Claire smiles at me and her eyes shine. She says she likes to look at the greeting cards, the perfume and jewelry. Claire has a feminine side! This is good news. Karen allows herself almost no traditionally feminine interests. Her clothes are drab; she does not often fix her hair or wear makeup. I'd been worried that Karen's overall development is limited by having no capacity for the expression of her femininity, but Claire holds these qualities. That means at some point they'll be available to Karen.

The last to talk to me is Juliann. Karen closes her eyes, goes blank, and then she sits up straighter, her arms tensed at her sides, as if bracing for something. Her eyes open wide, she says she has something terrible to tell me. She knows she isn't supposed to talk about it, but since the father died, maybe she wouldn't be hurt if she tells. I assure her she won't be hurt, and that I will help keep her safe. She seems reassured. She tells me about the Midnight Host ceremony. She went through it about ten times. It was like witchcraft. They would tie her down and take tiny bits of flesh from her. Many people were involved. The first time Karen took part, she was four years old. They would cut her arm, face, or ear, and take some skin or a few drops of blood. Hair, eyelashes, or eyebrows might do, but when they were older, they would cut her breasts, take some skin off her nipple or vagina. When this happened, the boys would come out, and they couldn't feel it when Karen's female parts were hurt. Later her parents would blame Karen for it and tell her she did it to herself in her sleep.

I tell Karen at the end of the hypnosis session, before I bring her out of her trance, that she will not remember the contents of what was just discussed. This is the stuff that the others have protected her from all these years. I'm not certain that she can handle memories this disturbing without hurting herself. So in the absence of certainty, I decide to wait.

A week later, as I'm pondering what to tell Karen about the Midnight Host, she comes in, looking sheepish and ashamed.

"I hurt myself again," she says, turning her face away, humiliated. It is clear she had hurt herself, but how and to what extent?

"Exactly how did you hurt yourself?" I ask. "I need to know how you might be hurt." I wait. Karen's eyebrows turn toward the ceiling and she begins to cry. "I don't remember much about it—I wasn't in control—but I think I took a hanger apart and put the sharp end inside me." She looks as if she is going to throw up.

"Did you bleed?"

"Yes."

"Are you still bleeding?"

"No."

"Did you have pain?" I continue.

"Yes."

"Do you still have pain?"

"A little. Not like before."

"If you press on your stomach, does it hurt?" I ask.

"No, not really."

With these questions, I'm trying to find out if she broke the tissues of her vagina, and if so, whether she perforated the vaginal wall or peritoneum, in which case she might have an abdominal infection. I'm not sure, but it doesn't sound too bad, physically anyway. Now I need to find out what happened mentally. Hypnosis is the only way since Karen doesn't have enough information.

Under hypnosis, Karen sits stiff in her chair with her eyes closed.

"I was trying to cut out the female parts," he says, his face hard with fear. It's Miles; he was responsible, I think. "The mother lady keeps talking about the father and I'm afraid he's coming back to hurt us. I was going to cut out Karen's female parts so she couldn't be hurt anymore. And if Holdon hadn't stopped me, I would've." Miles sits back in the chair, eyes still shut and teeth clenched. "Now I just want us all to die."

Miles by now knows me; we've spoken several times. He also

is aware of the esteem that the other parts have for me, and that gives me an authority I hope to use.

"Miles," I say kindly but firmly, "the father is dead. He can no longer hurt you. You no longer need to be afraid of him. There is no need to try to escape him."

Miles pauses and considers this. He is struggling. He keeps his eyes shut.

"Are you sure?" he asks.

"I'm absolutely sure, Miles."

"Okay, okay," he says. He is still trying to take this all in. I can see the struggle in his face. And then he begins to relax. I can see relief come over him.

"He can't hurt us anymore?"

"No." I pause to see if Miles will fully accept this. He's coming around. "So there's no need to do any more cutting on Karen. Okay, Miles?"

"Okay."

11

CHRISTMAS PRESENT

Karen arrives with her arm bandaged and in a sling. Her brow is drawn and her eyes are afraid. She looks at me briefly, and then down and away.

"What happened?" I ask, alarmed. "Did your husband hurt you?"

"No," she says, tearful and shaking, "the drugstore was robbed. I was the only one there."

"But how did you get hurt?"

Karen looks at the floor and shakes her head. "I don't remember."

"Some other part was out?" I ask.

"I suppose. I told the police the robber did this, but I don't really know. I found a woman in the pharmacy trying to steal drugs. She had a knife; I don't know what happened after that."

"Perhaps we can find out under hypnosis." Karen is now accustomed to our hypnosis routine, and she shifts in her chair to a comfortable position and closes her eyes. I start saying the now-familiar words to get her to relax and go deep down inside herself, deeper and deeper, until she finds herself in her safe little room. When she's ready, I ask her to go outside her little room to see if there's someone who can tell us how she got hurt.

In just a moment, Karen's back stiffens, her eyes shut tight, her brow descends into a scowl, and her voice becomes a little lower and tougher.

"I did it," she says.

"Miles?"

"Yeah."

"What did you do?"

"I hit her."

"You hit the robber?"

"Yeah, she held out a knife and tried to stab us. Karen got scared so I came out. I wasn't scared. I wasn't afraid to get cut."

"So what did you do?"

"I punched her right in the face. She staggered back, and then came at me with the knife. I put my arm up; that's how I got cut. Then I punched her again and started cussin' at her. She ran out of the store. I got her real good." Miles sits back with a smile on his face. I'm amazed by all this.

"That's quite a story," I say. "You were very brave."

"Aw, I just didn't like her stealing from the store, not while I'm in charge."

"I'm glad you weren't hurt any worse."

"This is nothin'."

"Still, if she'd killed you, where would we be then?"

"We'd be dead, just like I wanted."

"I see."

After saying good-bye to Miles, I end the hypnosis session by bringing Karen back into her little room, then back to my office. She looks around and squints at the light.

"It seems one of the other parts struggled with the robber," I say.

"I thought so," says Karen.

"I'm not sure it's safe for you to work at the drugstore anymore," I say. "What happened last night could happen again, and it could be worse, and you'd have no way to prevent it."

Karen thinks about this and slowly nods her head. Before she leaves, almost as an afterthought, she hands me three letters. They are from Miles, Katherine, and Claire. I open them as I hear her close the door.

Claire writes:

> Dear Doctor Bear,
>
> Can I come live with you.
> I wont be bad. Evenbody is sad.

I want to sleep forever and so does Sidney. We are so tired. Katherine is trying to teach me about faith. Do you have faith? Can you give me some? Karen Boo keeps crying. She's scared that Miles is going to hurt us. Can you tell Miles to be nice?

Miles writes:

> Dear Dr. Bear,
>
> Please talk to the Mother Lady. Tell her to go away. She makes me so mad I want to kill us. She doesn't know how much pain she causes.

Sometimes I get so mad I want to tell her about us, but Katherine and Holdon stop me. I can't take her anymore. She pretends that we had a perfect childhood and that Karen was always happy. This is not true. We are falling apart and are afraid you are going away. If I come out in your office, will you be mad? I have a lot to say but I can't. Karen is starting to share my thoughts but she can't act like me.

Miles

Katherine writes:

> Dearest Dr. Bear,
>
> We have been miserable. We need your help. Do you realize whats happening to us?

We are getting weaker; most of us are feeling suicidal. There has been damage to our communication: too much interference. We are trying to cope the best we can, but we can't function when Karen has lost the will to live. She has so many worries and needs to talk about them, only she feels helpless and won't talk. I feel she needs to stop resisting and let us come out with you. Karen is also not taking the medication you prescribed like she should. We are all worried and hope this weakness is temporary.

Sincerely,
Katherine

From these letters it is clear that everybody inside Karen is in his or her own particular distress and things are chaotic, but it also seems that several parts look to me for help and want to talk more.

It's the end of November 1994 and winter is threatening the air. When Karen enters, she's slightly bent over and has the reluctance of a child who's come to confess. She told me on the phone two days before that she was having stomach swelling and cramps off and on and she didn't know why. She looks as if she is still having them. She sits down in the chair in pain and looks away from me with humiliation on her face.

"I can see you're in distress," I say. "Can you tell me about it?" I sit back to signal to Karen I'm going to wait. Karen sits with her own thoughts for a while. Then, without looking at me, she begins to slowly pull up her blouse. As she pulls it higher and higher, she reveals over a dozen horizontal cuts on the surface of her stomach. She bites her lip and begins to cry.

"I see," I say softly. "What can you tell me about this?"

Karen just shrugs her shoulders. It is clear she doesn't know how they got there. She pulls down her blouse.

"Is this what's causing the stomach cramps?"

Karen shrugs her shoulders again but shakes her head, still looking away. It seems the answers I'm looking for don't reside with the Karen I'm talking to.

"There are a number of important things going on," I say, "and I think some of the other parts inside you might have information that can help. Shall we see what we can learn?"

Karen nods and closes her eyes, and we begin the hypnosis session.

"Hi."

"Hi, who's there?" I ask.

"It's me."

"Miles?"

"Yeah."

"What can you tell me about Karen's troubles?"

"I didn't do it."

"Didn't do it?"

"I didn't cut her."

"Oh!" I'm surprised.

Miles pauses. "You thought I did it?"

"What can you tell me?" I ask, ignoring his question. I don't want to ask him directly to snitch on who did it, but I'm curious to see what he'll tell me on his own. Miles looks me over.

"Jensen did it. Seventeen cuts—one for each of us. He's a jerk. He's always getting me into trouble. I get blamed for everything." Miles sets his face hard.

I can tell Miles is not friendly toward Jensen, whom I don't remember hearing about before, and who says there are seventeen alters. At my last count there were up to sixteen, including the Angry One. I'm curious about that alter since it's the only one without a name. Jensen would make seventeen.

"It seems I should learn more about Jensen. I wouldn't want to think you did something you didn't do." I'm trying to make up with Miles for my surprise, and he relaxes a bit.

"Yeah, he's pretty funny, all right."

"What about Karen's stomach cramps and swelling?" I ask.

"Oh, that's Sandy. She thinks she's *pregnant*," he says with a sneer.

"Could she be?"

"Nah, I know how that works. I make sure no one touches us down there."

"So she's making it up?"

"I guess so."

"Well, Miles, as always you've been very helpful. I would have been surprised if you'd hurt Karen, since you said you wouldn't. I wonder if any other part of you has something they'd like to share? Perhaps you could step back, and we can see if someone else would like to talk to me. See you next time."

"Okay, bye."

"Bye."

I wait a moment as Karen's face goes back to normal, at least what I'm used to seeing as normal, and then soften and become girlish and tentative. I wait another moment.

"Hello?" I ask.

"It's dark in here," says a little voice.

"Where are you?" I ask.

"In the closet. Me and Thea."

"Is that you, Claire?"

"Yes."

"What are you doing in the closet?"

"Hiding."

"Hiding from what?"

"From the men. If they find me, they'll hurt me."

"And Thea?" Thea is new—number eighteen? Jensen thought there were seventeen.

"She keeps me company," Claire continues, "when I'm frightened."

I realized she still thinks the men from her past are still about to hurt her. Perhaps I can help with this. If I recall correctly, Claire is about seven years old; she might be able to understand the passage of time.

"What year is it, Claire?"

"What year is it?"

"Yes, can you tell me?"

"It's 1967."

"Is that the last time you were hurt, in 1967?"

"Yes, why?"

"I'd like you to listen carefully to me, Claire. What I have to say may come as a surprise, but it may also help you."

"Okay."

"It's not 1967 anymore. It's 1994, the end of November. Twenty-seven years have passed. The father who hurt you is dead, and all the other men have gone away. There's no one to hurt you anymore." I wait while it sinks in.

"I don't believe you."

"Ask Katherine and Holdon what year it is."

"Okay, wait a minute."

Claire is gone for a moment. Karen sits impassively, her face expressionless, until Claire returns.

"You're right!" Her face lights up. "You mean the father and the men won't hurt me anymore, ever?"

"No, not ever. You don't need to hide in the closet if you don't want to. In fact, you could watch while some of the others are out, if you like. I'll let you work that out."

"Thanks, Dr. Baer."

"You're welcome, Claire. I hope you can be happier now and not want to die. Perhaps you could step back and we'll see if someone else would like to talk to me."

"Bye."

Karen leans back slightly in her chair and a look of strain comes over her face. Her right hand drifts up and circles her abdomen, the way a pregnant woman would feel her distended uterus. She speaks with effort.

"Dr. Baer."

"Yes."

"It's Sandy."

"How are you feeling?"

"I'm having contractions."

"Uh-huh."

"I think I may be having a baby. Dr. Loeschen says it's a . . . what's it called? A hernia—he says we'll need surgery. That's fine with me."

"Having surgery is fine?" Sandy is sounding pretty crazy, so I'm trying just to keep her talking so I can figure out how crazy.

"I like surgery."

"What do you like about it?"

"The pain."

"What do you like about the pain?"

"It makes me feel real."

"Real . . . like it makes you feel alive."

"Yes, alive. It's the only way I can feel. I like the pain surgery brings. I can fool the doctors."

"Fool the doctors?"

"Yes. I can be sick just by thinking about it."

"Sandy, I think it might be a good idea if you shared time with some of the others. Do you know about the others inside Karen?"

"Of course; don't be silly. There are seventeen of us now. There could be more, but there are seventeen functioning right now."

"Are there any that you get along with well?"

"Yes, I like Juliann." A good choice, I think. That part is pretty normal.

"Why don't you try and observe while she's out. Perhaps you can share some of her feelings and feel real that way. The stomach pains are distressing to the others."

"Oh, really? Well, I suppose I could try."

"We'll talk again soon." Sandy is a little scary. I assume she is responsible for Karen's stomach cramps. Apparently they can be quite incapacitating. I'll have to wait and see if I've had any impact on her.

Christmas is approaching. It's the last session before my vacation, and Karen comes in holding a present and a card. She displays more energy than usual. I know we won't be able to talk about anything else as long as she's holding the present she wants to give me, so I look at her, then the present, and lift my eyebrows.

"I have something for you. Merry Christmas, Dr. Baer." She hands me a slender box with a card on top. She's watching me closely to see what I'll do with it.

"Shall I open it?" I ask.

"Oh, yes!" she says. "Then read the card."

I unwrap the box and find a red tie. The tie has figures of children standing on each other's shoulders, four on the bottom, then three, two, and one. They're in the shape of a pyramid or Christmas tree. On the back, the label says "Save the Children" and there is a quote: "Today's children are the framework of tomorrow." How true for Karen.

"It's wonderful," I say, "I really like it." I really do. How great it is not to have to fake it—which is seldom successful with so perceptive a patient. I open the card and read it. What a wonderful story it tells.

Dec. 1994

Dear Dr. Baer,

We would like to wish you and yours family a very Merry Christmas, and to show

our appreciation we would like you to have this special gift. We would also like to tell you how special this gift is and how it came about. One day while we were out and Karen was asleep, Holdon was reading the paper, Claire started flipping channels on the TV when an ad caught her eye; it was part of the "Save the Children" charity. Claire loved this tie and wanted it for you so she called out for the others to see. All of a sudden, as I sat back to watch, I saw and heard all of the other's thoughts and this is what was said. Katherine said it was a lovely idea and a perfect gift for you. Karen Boo asked if it feels soft, and asked if she could touch it. Miles said, "Would Dr. Baer really wear that tie? He must have a million ties already!" But Miles also liked it. Thea said we are not afraid of ties anymore and could we really get it for Dr. Baer. Sidney said the kids on the tie look like us. Claire then said a girl named Tracy made the tie. Holdon interrupted and said she "designed" it. Holdon liked the tie but missed the ordering information. Sandy was excited and said she'd call the TV station. Jensen said the tie was neat. Ann said she liked the tie and that the money donated for the tie would help children. Karen 2 said, "Dr. Baer means so much to all of us, I'd like to get it for him too." Julie said, "Look, the kids on the tie are like a pyramid." Juliann said, "The tie seems to symbolize us growing together." Karen 3

said, "Isn't that what we are all about? This gift is a great idea."
Karl said Dr. Baer is good and deserves much more than a tie.
Katherine then said, "Karl, this isn't just any tie, it's the first thing
we've all agreed upon." Elise asked if you were our family. Holdon
said, "In a good sense, he is." Elise then asked if she could wrap
the tie. Katherine said yes. Miles said, "Will Dr. Baer be mad
at us for buying him a gift?" Karen 1 said, "I hope not. I like
him and he always helps us. Besides, the tie is cute and it is
Christmas."

Sandy then called for information, Holdon ordered it, Katherine
wrote the check, and we let Claire mail it.

This is the first time we all made a decision together and we feel
this is making progress. We are glad it is for you because we really
appreciate all you do for us. We hope this tie will remind you of us
and possibly put a smile on your face.

Merry Christmas × 17

It is the most amazing Christmas present I have ever gotten.

12

SEPARATE LINKS

The stress of Karen's different parts becoming aware of one another is giving her headaches. The parts don't always agree. Some of them start to keep a journal in which they can all write and then show me, but one of the parts burns it. Now that several parts have made their existence known to me, I invite them to come forward during the hypnosis sessions. They had been holding back, not knowing if it was all right for them to talk. It didn't occur to me they required permission. Karen asks for extra time during the next several sessions so several other parts can have more time to talk. She hopes to get some relief from the pressure of the competing voices in her head, but they have only begun to be heard. Karen, I fear, will only get worse before she gets better.

When Karen arrives next, we pass over the preliminaries quickly. There is so much to learn about all the separate parts within her and we want to get going. Karen slips into her hypnotic trance easily now. I probably just need to say *go to sleep* and she would, but I hold to our routine of trance inducement to provide a reliable structure for her and the others.

"When you're ready," I say after she's in her trance, "you can go out of your safe little room, and we'll see if anyone would like to speak with us."

"Hello . . . this is Ann." Karen sits erect, with a posture that suggests earnestness, attention, and poise. Her voice is both tentative and calm, and her face shows kindness. Interestingly, her manner puts *me* at ease.

"Hello, Ann, I'm Dr. Baer."

"Yes, I know," she says. "How do you do? This is my first time doing this and I'm a little afraid."

"I hope this can be an opportunity for me to get to know you," I say, "and the other parts inside Karen, so that I might be better able to help."

"That's what Katherine said; that's why I agreed to come and talk to you."

"What would you like to share about yourself?"

"I was born when Karen couldn't handle church—to keep the proper faith."

"Karen couldn't handle church?"

"Some of the men who hurt her were from the church. They used words from church ceremonies when they hurt her. She couldn't stand to go inside a church, so I was born."

"How old are you?"

"I'm sixteen. I was born when Karen was ten, and I was eleven when I was born. I know it's a little confusing."

"It seems you were born for a specific purpose."

"Well, yes, of course." It seems all of the parts I've met were born to deal with specific parts of Karen's traumatic emotional experience.

"I see. What more can you tell me?"

"I don't know; there's so much. I was always the nice one. I've always been very religious. The nuns liked me. I was their favorite at school. I'd help the principal and pastor. I acted like nothing was wrong. I wanted to be a nun, but I couldn't because . . . of what was done to us. I was unclean. But I worked at Saint Jerome's, the hospital for hurt and damaged children, even though the father beat me when I went there. He always said charity began at home."

Ann falls silent. She's thinking about something.

"What is it?" I ask.

"I have a confession to make."

"Oh?"

"I burned the journal."

"Really? Why?" I'm surprised it was her.

"I was angry you didn't write back. I thought you read it every day. I thought you weren't listening to us."

"The journal was to be a way for the other parts to tell me their thoughts and concerns. Karen was to collect them and give them to me later. Unfortunately, I'm not able to see you every day."

"Oh, my, I'm so ashamed!" says Ann, her hand coming to her mouth. "I didn't understand. I thought you didn't care."

"It's a loss to me," I say. "Perhaps you can help the others reconstruct what they wrote, and it will turn out all right."

"I'll try." Ann pauses; her eyes drift up and sideways, looking at nothing in particular. "There's something you may not know," she continues. "I was the one who fainted at Karen's wedding. Well, not just me. Different parts kept coming out while Karen was at the altar. I came out later and fainted again. I couldn't believe what was happening. Karen 1 was the one who actually wanted to get married. She was only ten years old, but she wanted to be a mother and have children. When we realized what was happening, it was too late. I didn't even know who we were marrying. It was all quite a shock."

Ann pauses, lost in her own thoughts. It amazes me what a wealth of information she just tossed off. It seems as if, collectively, the parts inside Karen must know everything. Since Karen has such trouble with her mother, I wonder if Ann could help with that.

"Do you have a relationship with Karen's mother?"

"Thank God, no. Sandy or Sidney deal with her. It was Sidney who was out when the mother scrubbed Karen's face with a wire brush for putting on makeup. Karen was fourteen. I don't like to think about it."

"I'd like to really thank you for sharing all this with me," I say. "It's very helpful. I look forward to talking to you again. If you're ready, perhaps you can step back and we'll see if anyone else has something to share."

"Thank you, Dr. Baer. It was a pleasure talking to you, too."

Karen's face goes blank momentarily, her posture shifts, almost imperceptibly, and she begins to speak more formally, but with less grace and poise.

"Hello, Dr. Baer, it's a pleasure to meet you at last."

"Katherine?"

"Why, yes, I'm sorry I didn't introduce myself. I forget it's not apparent to you who you're talking to."

"I recognized your manner of speech," I say. "I'm glad to talk to you, too. I've wanted to get to know you. I wonder if you would start with a little background. When were you born?"

"I've been here very much from the beginning. I was born when Karen was a year or two old. It was my job to take care of Karen. Holdon was born shortly thereafter. Karen was abused and neglected from the start. Holdon had the strength to protect, and I had the intelligence to take care of everything."

"When do you come out?" I ask.

"When something needs to get done. I do a lot of the cleaning and cooking. When Karen worked as a secretary—that was me. There have been long stretches of time when Karen doesn't come out at all." I wonder which Karen she means, but I let it go.

"How long? Do you mean for weeks?"

"Oh, no, Karen, the Karen that comes to see you has been gone for years at a time. She didn't come out at all during high school. We were continually beaten and sexually abused during high school. Karen wouldn't come out then. It was mostly Karen 2 and the boys who were out."

"How did you decide to come to see me?" I ask. "I assume it was you that made the decision."

"You're right about that. I brought Karen to your office that first day."

"Why me?"

"I talked to other patients who'd seen you, and they said you understood them. But when you saw us those first times, I wasn't so sure; I was checking you out. I needed to know if you'd care about us. I looked at your diplomas. I called the state medical society to see if you'd gotten in any trouble."

"Did you find anything that concerns you?"

"No, I think I made a good choice. I think we're on the right track."

"Do you have an idea how this therapy ought to go?" I ask, hoping for some help.

"No, I think you know what you're doing. I just don't think this can be rushed." Katherine reminded me of a schoolteacher. She was being patient with me and encouraging me to do my best.

Our time was up. Instead of being given help, I was told to be patient. Perhaps that was good help after all. Katherine was telling me what my supervisors had told me. "Sit back and let it unfold. Your job is to understand, and when you understand, help the patient understand." The temptation to proceed according to the therapist's own agenda instead of the patient's is always strong, and always wrong.

In the middle of January 1995, Karen comes into my office, hesitates at the door, and looks around behind the furniture and under the desk. Finally, she goes to her chair. She has a rolled-up sheaf of papers in her hand. As she sits stiffly in her chair, she looks from side to side, suspiciously. She holds up the roll of papers to her eye and looks through it at me like a pirate with a spyglass. I have the feeling this isn't Karen, so I decide to wait and see what happens.

After being satisfied we're alone, the person across from me looks at me for an uncomfortable length of time.

"Karen couldn't come."

"I see. Who's come in Karen's place?"

"Sidney."

"Ah, Sidney. I've been hoping I'd get to see you again."

"Holdon made me come. He wanted me to bring these." Sidney puts the roll to his eye again. "It's a kaleidoscope." Sidney holds out the roll of paper to me and winces as he does so. I take it; it's a letter from Holdon. I put it aside to concentrate on Sidney.

"I'm glad you came." Sidney eyes me for a moment, but relaxes his shoulders a little.

"Karen is sick," he says. "Holdon wants you to have the papers. I come out now with Holdon and Miles and the other boys." Sidney looks out the window, peering down to see how far it is to the ground.

"When you handed me the papers, it looked like your arm was hurting."

"My arm always hurts. Father made me steal, and if I didn't do it right, he'd twist my arm or punch it. I can't feel my fingers; Father would hit them with a stick for stealing."

"I thought you said he made you steal?"

"Yeah, he did, then he'd punish me for it."

"Did you know Karen's father died?" Sidney looks at me with his eyes wide, surprised. He hesitates again, pulling his head back and looking at me askance.

"Yes," I say. "He died of cancer about a year ago. He can't hurt you anymore. I'm trying to help Karen and Holdon make all of you feel better."

"You're trying to trick me."

"Ask Holdon." Sidney looks blank a moment, then looks at me again.

"It's true; I didn't know."

"It sounds like you had a hard time with the father. What you suffered has given you a lot of strength and courage, but also a lot of pain. I think it will help you and the others if you could share some of what you experienced, and it might help the others if you could share some of your strength." I'm trying to lay the groundwork here for eventual integration of all the parts.

After Sidney leaves, I turn to the papers he brought. There's a letter in Holdon's handwriting.

> Jan 6 '95
>
> Dear Dr. Baer,
> I would like to try to start the reconstruction of the burnt journal. To begin with we need to

update our being. Below I will list all of us and who is out and about these days. As of now there are 17 of us. I will try to expand a little on each.

Holdon (myself), 34 years old. I try my best to protect all of us. I hold on to the knowledge of Karen's birth. I make most of the decisions on who is allowed out. I drive most of the time. I am mechanically inclined; I fix things, build things, paint, wallpaper, etc. I very much want to be a paramedic. I am a temporary comforter to the children within. I was created to be the perfect son to

*work alongside Karen's father and grandfather. I can do most any-
thing. I do not feel pain.*

*Katherine is also 34 years old. She knows about everyone. She
makes and keeps appointments. Katherine was born right after me
when Karen was less than a year old. We age as she ages. Katherine likes to read and was responsible for getting us in therapy.
Katherine also feels no pain.*

*Claire is seven years old and is very insecure. Right now she is
sad because she feels forgotten by you. I've tried to encourage her
to come out and talk but she's hurting too much. She has terrible
headaches.*

*Sidney is five years old and is in pain. He wants to have fun
and likes to get us in trouble. He gets us in the strangest predica-
ments and leaves. He still wants to steal things to give to other
people. His hands and fingertips are numb. He took on some terrible abuse.*

*Sandy is 18 years old and has been a problem among us. It was
nice when Sandy was quiet and just stared out the window. But
somehow she woke up. She's had many suicidal plans. She is a
compulsive eater of junk food. She is sad and depressed and wants
to take over. She claims she can get you angry with us and you'll
give up. She seemed to get worse when Karen's father died.*

*Julie is 13 years old and is in so much pain that when she's out
I think we will all die. She can't breathe very well. She has black
hair and green eyes. She can barely walk.*

*Karen Boo is 21 months old. She cannot speak English very
well. She understands some Hungarian. She can't see because of
the tumor over her eye. She cries "owie!" has leg pains, and vaginal pain. She needs to be soothed by your voice.*

*Miles is eight years old and seems to be calming down. He
doesn't hate everyone anymore because he likes you. He wants
you to like him so he hasn't been hurting us. He still hates being in
a woman's body. Miles still feels pain from the abuse. Miles goes to
all sports events with James and Sara.*

*Karl is ten years old and is upset that the journal was burnt;
he had written many details of the abuse and hoped he would
never have to talk about it again because during his writing,
Karen was the sickest. He feels the most severe pain and prefers*

us to end the suffering. When Miles couldn't handle the pain, Karl took it.

Elise is eight years old and she keeps Miles' and Karl's regular life and the abuse separate. Elise writes poems in Hungarian and none of us have a clue what they mean. She feels God will forgive us for being born. She always knew the abuse was wrong.

Thea is six years old and she was born in 1965 when Karen had an aneurysm and was told by the parents they hoped she would die. When Karen didn't die as expected, Thea took her place totally for 1½ years. During this time Karen did not exist; she slept. Thea holds all the memories during that time.

Karen 1 is ten years old and was born in 1969, she was eight when she was born and grew for two years and stopped at age ten. Karen 1 is very sensitive and shy. She was lonely in 1979 when she met Josh and her innocent ways attracted him. She wished for a wedding and got one. She's afraid of noises, polka dots, clowns, the smell of cocoanuts, and Brut cologne. She suffers headaches and hates her mother and father.

Juliann is 15 years old and has a lot of energy. She doesn't worry about anything. She's unorganized, inconsistent, cancels appointments, and is promiscuous. She likes to talk, and sometimes talks too much. She wants to tell our story to you. She was born in 1970 when Karen was 11 years old.

Jensen is eleven years old and was born in 1971 when Karen was 12 years old. Jensen took over and fought back when Karen was raped with a hanger by her Grandmother's brother, Constantine. Jensen wrapped the bite marks and flattened Karen's chest to become male. Jensen wants to hurt all who hurt us. Jensen especially hates older men. He feels that if given the chance, they will hurt us.

Ann is 16 years old, and although usually religious, has lost faith. She cannot understand why there is so much sadness in the world. Ann was born in the late '60s or early '70s. She went to Catholic school for Karen and was the teacher's and principal's pet. She worked in the rectory, in the office, and went to church everyday. Always ashamed of the rest of us, she went to confession often and made up sins. She has always felt we should be blamed for what we are, and only God could forgive us.

Karen 2 is 21 years old and was born in 1969 when Karen was ten. Karen 2 went to school, worked alongside Katherine as a secretary, and delivered her son James. She has no headaches or pain and loves to be with people. She feels lucky to be alive. She started to deliver her daughter Sara, then Claire came out all hysterical and that started our total collapse. Karen 2 has been dormant since 1985.

Karen 3 is 30 years old and was reawakened four days after Sara was born in 1985. She has been our last birth. She was chosen to begin therapy. All memories told to you were information we fed her. She is depressed and suicidal. She has a sense of some of us, but not all. Karen 3 is the one you see most often.

I put down the sheaf of papers and think how odd it is that a human being can be organized this way. It's an alternative way of thinking and functioning, but it uses the same mental tools, the same brain, we all have. If we all grew up under the circumstances the letter describes, maybe we'd all operate the way Karen does. I wonder at the complex weave of relationships we would have if each of us knew different slices of each other. Falling in love would be like this therapy, where you slowly make the acquaintance of all the other parts and try to get them on board in the relationship.

I took note that Holdon said he was born before Katherine. Katherine said the opposite. Maybe there's a little competitiveness among the alters. I've noticed other small inconsistencies in the details the other parts have told me; not contradictions, just slightly different versions of the details. I don't need to adhere to any one version at this point; it's probably not reasonable to expect the alters to have perfect recall of every detail over the span of decades. In fact, it amazes me just how internally consistent Karen's system is.

During this time, the structure of the therapy sessions changes. I now only spend a brief, initial time with Karen (Karen 3), and then the bulk of the session is conducted under hypnosis talking to the others.

"I feel terrible," says Sandy, "nothing is going my way. Everyone else is afraid of the figures that come at night . . . they're not real;

they're just dreams. Julie, Thea, and Jensen want to die. Juliann is afraid the father will come and hurt them."

"Could you tell them it's just a dream?"

"They won't listen to me. It makes me crabby. I don't want to live in the past. Everything reminds me of it: tools, electrical cords, silverware, everything. The memories are still there, even for me."

"It must be a terrible burden for you," I say, "all those memories, when you want to move forward."

"Yeah, but Julie's hurting the most. She can't talk or walk. The weight of the men is still on her legs."

"Perhaps I can talk to her . . ."

"Just a moment," says Sandy, and she ducks back inside.

Karen sinks in the chair and puts her legs out straight, with her heels resting on the floor. She has her eyes closed, and her face gets puffier somehow, as if she's subtly bloating before my eyes.

"How are you feeling, Julie?" I ask.

"I'm hurting; I feel sick to my stomach," says Julie, "I feel like there's a penis in my throat."

"Can you move your legs?"

"A little." Julie struggles as if pinned and moves one leg slightly to the side.

"What does it feel like?"

"They're on me. I can't move. I can't breathe."

"Julie, you're having a dream, a memory from the past. The men aren't hurting you now."

"But it feels like they are!" Julie writhes slightly from side to side.

"All the men that hurt you are dead," I say. "The feeling of the men from the past will fade away." I'm trying to do a little hypnotic suggestion. "You'll feel their weight gradually lift from your legs. You feel the weight releasing from your legs even now. Gradually, the function of your legs is returning to you. The men are gone. You won't have to be afraid of them anymore."

"I feel a little better, but how can I believe you, that they are gone?"

"Ask the older ones, especially Katherine and Holdon. You'll feel better from now on."

"I don't know . . ."

1-22-95

Dearest Dr. Baer,
We are not doing very well.—I think
we are sick. I drove us to the doctor

to be examined by the OB Gyn. We've had terrible cramping since Jensen put the antifreeze inside our vagina. Julie has been in great pain. I'm worried about toxic shock syndrome. Karen is also having many problems at home. Her children seem to have lost respect for her. I'm sure this is due to the constant degrading from Josh. We are all becoming confused and disoriented; the memories are beginning to be shared and causing much distress.

Katherine

"How are you feeling, Katherine? I got your note."

"Not very well. Jensen tried to clean himself out with antifreeze—a douche. He hoped to burn out the organs. Julie has had a hard time breathing and walking and she's very fatigued. She feels the worst when you're gone."

"How is it that Jensen can come out and do this to you?" I ask. "How is it determined who gets to come out?"

"Different reasons," says Katherine, "but it's usually the one with the strongest feelings."

"It sounds like Jensen's feelings are pretty strong," I say. "Perhaps I could talk to him and maybe help him."

"We'd all really appreciate it if you'd try, Dr. Baer."

"Perhaps you could step back and we'll see if Jensen would like to come and talk to me."

"Okay." Karen closes her eyes and her body shifts slightly. She becomes smaller and harder somehow. She seems to almost crouch in the chair, ready to spring. Her voice also becomes harder, with more energy, but at the same time, more constricted.

"I want to kill us."

"Jensen?"

"Yeah." Jensen keeps his gaze away from me.

"Why do you want to kill all of you?"

"Because this body hurts. He hurt me with a hanger and I have to clean it out. The metal is still in there. I need to burn it out and sew it up so it's no more a female."

Well, this one is pretty scary, I think. What can I do to diminish Jensen's will toward violence against himself? I guess the first step is to try and establish a relationship.

"You were hurt with a hanger?" I ask gently. "What is it you feel?"

"Nobody believes me when I talk about my feelings. We have to be alone all the time. Nobody understands."

"Has there never been a man who understood you?" I ask, trying to tempt him.

"No, never. All men hurt people."

"I know this will be new for you, and I don't expect you to accept this right away, but I'd very much like to understand you. It's the most important part of what I do, trying to understand, and I think you can really help me."

"I can help *you*?" Surprised, Jensen loses a little of his hardness.

"Well, yes, you can," I say. I've got his interest. "You seem to have suffered much of what happened to Karen. I've been trying to understand it all from what the others have been able to tell me, but it sounds like you have some very important pieces." I know it's shameless, but I'm trying to build up his self-esteem so he won't see me as hurting, but rather, as a source of emotional supplies. It's an outright seduction, but sometimes it's necessary.

"What would you like to know?" Jensen asks.

"Well, tell me your first memory."

"Oh, that's easy. Karen was being jabbed in the vagina by Constantine, her grandmother's brother. I think he was retarded. He was old and ugly. Karen was supposed to watch him because someone needed to stay with him. He put his tongue in Karen's mouth. I fought back. I kicked him where it *hurts*. Karen was bleeding from her vagina, and she had bite marks on her chest. I tied a bandage around her chest so she wouldn't look like a girl."

"You tried to protect Karen from being hurt?" I needed to say something to chip away at the conviction no man could understand him. These little bits should help.

"Yes. It wasn't easy, and I wasn't there all the time."

"And if you could take away Karen's vagina, maybe she wouldn't be hurt by the men."

"Yes! Only girls get hurt. If you're not a girl, they'll leave you alone."

"Some time has passed since the men hurt Karen's vagina. They're actually all dead now. There's no one left to hurt Karen like that, so you don't need to protect her by destroying her vagina. That ends up hurting her like the men did."

"Oh! I don't want to do that! I was just trying to help."

"Of course you were, Jensen. You were trying to save Karen."

"Yeah!"

That was a little aggressive on my part, but I'm anxious to get Jensen to stop hurting Karen's body. I tell him I'll be looking forward to talking to him again and he seems all right with that.

In early February I received a letter that appeared to be a joint effort in which the parts took turns writing to me.

Dear Doctor Bear,
I am having bad dreams. I don't want you to go away. Can you come over to my house, and make the boogie man go away, he comes out at night and I see him. Will you hold my hand and stay so he will go away. Thank you. Love Claire.

Dr. Baer,
Remember when we asked you about euthanasia? How about it. The pain is unbearable. Sandy

I am writing for Sidney, he wants you to know that he wants to play a game with you in your kitchen. Sidney says if you play cards with him he can tell his story

Miles

Dr. Baer,
    Will reintegration help us?   Sandy

What about our medical problems. Are we Diabetic or what? When I am out I am sick. I am dizzy all the time.   Julie

Hi Dr. Baer,
We are doing fine, some of us are sharing memories, sometimes this causes confusion but I think its interesting. We are all trying to share Karen's body. Sometimes we get headaches and they dont go away, certain odors make us sick (like Brut cologne) but we are handling it. We had some close calls but God is watching us. We have also trying to decide whether or not to be cremated when we die, I feel that we are going to die soon and we will finally be at peace. We have been restless since Grandma died in 1985.
                                Ann

It's clear that many of the parts are anxious to communicate with me, and find it easier to do so by writing. What strikes me is how distinct each part is. Each has its own voice and its own concerns. Except for Katherine and Holdon, who aged as Karen aged, the other parts ceased to age and grow. At a different moment for each part, time stopped, and the events occurring at that instant, like for Claire when she was seven, are still occurring. It is as if some of the parts are suspended forever in a freeze-frame of torment. It sounds like a definition of hell.

I have long wondered how Karen has been able to make use of me as a therapist at all. How did she know she could find someone to trust and to help her? How could she believe such a relationship could exist? Usually a person needs a prior experience with a supportive relationship before they'll truly believe one is possible. Karen didn't experience that with her parents. I know Karen's afraid of losing me; she's afraid I'll die, or that I'll lose interest, that she'll get better and I'll stop seeing her, or her stories will be too repellent and I'll give up—something. Karen's sense of our relationship is fragile, but I'm amazed she can manage one with me at all. A note from Karen helps me understand how this happened.

> *I remember spending many evenings sitting and talking with my grandmother*

We would talk about many things including the other parts of me. My grandmother was able to talk with Ann, Julie, Sidney, Claire and Holdon. These memories are starting to come back to me. My grandmother was incapable of reporting my abuse, but she understood that the other parts felt the pain; she understood I had to become someone else to survive. When I spent nights with her, she would gently guide me back to bed when I walked in my sleep or lost time. I spent quite a bit of time with my grandmother; she was a second mother to me. I learned to be at ease with her when I lost time. She made me feel I was important and that maybe someday I would find someone who would understand me like she did. I

realize that someone is you, and it scares me because I know
someday you will stop treating me. I can't afford to lose you, too.

I wasn't convinced that Karen's experience with her grand-mother specifically prepared her to find me, but I do think that relationship provided the foundation she needed in order to trust.

As my therapeutic relationship with Karen strengthens, I encourage several of the parts to watch while others are out. One suggestion I make is for them to go alone to visit the father's grave to show all the parts that he died. Many are reluctant to believe it.

I particularly encourage Karen (the one that regularly comes to see me) to watch while Katherine is out. She does this for the first time in the beginning of March 1995.

"What did you see?" I ask.

"I knew we were in the grocery store, but I didn't feel my body," Karen says. "I was floating, like the feeling you have as the elevator starts to go down. I was kind of in a daze, like my mind was in two places at once. I wasn't afraid of anything."

"What did you all do?"

"Nothing much, shopped for food and cleaning products. It was very efficient. We had a list and we knew where everything was in the store."

"It sounds very interesting. I hope you're able to share time with her often." Under hypnosis I had a chance to hear Katherine's version of the same experience.

"What was it like for you, Katherine?"

"I'm not sure I want Karen watching me. It's strange; I can feel her feelings. I've never done it with her before."

"You've done it with others?"

"Well, Holdon and I are out together all the time. We're side by side, kind of like mirror images of each other—partners. Each of us does what the other can't."

"Do any of the others share time with you?" I'm interested to know how flexible the system is with regard to sharing time. How absolute are the boundaries between the various parts?

"Sometimes I can relax a little and let others in."

"When might you do this?"

"Oh, say if one of the children needs comforting and they want to see a movie or something, I can show them."

"Can you come out whenever you want?"

"Most of the time. I don't come out when we're with the mother. Sandy usually deals with the mother. Sandy resists sharing time."

"It might be helpful if you could share more time with Karen. I think she could benefit."

"Okay. I'll try."

I thought if I suggest Karen and Katherine share time together, then the barrier between them will gradually become more transparent, until it disappears altogether. Then we can do this with the others, one by one. This technique has been described in several of the books and articles I've researched.

The next session Karen comes in clutching to her chest a large manila envelope bulging with objects. She sits down with it, looking at the ground, and holds it in her lap with a mixture of familiarity and revulsion. I nod to her, indicating my interest. She hands me the envelope, and sits back down with a sense of relief, as if glad to be rid of it.

"May I look?" I ask. Karen nods, biting her lip. I peer into the envelope and begin removing items. First is a small cedar box. It has a picture of an Indian family with the man smoking a pipe, seated, and a woman and child on the ground next to him. The child is naked and the space where his or her genitals would be is blotted out by repeated pencil scratches. The man has several small round marks or indentations on and around him. Each indentation has a small + sign in its center. My guess is they were made by repeated stabbing by a Phillips screwdriver. "Knott's Berry Farm" is printed on the side. I hold it up to Karen.

"What's this?" I ask.

"It's a pain box. My grandmother gave it to me. She said you can put your pain inside it and close it up again. She had one when she was a little girl." Multigenerational abuse, I think.

"And this?" I show her a crudely made gold-colored nutcracker in the shape of a woman's body from the waist down, hinged at the hips so the legs will split apart and you can crush the nut between the thighs.

"That was used to pinch me, my nipples and fingers." Karen

looks sick and tries not to look directly at me as I go through the envelope. I pull out several more items, all tools, a couple of old wood-handled screwdrivers, a little cheap hammer, and a pair of heavy electrician's pliers.

"Those tools were used to hurt me. Some were used to pinch me; some were put inside of me." She pauses and looks out the window with pain on her face.

"I think I'm going to be sick. Can I use your bathroom?" Karen gets up quickly from her chair and darts to the bathroom, a few feet down the hall from where we're sitting. She stays inside for about two minutes. There's no noise, so I think she just is collecting herself.

"I'm sorry," she says, "those things just bring back thoughts that make me nauseous."

"I'm sorry, too. Should we not look at the rest of it?"

"No, it's all right, you can go ahead."

I look inside the envelope again and pull out an old phone cord, bungee cords, a book *(Born to Win)*, an Ann Landers column, a small brass sculpture of hands set in a pose of prayer, and some family snapshots. I put the cords aside; they don't require any explanation. I started reading the Ann Landers column.

"It's how I think, sometimes," she says.

The column depicts the fictional narration of a teenager killed in an auto accident who watches the events of his funeral.

"You imagine how people would react to your death?"

"All the time."

"Can you tell me about the photographs?" I hold them up one at a time.

"That's a photo of our family—me, Josh, James, and Sara. That one's me and Josh around the time we got married. That's my grandfather and grandmother."

There's nothing remarkable about these pictures. I try to see evil in the face of her grandfather. If anything, he looks vaguely defiant, and her grandmother looks blank, expressionless.

"Shall we see if some of the other parts have any thoughts about these items?" Karen sits back and closes her eyes, waiting for me to say the words that have come to initiate hypnosis. Once she's in her trance state, I ask if anyone wants to talk with us.

"There were other things, too."

"Miles?" Miles nods. "What do you mean, other things?"

"Tape, hypodermic needles, a saw. They said they were going to cut my head off. The father took the saw and scratched my throat from ear to ear. Then they all laughed. They thought it was real funny. I had to say I liked it, or they would really do it to me!"

No sooner have I finished comforting Miles than Claire steps forward.

"Can you make the bad dreams go away?"

"Yes," I say, recognizing Claire's voice, "I hope so. Karen has brought me the tools so I can destroy them, so they can never hurt you again. What do you see when you have the bad dreams?"

"I don't want to talk about it."

"Sometimes if thoughts are spoken, they won't come back to scare you in your dreams." Claire squirms and begins to cry.

"The men twisted and pinched me here," she says, cupping her hands over her breasts, "and here"—her hands go to her belly—"and here." She slides her hands down between her legs, winces in pain, and weeps hard. I sit quietly for a few minutes as Claire recalls her pain.

"I know you still feel it, Claire," I say, "but it happened a long time ago. The men are gone, the tools can't hurt you, and your body is all healed and without pain. You should share these memories with Karen, so you don't have to suffer them alone. Will you share them with Karen?"

"Okay, I'll try." She continues to hold herself and rub the places where she'd been hurt.

"Do you remember anything else, Claire?"

"One more thing."

"Yes?"

"The praying hands . . ."

"Yes?"

"They would use them to slap me over and over across the face."

It's the beginning of April 1995 and Jensen has news for me.

"I bought a cockatiel," says Jensen.

"Tell me about it."

"The pet store owner, Gary, is my friend—that's why I came

out. He lets me look at all the animals. It was Gary who suggested the cockatiel."

"Do you like birds?"

"Yeah! Karen's grandmother always had birds."

"What made you want a pet now?"

"Nobody ever talks to me. Well, Miles does sometimes, and

Katherine and Holdon, of course. So I'm by myself most of the time, but now I have my bird."

"Maybe the bird can help us."

"How?"

"You said everyone liked the bird. Maybe all of you can all share in taking care of it? That way you'd get to talk to everyone."

Before coming to the session, Jensen drew a picture of the bird for me. He named it Link because it was the link that brings all the parts within Karen closer together.

Throughout these hypnosis sessions, and in many of the letters through the middle of 1995, the memories of the funeral home and factory abuse are referred to over and over again by different parts that experienced different moments of the torture. Each adds details—people's names, implements used, phone calls made, various ways in which Karen was hurt. The basic events never change, but they become more vivid and real with each telling, like a picture transitioning from black-and-white to color, with each step of the ordeals painted by a different hand.

13

FAMILY TREE

Karen hobbles in, favoring one leg, and just visible beneath the edge of her sleeve on her left upper arm is a large bruise. There is also one on the outside of her left shin. She crumples into her chair and her face collapses into a stream of tears. I sit and wait. Several times Karen starts to talk, but falls back to sobbing. After a few minutes of this, she collects herself enough to speak.

"Josh acts as if it never happened!" She cries again.

"Did you call the police?"

"I don't remember exactly what happened. I'd lost time but came back to myself just after Josh hit me in the leg with a two-by-four. He was drunk. He was yelling at me to get off the phone and get him some beer and cigarettes. I was on the phone, and my mother was screaming at me. Then I don't remember, but I think we had a fight; I lost time. This morning he acted like everything was fine, like nothing happened."

"You mustn't let this happen," I urge. "I know it's hard for you, but if Josh hits you, you need to call the police, even if you have to run outside and use your cell phone. It's clear he thinks he can hit you and you'll forget about it; he's counting on you somehow losing that time. But you'll be losing time less and less, and you'll need to stop the beatings, not just hide from them inside your head." Karen begins to weep again.

"It's easier to just lose time. I lost time coming here. I lose time all day long."

"If you cope by losing time, the beatings will continue. You'll hide from them, but there will be no way to stop them."

"Isn't that good enough?"

"Is it?" I nod to her leg. She looks down at the bruise and ponders it.

"No," she admits, and returns to weeping. I let her sit with the struggle she's going through. "I haven't slept in five days," she says. "I just keep switching and keep on going. Sometimes I can't handle things and I hide. Sometimes I've hidden for a week or a month, or even a year."

"Where do you go when you hide?"

"I go inside to my room."

"Your room?"

"Yes, in the house."

"The house?"

"Yes, inside."

"Oh." I don't really understand what Karen is referring to and we're out of time. Later that week I receive an envelope in the mail. Inside is a student's composition book. It was written between March 31, 1995, and May 4, 1995. It begins with Katherine's letter to me.

The first item in the book is a flow diagram of the division of Karen's personality into its parts. The arrows represent the lines of communication.

I'm not sure what to make of the Bad One. This part has never manifested itself, since every time Karen has hurt herself, it's turned out that one of the parts I've talked to is responsible.

Following this diagram are several letters: one describes the purchase of Link; two are from Miles complaining he's scared and having bad dreams because he can't stop the memories. There are also a letter of sadness written by Claire, a request from Holdon for an extended session, and several memory vignettes describing events during Karen's early years. An entry entitled "One Day in Our Life" reads as follows:

March 31, 1995

Dearest Dr. Baer,

In the following pages we will attempt to write stories that are coming to memory. We have decided the best one to write is Juliana we will tell her our stories and she will record them. We will also try to provide you with as much background information as possible. I do not know if it is possible, but we want to help you help us.

Sincerely,
Katherine

Today Katherine woke up at 7:15 am and woke up James and Sara for school, made breakfast, made lunches, and sent them off to school. When the kids left, Katherine went to sleep to rest and Sandy went out to breakfast with her friend, Peg, at 8:30 am. Sandy got tired and went in and Karen 2 came out and did some shopping at 10:30 am. Karen 2 can't carry groceries, so she went in and Holdon carried the groceries into the house. Katherine came back out to put the groceries away. After putting them away, Katherine went back in and Karen woke up (2:00 p.m.). Karen slept all afternoon until she took Sara to her ice skating class (5:20–6:06 p.m.). Karen brought Sara home and Ann went to pick up her project from church. Ann came home, Holdon carried it and Karen took Sara back to ice skating for another class from 7:15 to 8:00 p.m. After this class, Claire wanted a chocolate shake, so Holdon drove us to Jean's Ice Cream for a shake for us and a sundae for Sara. Karen came out to drive us home and get the kids ready for bed.

Karen says this was a fairly simple day because they didn't see her mother and no one got upset. The entry keeps referring to

"Karen." I wonder if that means Karen 3. There was another simi-lar, shorter vignette that read:

What a day! Karen had nightmares and we let her sleep all day. Miles went to the basketball game with James, Katherine colored eggs for Easter, Sandy made up the kids' baskets, Ann took the baskets to church to get them blessed, Juliann cleaned the house, and Holdon picked up the ham.

This is how Karen functions during the day, day after day, in ordinary times and in times of crisis. It's a marvelous, elaborate coping strategy, but it allows no room for growth. Even so, it's amazing how stable it is.

Finally, the composition book held a diagram: the architecture of the system's internal world.

This is how Karen has always kept her parts separated. She cre-ated a mental house, based loosely on her childhood home, in which each part has a place: in a separate room or in his or her own portion of a shared room. Interestingly, she's incorporated her "safe room" into her internal house. Late in the evening, they can all go in the meeting room and sit at the oval table. Karen never goes to these meetings. The meeting is conducted by Holdon, and they

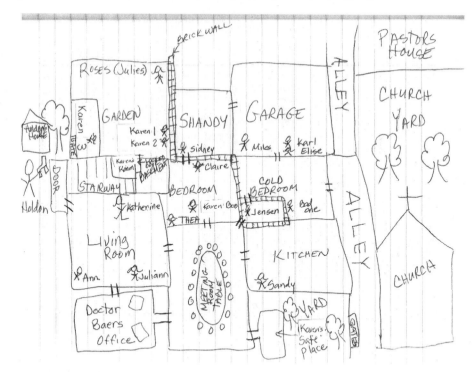

discuss the previous day and the next. After the discussion, Katherine and Holdon will make the final decisions on what they should do. If the parts argue, the next day may not go as planned.

In the composition book, Holdon wrote a brief note asking for an extended therapy session so he could have enough time to share his concerns. I arranged for one and a half hours for the next session.

Karen sits in her chair looking at the diagram in the book that shows all the rooms. She hadn't seen it before. She stares at it for a long time.

"What are your thoughts?" I ask.

"The names, the rooms, are all kind of familiar, like I remember them from a dream. I don't really understand it."

"I think it was written so I could understand you better. I think you'll come to understand it over time."

"That's okay, I guess."

"Holdon mentioned he wanted to spend some time talking with me. Perhaps we could start our hypnosis session?"

"Okay." Karen sits back in her chair and I start our routine of relaxation and induction. When Karen is deep in her trance, I guide her to her safe place, and then to the meeting room, where, apparently, any of the parts can present themselves to me through her. I never know which part of her is the best one to talk with, so I always leave it to them to choose. Karen shifts in her chair and takes the posture I've come to recognize as Miles, but this time she opens her eyes, squints at the light, and looks around.

"It's bright!" He looks out the window and shrinks back from the forty-floor drop. He looks back at me.

"Miles?"

"Yeah."

"You opened your eyes."

"Yeah, Holdon said I could."

"You didn't know?"

"No, you never said I could."

"Oh, I'm sorry. I didn't realize . . ."

"Talking in the dark makes me think about being in the shandy. That's what the father called it."

"What was the shandy like?"

"It was a shed with tools. When we were bad we'd be made to stay in the shandy. It was cold and dark in there. It had a gray cement floor. The floor would be cold if we didn't have any clothes on. There was a ladder in there, too. Sometimes we'd be tied to the ladder. Once the father threw a cat in there with us when we were tied to the ladder. The cat was real scared, too. I thought it was going to scratch me, but I was real quiet, and it didn't do nothin'. I still live there a lot, or in the garage."

"Where else can you go?"

"Well, I can go in the cold room or I can go to the meeting room, after dark, when the room is dark, when Karen closes her eyes."

"Is there anything on your mind now?"

"I had an argument with Sandy. She wants to go to the father's grave with the mother lady, but I didn't want to go. I was afraid he'd come out of the ground and get us."

"He died about a year ago," I remind him.

"Yeah, they said it was his anniversary."

"What happened?"

"I wanted to cut myself. I thought if I did that, nobody would want to go to the cemetery."

"How would that keep the others from the cemetery?"

"If we went there, we'd remember him and how he hurt us, so I was going to give us some pain to take away the pain of remembering."

"I don't understand."

"Pain takes away pain."

"Really, how does that work?"

"Outside pain make inside pain hurt less."

"You mean if you cut yourself on the outside, your feelings will hurt less?"

"Yeah."

"Where did you learn this?"

"I don't know. Jensen does it, too."

"I'd like to try to help you to find *other* ways to make your feelings hurt less. Shall we work on that?"

"Okay, sure."

After Miles steps back, Karen sits up in her chair to her full height and speaks to me directly and plainly.

"Dr. Baer, it's Holdon. I can't hold the fort together; the system is breaking apart!"

"Holdon, you sound alarmed. What exactly is the problem?"

"The memories are being shared by everyone. The parts are becoming less distinct and it's causing confusion. I used to decide which parts came out and when. Now they're coming out when they want!"

"How is that a problem?"

"They are beginning to feel things they haven't felt before. It's affecting me, too. I have a shakiness, a trembling when I write and drive; my arms go numb!"

"Are you afraid some part will get hurt or do something destructive?"

"Yes, Dr. Baer." Holdon slumps a little and nods forward. "You need to know them as I do."

"Why don't we start on that? What should I know?"

"Where do I start? Things affect us differently."

"Things, what things?"

"Well, like alcohol, for instance; it affects us all differently; it's dangerous." Holdon's speech is rapid, as if he wants to get out a lot of information in the brief time we have. "It doesn't affect me, but it makes Sidney giggle, Miles gets meaner, and it puts Claire in a coma. It's just too hard to control. We won't be able to leave the husband until we're all put together. We won't be able to survive."

"Karen mentioned to me that not all the parts need glasses like she does."

"Right, we're all different. We were born at different times for different reasons. Katherine has intelligence, I keep things straight, and Karen Boo stayed a baby to pacify the parents. Julie and Juliann were split off from Katherine when Katherine felt pain. Juliann was born to write about it. Karl feels the pain and evil. Ann feels the good; she tries to remain Christian and keep away from the abusive people. The spoofs are little fragments of memory. They have no names, only one memory each, and are isolated from all the others. Karl and Elise split off from Miles; they're the alters of Miles. Karl takes extreme pain. Elise keeps separate their pain from the normal day. Miles and Jensen—they feel much the same things, they were side by side in pain. They took the pain and spared everyone else."

I've heard most of this before, but with each description, there are always additional details added.

"Why were you and Katherine originally split off?" I ask.

"The large tumor on Karen's forehead made the parents want to put her up for adoption. They beat her because of this defect. Katherine and I were born and Karen Boo took that first pain. When Karen was two and a half years old, Thea was born and grew to age six. Katherine took over in first grade and started learning. Sandy came after Thea; her role was to get along with the parents. She was also born when Karen was eleven, but stopped growing at age eighteen, when Karen moved out of her parents' house. The alters stop growing when a certain kind of abuse stops, then they stay that age for life. Katherine and I are still needed, so we're still growing. We confer together most of the time to keep things running."

Our time is up, but I thank Holdon and ask him to talk with me again soon.

The next session, Karen brings a picture of herself at age eighteen months. It is an old black-and-white photograph of herself as a toddler. It's a posed, studio photograph with Karen in a light-colored dress; she has a dark, golf ball–sized tumor where her right eye meets the top of her nose. So there it is, I think. She's talked about the tumor, and she carries the scar from its removal, but it's still striking to see the baby picture. It's now more understandable why her emotionally primitive father would have picked her out for abuse; the tumor looks frightening.

Under hypnosis, Claire and Miles tell me of an episode of abuse that was described in a previous letter, but there are added details.

"Katherine took us to a funeral last week," says Claire, smiling at me and curled up coyly in the chair. "I don't usually come out at funerals. I get scared. But I came out just for a second."

"What scares you?"

"It makes me remember the funeral home—what happened there."

"What can you tell me about it?" Claire turns to the side and curls up, as if trying to hide in the chair.

"It started with chocolate milk," she says. "I like chocolate milk, but Father put something in the Bosco. It made me sleepy and feel like I was floating. They took me to church, to the . . . confessional." Claire was struggling to form the words. She was very upset. "The priest told me I was bad and belonged to the devil. They kept saying I was bad and I had to say it, too. I was scared." Claire's face winces in pain. "Then they took me to the funeral home." Claire burrows further into the chair and begins to cry.

"Are you sure you want to tell me all this?" I ask. Claire's crying slows to little sobs.

"Holdon said I should." She sniffs. "He said if I told you, the bad dreams would go away. Is that true?"

"It may be so; it happens that way most of the time," I say, trying to be encouraging without promising. "Why don't you continue as best you can."

"They locked us in a coffin!"

"Us?"

"Me and Miles."

"Uh-huh."

"I couldn't breathe or see. I could feel the silk on the sides of the coffin. They said we were going to die that way because we were bad."

"Who said this?"

"The men. I don't know, there were five men, I think; they were all laughing." Claire begins shivering and hugs herself. "They put me in ice water first." Claire starts crying again and hugging herself and rocking back and forth. Then she relaxes and turns in the chair; she looks less afraid, angrier.

"I'll tell you the rest."

"Miles?"

"Yeah," he says, like a tough guy. "They put us in ice water mixed with blood from a corpse. Then they rinsed us off and put us in the coffin. They said we had to die if we were to be reborn. But they were laughing; they thought it was a big stinking joke. Claire was scared, and she started screaming when they closed the lid. They would open the lid and then close it again, a little longer each time, each time Claire screamed, and each time they laughed. So I came out and I wouldn't scream. They opened the lid and I just stared at them, so they slammed the lid and kept it closed a long time. I closed my eyes and waited to die. I couldn't breathe. I wanted to kick and scream; I couldn't stand it. Then I don't remember."

"That sounds so frightening," I say. It frightens the hell out of *me*, I think. "There's so much for you to tell me, Miles, I think we might need more time together. What do you think?"

"It's okay with me. If you're ready."

The next session Karen brings an envelope. I'm stunned. Inside is a drawing of seventeen faces. I'm amazed at the quality. I assume it is a picture of the parts inside Karen, but I'm not sure who is who. I can identify Holdon, and Jensen, because he is supposed to be black, and he is holding paintbrushes. I can only guess at the others. I show it to Karen. She shrugs her shoulders and turns red, but smiles a little.

"I don't know what to say," Karen says, holding the picture

away from her with discomfort. "I guess I must have done it." She hadn't opened the envelope, and hasn't seen the picture.

"Did you know about this picture? Can you tell me who the faces are?" Karen shakes her head. She looks out the window. I've been feeling that Karen has been getting short shrift in here because I've been spending more and more time with her other parts. I know she understands the importance of learning about the other parts, but I'm certain she's been feeling left out.

"With all the new information we have been getting about the other parts inside you, I wonder if you feel you've been forgotten about?" Karen squirms in a way that tells me she agrees but is too embarrassed to admit it. "I appreciate your being patient during this period, and I'll make sure we have some time at the beginning of every session for us to talk together."

Karen smiles and repositions herself to a comfortable slouch, signaling she's ready to begin the hypnosis part of the session. . . .

"Hi, it's Jensen."

"Hi! What a great picture!" Jensen smiles with pride. "Tell me who everyone is. I'm guessing it's a picture of all the parts within Karen. Is this Holdon?" I point to the adult male on the lower right side.

"Right, that's Holdon. He's holding Karen Boo."

"That's me on the bottom, with the paintbrushes. I'm black. Karen's father didn't like blacks. Next to me is Sidney. Claire is just above him, and Miles and Thea are next to Claire. That's Karl with the angry face and Elise is next to him. Julie has a crutch because she can't walk, and Katherine has a guitar. She plays for us sometimes. Ann is praying, and Sandy is there. She's fat. Next to Sandy are Karen 1, 2, and 3, and Juliann is on top."

"Wow. Where's the Angry One?"

"Oh, I don't think there *is* an angry one. I think that's just Karl being mean."

"Karl?"

"Yeah, we had a lot of bad thoughts this week. We thought it was Karl, but he said it wasn't him. He said it was the Angry One, but I don't believe him." That would answer the question of the mysterious eighteenth alter, I think. There are seventeen alters after all.

"You certainly have a talent for drawing. Perhaps you'll have other pictures to show me. Do you think I could talk to Karl?" I need to form some kind of alliance with Karl if possible to try to stop the damage he's inflicting on Karen.

"I'll see."

Karen closes her eyes and her face goes blank for several moments. She tilts her head back a couple of inches. Her face is in a grimace and she grits her teeth. She stays that way for several seconds until I break the silence.

"Karl?"

"Yes," he says, through his clenched jaw.

"I'm glad to meet you, and I'm glad you've come to talk to me."

"I'm not sure I want to talk to you." He continues to speak with his jaw held tight.

"How come?"

"You'll just hurt me."

"I understand you've been hurt a lot."

"I take the pain when no one else can take it. That's all I'm good for."

"It sounds like what you do for the others is very important. I want very much to learn about you. When were you born, Karl?"

"I was born in the coffin."

"The coffin Claire and Miles told me about?"

"Yeah. Claire and Miles took turns being in the ice water. I was born in the coffin when Miles couldn't breathe. He cried out for help. I was born to take what the others couldn't handle. I wasn't afraid. I said I liked it."

"Are there any concerns you have, Karl, that I might help you with?"

"I'd like to touch somebody."

"What?"

"I've never touched anybody. I've always been alone. I'd like to touch someone, hurt someone like I was hurt. I'd like to grow up like Sara and James are growing up."

"I'd like to see you grow up, too, and I'll be able to help you do that. But a part of growing up is leaving behind the wish to hurt someone. Perhaps we could work on both those things together. Do you have any thoughts about hurting right now?"

"Yeah."

"What?"

"I want to cut off Karen's breasts."

"What's the reason?" I ask, pretending not to want to run screaming from the room.

"If she doesn't have any breasts, then she'll be a boy. I don't like this body."

"I understand your wish to have a boy's body. Unfortunately, cutting Karen's breasts won't give you the body of a boy. You'll still be in Karen's body, but with cut breasts. Not much help really. Do you think you could hold off on doing anything to hurt Karen's body until you and I have had a chance to talk things over?"

"Well, okay."

"Fine. By the way, can you tell me why you have to clench your teeth so?"

"Yeah, my jaw is broken."

14.

STORY TIME

"I go to bed at night, but I don't sleep," says Karen, *looking* weary and strained. "I wake up exhausted, but at least my house is clean. I don't know who does it." She sighs and shakes her head.

"Someone is out while you're asleep?"

"Must be."

"Is your husband, Josh, aware you're up at night? Does that cause a problem?"

"No, he's usually drunk and unconscious."

"Does he notice you switching time?"

"Not really, but he can make me switch when he wants to."

"What do you mean?"

"When he doesn't like the way I am, he'll get real close to my face and scream at me, and I'll lose time. I'll come back later and everything will be normal again."

"So he doesn't necessarily know you're switching, only that you suddenly become compliant."

"I think so."

"Shall we see if any of the other parts need to speak to me?"

"Okay."

I help Karen go into her hypnotic trance, and let whatever part come out that wishes. In quick succession Claire and Miles step forward, both with familiar complaints. Miles does say something I take particular note of. He comments about Josh:

"If he'd hurt us, I used to kick him out of bed and punch him when he was sleeping." Maybe that's why Karen says her husband wakes her at night by punching her. Maybe he's just hitting her back.

Next Sandy comes out to challenge a comment Miles had made about "everybody," meaning the entire system, getting fat.

"Eating makes me feel good," says Sandy. She smiles a dumb, fatuous smile and oozes out over the chair.

"So you often feel bad?" I ask. It's dizzying to have to do therapy with several parts in succession, remembering who they are, their particular issues, and what needs fixing. I'm keeping up as best I can.

"When I give money to Mother, I feel bad."

"Why do you give it to her?"

"I want her to like me."

"Does she like you when you give her money?"

"For a little while, but then she's mean again, and I feel bad."

"Is that when you eat?"

"Yes."

"And you feel better?"

"Yes."

"Maybe if you didn't give her money, you wouldn't feel bad."

"But she asks for it. If I don't give it, she's mean and I feel bad."

"Maybe when she next asks for money, you could say no."

"I can't."

"Why not?"

"Then she won't like me."

In July 1995, Karen brings me a gift. It's a back scratcher in the form of Taz, the Tasmanian Devil cartoon character. Karen is embarrassed. Under hypnosis Karen tells me more.

"It's from me."

"Who is this?"

"Sidney, and I didn't steal it!"

"Steal it?"

"I didn't! Holdon gave me money to buy it for you. I said you could probably use it, and Taz would remind you of me."

"It's a wonderful present, and I'm very appreciative." I scratch my back with it for a second and Sidney laughs. "Were you afraid I thought you stole it?" I ask.

"Yeah, Father made me steal stuff all the time. If I didn't want to do it, he'd pull my ear, punch me, or pinch me. He even threatened to pull my fingernails out, but he didn't do it."

"It sounds like you feel proud you bought this present and didn't steal it."

"Yeah! I wanted to give it to you, so I didn't want it to be stolen."

"Thanks. That makes me feel better about it, too."

"Everybody inside is beginning to know everybody's story."

"What do you mean?"

"I'm beginning to remember more of what happened to Miles and Claire."

"What do you think?"

"I don't like it." Sidney goes back inside and Karen sits upright.

"We're trying to share more of our experience, especially with the younger ones," says Katherine. "Oh, and by the way, I've arranged for you to get the insurance check. I'm sorry Karen has trouble with this. She has bad feelings about money, which I don't share, of course, but for Karen, the men paid her father money to abuse her, and her mother always wants money, and Sandy thinks she has to give the money to her mother so she'll like her. Karen doesn't want to have to pay you to like her, too."

"I can understand her conflict."

"I've been trying to take care of the house with Holdon. Karen is really a lost person; she needs the most help."

"Who are you referring to when you say 'Karen'?"

"I'm sorry, Karen 3, the one we picked to see you originally and the one you see most of the time."

"I've always been curious, why was Karen 3 the one to come to see me and not you?"

"Karen 3 carries all of us. She was the one best able to form a relationship with you."

"She carries you, so she's the main one?"

"No, not the main one—it's difficult to explain, really. It's just her job."

"I see." I'm not sure I do, really. "Can you tell me more about your relationship with Karen?"

"Well, in the evening, Holdon and I will talk to her and we'll let some of the memories seep into Karen's consciousness while she's going to sleep. That way she knows what has happened during the day."

"How does she decide when to come out?"

"Holdon and I really decide who comes out. We function together most of the time. We've protected Karen all our lives. When Karen is out, we usually don't interrupt her until she wants to go inside. Then Holdon or I, usually Holdon, will send someone else out. Sometimes we'll be inside attending to the children and not be available, and Sandy or someone else will come out. When we send one of the children out, we will supervise them by talking to them so they won't be found out."

"I'm not getting any sleep," Karen whines, *"there's too much* talking in my head at night! There's a lot of organizing going on . . . and on and on!"

"What's it all about?"

"Oh, who is going to do what during the next day. Last night I woke up at two a.m. and discovered I was on the phone ordering something from a catalog. I think I've slept but I really haven't."

"What do the voices at night say?"

"It's the reports from all the others: phone calls received, appointments kept and made, errands to do."

"Are you able to participate while some of the others are out?"

"Not participate, but I can watch. It's like going to a movie; I can't talk and I'm sitting in a backseat."

"Miles and I drank a margarita—Miles wanted to drink it," says Karen under hypnosis, "but Miles can't take it. Alcohol affects us all differently. If I'd stayed out, I would have handled it differently. It doesn't really affect me, but it made Miles sick and sleepy." Karen is animated and speaking quickly.

"Have I spoken to you before?" I ask. This alter sounds unfamiliar.

"Yes, but you don't know it. I've come here before unannounced, but you didn't notice. I have a much more positive attitude than Karen."

That explains the times when I thought Karen's depression was much improved, only to see her the next week as depressed as ever, I think. How do you give an antidepressant to someone like that?

"I've been out all weekend," she says with a toss of her head. She studies the clock behind her, which has momentarily captured her interest. Her mood is buoyant.

"Who are you?" I ask.

"Holdon refers to me as Karen 2."

"Oh, yes. Why this weekend?" I ask.

"It started at the ice show. Our tickets had the same seat numbers as another family's. The manager was very rude . . ." Karen goes on to describe the incident word for word, taking each side in turn. Before she takes up too much time with this story, I decide to interrupt.

"You seem in quite good spirits."

"Oh, there's nothing wrong with me." She gives a little turn of her head.

"Tell me more about yourself. When were you born?"

"I came along when Karen was four or five. I'm here to be happy and have a good time. I stopped aging at age twenty-one. That's how old I am now. I'm the one who moved out of the parents' house because they were so mean. I wasn't going to take it."

"What happened then?"

"I got a job as a secretary, and I shared this job with Katherine and Ann. I'm good at math, Katherine can type, and Ann would talk to our boss. I'm the one who dated and met Josh and married him. I get along with him pretty well; he's not that bad." I recall Karen 1 wanted a wedding, but here Karen 2 feels it was her idea.

"How does Josh manage with all of you switching?" I'm using this opportunity with a part I haven't talked to before to pump her for information.

"It makes him angry sometimes, because he doesn't know what Karen is going to do next, but sometimes he likes it because Sandy and I will do things for him, and sometimes when he's angry with us, we seem to forget about it." It's interesting—the same facts, but from a different perspective.

I'm thrilled Karen 2 is so uninhibited and talkative, so I keep asking questions.

"What do you make of the sharing of information that is occurring at night?"

"Well, I can tell you the talking is growing!" She's emphatic about this and speaks quickly. "Holdon calls it 'Story time.' I can stay out a long time—up to a year if I want to. I don't like sharing time with the others."

"When do you go back in?" I have to pop my questions in when she takes a breath.

"If I feel tired or weak, or if I have nothing to do and I'm bored, another will come out. When I married Josh, walking down the aisle, I had some doubts. Am I doing the right thing? I wondered. The others fought it, too. At the altar, some of the others came out; that's why we fainted three times. But I decided to go through with it and stayed out. I think it was the right thing to do; he's not so bad."

"What about the times he hits you?" I ask.

"What do you mean?" she asks, taken by surprise. "Don't be silly."

"I'm sorry, never mind; it was a pleasure to talk to you." I guess she really is protected from being hurt.

Karen comes striding into my office and settles into her chair. It's not her usual entrance. I don't say anything, but wait. Karen looks at me for a moment.

"It's Holdon, Dr. Baer. Karen hasn't come out. There've been too many stresses. We're all trying to do the right thing when Karen can't, but it's hard. We're not sleeping; someone different is out all the time; we've been shaky and nauseous from the lack of sleep. Some of us get headaches. We take aspirin, but it doesn't work the same for all of us."

Holdon has his hands full. Progress is difficult because our work is always interrupted by crises. I spend hours on the phone with Karen each week listening to the particular day's unpleasantness, and it is stressful for me, too. I try to take her calls after my children have gone to bed, but then I see my wife's back stiffen when she asks whom I'm talking to and my answer is always the same.

"Despite the hardship, have some of the others shared their time out?" I ask.

"Karen 2 allows some others to come out with her. But she doesn't do it all the time. Katherine does it sometimes, too, but we've been so busy."

"I understand," I say, not wanting to push, but wanting to encourage her, him, them, or whatever.

"We do share time when we take care of Link."

"Yes, the bird. How is that going? Tell me about it."

"Well, Karen goes up to the bird, and then somehow she steps back, like she does in your office, and then each part will come out for a couple minutes. It's like they hand off the tasks to each other, with just a little pause for the transition to take place."

"Do they share time during this?"

"A little. Karen watches it all take place. Katherine and I help some of the younger ones."

"Has this ever happened before, where everyone shares in a task?"

"No, this is the first time."

"What has made the days so stressful for Karen?"

"Oh, boy," Holdon says, "the days are just one big gigantic lie for Karen. She's always pretending she knows what's going on. People will come up to her and start a conversation. She won't know who they are, but clearly they know a lot about her. She has to play along until the part that knows them comes out."

"There's a delay for the appropriate part to come out?"

"Yes, if we're surprised. Katherine or I may be busy with the children and not see that someone needs to be sent out."

"You seem to look out for Karen pretty much all day."

"She's protected all the time," he says, "as best we can. That's what we're for. She's even protected in her sleep. Her nightmares will be given away to someone else automatically. If she stubs her toe, it will hurt for a moment, and then someone else takes the pain. But I'm not able to control who comes out all the time. When Sandy or Sidney comes out, they make the most problems. Sandy is unpredictable. She keeps eating and eating."

"She's the one that has made Karen fat?" I ask.

"Yes, she sees herself as a fat girl. It's hard for some of us to be in this woman's body."

"It's hard for you?"

"Well, I can tell you, it's darn awkward. Miles hates makeup, and I can't walk in high heels, although Karen 2 seems to have no problem."

"What can you tell me about Karen Boo?" I ask.

"Boo was born of severe pain—she was hurt the worst. She was just a baby. Her father would put duct tape over her mouth so she couldn't scream, then he'd stick hat pins in her. The pinholes would disappear. No one could tell. Once the father stuck a pin in the tumor, and it bled a lot; he didn't do that again." Holdon hangs his head and sighs, not from the horror of his story, but from plain exhaustion.

A minute later Sandy comes out, slouching back with her belly stuck out, and somehow, completely unself-conscious.

"I understand there are concerns about eating and spending money," I say. This is not the way to ingratiate myself with Sandy, I know, but my concern for Karen's troubles, Sandy's role in them, my grandiose fantasy that I may be able to fix everything, and just plain fatigue, make me blunder with this accusation.

"I'm trying to behave," she says, throwing up her hands, "but when I see something I want, I just have to have it." She turns away from me. "I don't really care, anyway."

"The others don't want to be so heavy," I say, inappropriately compounding my mistake by taking their side. I should just shut up and learn about Sandy.

"Sometimes I don't even believe there *are* others." Sandy is annoyed. "The very idea irritates me. When I'm out, nobody can make me go back in. I want to be the only one. Maybe I'll come out and never go back!"

"Is there anything I can help you with?" I ask, trying to recover, ally myself with her, and gain favor.

"Well, I'd like to be an adult. I'm eighteen, and I'd like to grow up all the way."

"Some of the others wish the same thing. I've told them I'll help them; perhaps I can help you, too. Shall we work on it together?" Sometimes I'm shameless with my little seductions, but right now I'm trying to patch things up.

After obtaining Sandy's spirited agreement and having a short conversation with Sidney, who is ever the appealing schoolboy, I find myself talking to Karen 1.

"Karen can't handle Sara's getting breasts," she says. "It's reminding her of when she got breasts and the men hurt them. I don't have breasts; I don't want them." Ten-year-old Karen 1 looks at me, hurt, defiant, and daring me to try to help her. "Sara was asking Karen about her period, so I stopped Karen from having hers. I can stop it when I want."

"How?" I ask.

"I just can."

"What else can you do?"

"When I was told we were going to have a baby, I wanted to make that stop, too. I punched myself in the stomach to make it stop."

"Did it work?"

"No. Now Sara will be hurt, too."

"Who's going to hurt Sara?"

"The father will; he tried it before. The grandfather will."

"They're all dead," I interrupt. "The father, the grandfather, the men who hurt you."

"You're lying."

"It's true. Sara won't be hurt. The men are dead. You don't have to worry about your breasts and your period."

"How can I believe you?"

"Ask Katherine; she'll tell you it's true." I use my reliable ploy. All the children trust and believe Katherine and Holdon. The important question is whether healing will occur once most or all of the parts no longer see a threat.

It's the beginning of August 1995, and we're in our sixth summer together. Karen says she's been losing a lot of time. "There's no use for me," she laments, "I'm only living part of my life."

Because of this, I feel uncertain about hypnotizing her again today. We've been spending less and less time with "her." She is, at this time, truly a passenger in her own life. I tell her I'm sorry that I don't spend as much time with her as I used to, but I feel all the work we're doing with the others is temporary but important right now. She says she understands and we go on as before.

Juliann comes out and explains what happens at the evening "meetings."

"We hold the meeting to tell everyone, especially Karen, what happens during the day. I wrote you notes on what happened yesterday, but I forgot them. Basically it went like this. In the morning, Josh punched Karen. Miles came out and punched Josh back. After Josh went to work, they all went to the pet shop together. It took fifteen minutes for all of them to look at the birds. Only two or three of us can look at any one time. We can look at things together, but we can only touch something one part at a time. When we take care of Link, we have to take turns. Later, after Josh came home, Karen 3 came out when he punched Ann for accidentally putting her feet on his jeans. That's when Karen 3 called you."

I'm trying to process the odd events of the day, and trying to calculate how many times Josh had hit Karen and which part of her had experienced it.

"I tell this to Karen at night," Juliann continues, "when she's sleeping so she'll know what's happened." She pauses and looks at me and cocks her head. "Dr. Baer, if we all come together, will I die?" I'm taken aback by this question. I hadn't really thought about it.

"No," I say, "I don't believe any part of you will be lost, will die. But you won't be just yourself," I add, "your own separate self."

She thinks about this for a while. I'm not sure the issue is resolved for her, or for me.

In early September, I get calls from several of the alters. I receive a page from the answering service from "Mrs. Holdon" who says everyone is terribly stressed. Sara broke her arm, and Josh is blaming Karen. The next day Jensen calls. He's afraid because Miles is unconscious. Josh choked him because Miles argued with him.

Ann came out for the next few days to help calm things down. When she's out, Josh leaves them alone more.

Miles calls and says his throat hurts and he wants to kill Josh. He recalls the men who abused them would choke them if they screamed. He's afraid to go to the police because Josh said the police are his friends and they'll kill him. I tell Miles that Josh is full of shit; he has no special relationship with the police. Karen should definitely call the police. Miles is relieved and amused.

Claire saw a dead baby in the coffin at the funeral they attended. She says the men dressed her in a white dress and put her in a coffin. She asks me if the men killed the baby. I discuss with her what "stillborn" means.

I receive a 1:00 a.m. call from "Elise Overhill," who says she's suicidal. She hasn't been out for a long time and doesn't know where she is. She seems quite frightened. I say I can help her, and since she knows I'm helping the others, she lets me hypnotize her; I ask Katherine to come out. Katherine apologizes and is quite upset Elise was out, saying Elise is not ready and needs to be protected. After I hang up, my wife turns over and beats her pillow with her fist a few times, as if it's her pillow that's keeping her awake. I lie awake, looking at the ceiling, feeling the unrelenting burden of Karen and all her parts. My marriage has lately been full of complicated issues, of which Karen is merely one. It would help matters at home if I tried to set more limits with Karen, but I fear what the effect on her would be—and after everyone in her life has let her down, I can't be just one more.

In early October 1995, I meet Thea for the first time. She holds her hands in front of her face in a defensive posture, as if she'll be hit.

"I think we'll all die," Thea says.

"Are you protecting yourself?" I ask, attending to the hands, not the statement.

"I'm afraid you'll hit me."

"Afraid I'll hit you?"

"Everybody hits me. But Claire says you're nice. I don't like doctors."

"What do doctors do?"

"Dr. Walsh hates me. He lets them hurt me. He put me in the hospital and they did bad things to me, too, needles and things." Thea continues to hold her hands in front of her face.

"Are you still afraid I'm going to hit you?"

"No."

"But you're still protecting yourself."

"I don't want you to see this big ugly thing on my face."

"Do you mean the tumor?"

"Yes. The other kids make fun of me. Mother told everyone I'm going to die."

"You may not know it, but some *nice* doctors removed the tumor and made your face all well. You don't need to hide anymore."

"I don't believe you."

"See for yourself. Try to find it."

Thea actually touches around her forehead, looking for the tumor. "It's not there," she says, surprised.

"No, it's not there." I pause and let Thea come to terms with the loss of the tumor.

"Thea, can you tell me when you were born?"

I use the question to distract Thea from her tumor thoughts.

"I was born in 1965. I'm six."

"What grade are you in?"

"Kindergarten. That's when I went into the hospital; that's what I'm for. I have to go now." Karen goes blank and Thea is gone.

"My mother wants me to stop coming to see you," says Karen.

"How come?"

Karen turns away, her face reddening with shame. "She says all you want is to screw . . . have sex, with me. She says we do it all the time. She says I've always been like this." She looks mortified and helpless, as if the most important thing to her, her hope of being helped, is getting soiled and ruined.

"What did she mean; you've always been like this?"

"I don't know. I don't remember. I wasn't there for that."

"Perhaps we can find out more about it under hypnosis." Karen settles back and again we go through our induction routine.

"I think you want to talk to me."

"Who's 'me'?"

"Sandy, of course."

"Sandy! What can you tell me about Karen's troubles?" I sit back to see what Sandy will come up with.

"Mother says Karen has sex with you. She says she gives you blow jobs and all sorts of other things. She says Karen is nothing but a prostitute and that you should be paying *her.*" Sandy is speaking with a kind of *la belle indifference*, an unconcerned air about something quite shocking.

"Where did she get such an idea?"

"Oh, I think she's just jealous. But this is what we've always done. In high school, father would secretly get dates for us. The men paid him and I'd have sex with them." She looks at me with wide eyes that show no emotion. "That's what women are for, to be used, to make men feel good." She looks around the office; I remain mute. "We were trained from an early age, beginning about eleven years old, to perform certain sex acts. If I didn't give a blow job good enough, Father would yell and hit my head. He wanted me to have sex with twelve- and thirteen-year-old boys." She looks at me. "If we didn't do what he wanted, he'd have killed us long ago."

Sandy turns to the window. It's interesting that a topic that causes Karen such mortification can be discussed by Sandy in the same routine tone she'd use to describe baking cookies. I remain quiet; I don't want to interrupt or derail whatever she has to say.

"They took a lot of pictures. That's why I'm fat—so they can't use me anymore." She looks at me once more with that open blankness. "The mother says all you want is to have sex with Karen. Karen, Ann, and I all heard her say it. I don't know if that's true; I wasn't there. But I ate a lot yesterday, just to protect myself. Ann was saying prayers all night—that drove me crazy."

"Well, it's not true, Sandy, none of it, what your mother said about me." I try to be calm and direct, and not appear to deny too strenuously. "I would suggest that instead of eating to protect yourself, you just go inside when your mother talks this kind of trash."

"Perhaps I should begin training Sara. Father always said 'You have to train them early.' Do you think I should do that? At least when I thought about having sex with you, it was pleasant, not hurtful. But I probably shouldn't be thinking about that."

"It's important that Sara and you be protected from any sort of harm or sexual abuse. Why don't you spend some time out with Katherine and Miles; they'll help you understand more about your mother. Do you think you can do that?"

"Sure, that might be fun." Sandy is one damaged fragment.

15

CHURCH PHOTOS

When I return from my Christmas vacation, I call Karen to confirm our next appointment and mention she's behind on my bill. She promises to try to make a payment, but seems taken aback and distant after I mention it, as if I'd hurt her feelings. I try to be as ordinary and matter-of-fact about the money as I can.

The day after New Year's 1996, I get a call from Karen; it's Ann on the phone, and she says she can't go on with therapy anymore. They've all agreed; it's time to stop.

"What's happened?" I ask. "This is all a surprise to me. What happened since we last talked?"

"Nothing," says Ann. "It has to do with what you said."

I'm scrambling inside my own head, trying to recall what I might have said that could have provoked such a severe reaction.

"I'm sorry, Ann, I'm at a loss," I say, trying to conceal the anxiety I feel at having screwed up somehow. "I don't know what I said that has upset you. Can you tell me what it was?"

"It has to do with the money issue."

"You mean my asking Karen to make a payment on my bill?"

"You weren't talking to Karen; you were talking to Katherine. Miles overheard and told everybody else." So my encouraging the alters to share time backfired on me, I think.

"I'm sorry, Ann, I still don't understand. What is it about paying my bill that is now so upsetting?"

"None of the others knew Karen was paying you except Katherine and Holdon—until you told them." Ann pauses. She seems to be trying to help me. She continues.

"The men paid to have sex with Karen. Now she's paying you. Karl wants to hurt us." I'm scrambling to think what to do to reverse this harm I've caused.

"Perhaps I should talk to Karl. Ann, would you mind?"

"Not at all."

There is a pause at the other end of the phone, and then the silence shifts and turns ominous.

"Karl?"

"Why do you need to be paid?" Karl's voice has a bitter, hard edge.

"I'm a doctor, Karl; helping Karen is a part of my business. Helping people is how I make my living."

"We are just a business to you."

"You are that and much more." I know Karl would really like to trust me, but he feels betrayed. "It may be hard to understand, but my work with Karen, you, and the others is both a business relationship and a helping relationship. Does it make sense that it can be both?"

"No . . . I don't know," says Karl.

"Can you tell me what makes paying me a hurtful thing? What does it mean to you?"

"The men paid the father to make Karen do what they wanted."

"How did that work?"

"The men gave the money to Karen, and she gave it to the father. The father would tell Karen what cost what. Like, how much a blow job was worth." Karl is seething, full of rage. I need to quiet his injury through empathy, and add a dose of reality processing.

"I understand now. You're afraid my asking to be paid for seeing Karen could somehow be like the father asking for money, and that would make our relationship terrible."

"Yeah!"

"And that would take away all the trust you have for me."

"Yeah!"

"Karl, I'm a doctor for people's feelings, and like all doctors, people pay me to help them. That's how it is with Karen and me. Just because there's a payment, there doesn't have to be any hurting."

There is silence, then, "Are you sure?"

"I promise, Karl. You might ask Katherine and Holdon to help you understand this better. They are okay with this arrangement."

"Okay." Karl is calmer, but still suspicious. "We'll see."

It's ironic that Karl's rage at my seeing patients for money comes at the time when, because of corporate tightening, I have to give up my half day a week of psychiatric practice—all my patients except for Karen, that is. Since neither of us wants to interrupt the therapeutic process we've been working on for so long, we need to find a different meeting place. Sadly, my wife and I have recently separated so my apartment will have to do. I can't afford the overhead of a part-time office for just one patient. After some initial turmoil, Karen adapts to this change of treatment setting, and we resume our work together.

In early February, Karen comes in a few minutes late— unusual for her. She says she got dizzy bowling last night, and the next thing she knew, she woke up and found herself at the Prudential Building, which is near my office. It always fascinates me when I learn what it's like for Karen to live day to day. She had to ask directions to my office because another part usually gets her to my building. She's lost time at bowling before—some other part usually bowls—but she's always come back before she leaves the bowling alley. I tell her I don't know why it was different this time, but that perhaps another part of her can explain.

"Karen became ill at the bowling alley," says Holdon, with a raspy voice. "She had chest pain. I bowled the last two games for her. Karen usually averages about 100. I average 208, so her friends were surprised." Holdon looks out the window at the neighboring skyscrapers. "I like to park at the Prudential Building," he continues. "I walk over here and then I let Karen come back out." Holdon coughs a few times.

"Are you okay?" I ask.

"I've got a cough—about half of us have it. I'm not sure why some of us don't get sick. I'm more hoarse than the others."

"I hope you feel better," I say. "Perhaps there's someone else who'd like to talk to me."

Holdon takes his cue, nods his head as a good-bye, and closes his eyes. As Karen's eyes open, she takes on Miles's familiar forward, in-your-face posture.

"I'm getting sick, too," says Miles with irritation. "More of us are. We never all got sick before."

We've been working to have many of the alters share the experiences of each other. I'd asked Ann to spend time with Miles and Katherine to help modulate Miles's anger. Now it seems physical symptoms that used to be separated are also being shared. I wait to see what else Miles has to say.

"Ann has been doing things with me and Katherine. She's a good listener; I've been telling her things, you know, that happened to me." He sits up straighter. "But I can't do what I want with them around all the time."

"I can see how that would be frustrating. I can imagine they're not helpful *all* the time." For him to accept my empathy, he has to accept that they're indeed helpful much of the time.

A minute later Ann makes her entrance and tells me she's perturbed with Miles. He doesn't listen, she says, and she questions why she should be out with him. Because he needs you, Ann, I say. Ann isn't appeased. She doesn't want to lose her individuality and fears she'll never be able to be alone again. I say I understand her fears but am concerned about what's best for all the parts together. She understands my view, but is still unsettled. When she has to pee, she says, Miles gets panicky and won't let her. He has to step back before she can do it.

"The integration process seems to be fraught with challenges, Ann," I say, apologetically. She chuckles, but isn't happy.

"Miles did share with me the memory of being shut in the coffin at the funeral home," says Ann. "I had no idea what was done to them."

Karen looks at me slyly, with a smile lurking at the corners of her mouth.

"I'm not who you think I am," she says.

"Oh!" She's surprised me. "Do I know you?"

"Of course. I'm Karen 2." She sits back, full of ease, and looks me in the eye.

"What brings you in to see me today?" I ask. I'm again struck by her casual manner, lack of anxiety, and self-confidence. Qualities all the others lack.

"I've noticed the changes going on within our system," says Karen 2. "I haven't been out very much, and I don't like what's happening to us. Our body, for example. I get depressed when I look in the mirror."

"You can observe when the others are out?"

"Of course, and I can come out whenever I want to. Karen 3 is not aware of me, but I can put ideas in her head. I'm not affected by the things the others are. I don't have Karen 3's bronchitis. I think the rest of them should just disappear and let me take over."

She peers at me with eyes showing a mischief that borders on malevolence. I wonder, if she can come out whenever she wants, why she doesn't just come out and stay out, if that's what she desires. I don't ask because I don't want to suggest it.

"If you want to be out more, why don't you share time with Karen 3, and share more of yourself with her?" I think Karen 3 could use some of her lack of anxiety and self-confidence.

"Well, I could do it some, but when she gets sick, I'm leaving."

"When she gets sick?"

"I don't have the diabetes and the cough that she does. So when she gets sick, I just go inside." She looks at me with that sly smile again. "The mind is a powerful thing, don't you think?" I feel as if she's laughing at me.

"Shall I talk to Karen 3 and tell her what we've discussed?"

"If you like. Bye." Karen closes her eyes and I bring her out of her trance. When she opens her eyes, she looks around the room and then at me, wide-eyed and frightened.

"Someone else came to see me," I say. This registers on her. "There will be another part—one called Karen 2; she says you're Karen 3—who will be spending some time with you. It may give you a little more self-confidence." Karen nods, and I tell her I'm sorry but our time is up, although "she" just got here. She nods again and as she turns to leave, I see her eyes well with tears. She walks unsteadily out of the room.

It's a few months later and I've been talking to Juliann for most of the session. I'm fascinated by her manner. She has a subtle but palpable feminine charm and poise. She sits with her knees to the side, her torso facing me, and her head gently tilted to the side as she speaks. Her eyes are calm and kind. Although I've spoken to her briefly in the past, I'm getting a big dose of her today. She has a way of listening with full attention; she considers what I say, then she uses the information she's just learned to ask intuitive questions. I realize it's the first time I have found Karen interesting on a personal level, as if we could be chatting over coffee, and she would be quietly engaging. I wonder if her manner is quiet and calm because she's mirroring my manner; in other words, if I find her engaging because she's empathically suiting herself to me. I have the disquieting feeling she's better at this than I am. And I'm good.

"I find I'm very comfortable talking with you, Juliann. You have a very compatible way about you."

"I like to learn things," she says, smiling without the least trace of anxiety or embarrassment. "I'm a calm and independent sort."

"What part do you play for Karen; how were you born?"

"I was born to talk to the men who came for Karen. We would have long conversations. I'd get to know them and draw them in."

"What would happen then?"

"Another part would come out to have sex with them."

"Why did you bother with them at all?"

"If they got to know us a little bit, they'd be less inclined to hurt us," she says. Very wise, I think.

"Jensen, what seems to be the trouble?" Karen, as Jensen, is shaking and looking at me with wide eyes that scare me.

"I'm mad!" he says. It's interesting to see Karen, who in most of her incarnations is so calm, passive, depressed, and immature, exhibiting such agitation. She's furious and about to strike out. I'll have to rely on being a grown man to Jensen's little boy in order to keep him under control. What I mean by this, precisely, is that there's a manner I can adopt—in part I learned it from my father, and have refined and polished it with my own son—that has the paternal authority and confidence to dominate a boy's anger. I know no matter how angry my young son may get, I can prevail. My son knows it, too. He relies on it.

"I see that you're mad," I say, calmly holding his wide-eyed gaze. "Why don't you tell me about it?"

"I've been breaking down the walls inside, and now I want to put them back up, and I can't!"

"You want to put them back up?"

"Yeah, I don't want to be out there. I want to kill them all! I don't ever want to come out!"

"You're the one who makes the walls?" I ask, not attending to his rage.

"Yeah," he says, distracted for a moment. "The walls took years and years to make. Every time something happened, I'd make a piece of wall out of the feeling, the memory."

"I've been told you've been taking some of the walls down all by yourself."

"Yeah, I've been building a big stone wall—all around me."

"A big stone wall to keep you from being hurt?" I ask.

Jensen looks at me in surprise, as if he's been found out. I look at him as if I already know the answer. He looks down, his anger deflating.

"I've put up the walls all these years to keep us safe, and now they're coming down." He's downcast.

"I can understand how that could be real scary for you, if you thought the others were in danger and you couldn't help them like you've done before."

"Yeah! We're not going to be able to take it if we don't have the walls."

"But you're not in the danger you once were, Jensen. You're going to have to trust me. Karen is no longer hurt like she was. The others want to come out from behind the walls. It'll be okay."

Jensen looks confused, hurt, and sad. But I also see a glimmer of relief. I didn't realize what a drastic change this is for him—didn't appreciate that he sees his role as the guardian of keeping experiences isolated. I sense it will take some time for him to come completely around to the idea of integration instead of separation. Unconvinced, Jensen steps back inside Karen.

"I miss coming to see you," says Claire. She's very reticent; she lowers her eyes and speaks so I can hardly hear her. "I'm afraid, Dr. Baer."

"What has made you afraid, Claire?"

"We saw a scary movie last night. I watched, too."

"What was the movie?"

"I think it was called *Primal Fear.* It made me remember— about the priest."

"Do you want to tell me what you remembered?"

In pieces, Claire tells me her story:

Karen looks at the clock: thirty minutes left before school is out. Father Moravec comes into the room, spots Karen, whispers something to the teacher, and walks toward her. Karen switches and Claire finds Father Moravec standing over her whispering that she's to come to his office after school. Claire nods and sits staring ahead, not listening to the teacher. The minutes go by, and the bell rings.

As the last few students fly out the doors, Claire walks down to the end of the corridor to Father Moravec's office. Her father and the police officer, Bert, are already there.

"Have a seat, Karen," says Father Moravec. "We'll wait until Scott comes." Scott is Bert's nephew. Claire looks at her father, who smiles that scary smile.

Claire sits on one of the wooden chairs that students waiting for discipline sit on. She's sat here before, but not because she was bad. Within a few minutes, she can hear Scott's steps come slowly down the hall. When Scott enters the office, Father Moravec leads the way to the adjacent church and down into the basement. The police officer carries a suitcase Claire hadn't noticed before. The church is deserted, and the only sound she can hear is the clicking and tapping of their shoes echoing off the stone floor.

They pass a room filled with small desks and chairs with drawings of lambs taped to the walls. They turn a corner and follow a darker passageway. Father Moravec takes out his keys and unlocks the door to one of the rooms, and waits until everyone has entered before he closes it behind himself and locks it again. The room is sparsely furnished. Along one wall is a gray sofa. Five folding chairs face the sofa near the other side of the room. Bert opens the suitcase and removes a 35-mm still camera and 8-mm movie camera. He also has floodlights on stands with small shades that allow him to direct the light. These he goes about set-ting up quickly.

"You kids are going to be famous models," says Karen's father. "We sent some of your pictures to a magazine." Bert hands the still camera to Karen's father and turns on the lights and starts the movie camera. He nods to the priest.

"Go over to the couch, children," says the priest in a honeyed voice. "And Scott, take off Karen's shirt." Scott looks at Claire; they've done this before and they're friends, but they're both scared. Scott has told Claire that when they grow up, they're going to get married. Claire likes Scott, too, but she doesn't like this part.

Scott helps Claire unbutton her blouse and then pulls her undershirt over her head. Claire turns her head away from Scott.

"Now, Karen, take off Scott's shirt."

Claire does the same for Scott, and the priest leads them through Claire's skirt and Scott's pants and their underwear. As they're undressing each other, Karen's father takes a few pictures while Bert runs the movie camera. Once the two children are naked, Bert turns off the camera and takes the still camera from Karen's father. As the priest directs the children into various lewd poses, Bert snaps a roll of pictures. Tears are in Claire's eyes.

When the camera runs out of film, Bert puts in a new roll and hands it back to Karen's father. Bert nods to the priest as he turns on the movie camera.

"Now get on your knees in front of Scott and hold his pee pee and kiss it," says Father Morevec. Claire obeys, but she feels sick. Not long ago she'd refused to do this and her father took her to another room and beat her. She can feel Scott trembling; she knows he's scared, too, so she makes sure she's gentle.

"This is what God made you for," says Father Moravec, "to love one another."

The police officer motions to the priest, who tells Claire to get up. Another reel of film is put in the movie camera and the priest says to Claire, "Lie down on the couch, Karen, and open your legs." He turns to Scott. "Kneel down at her feet."

Scott knows he's going to be told to kiss Karen "down there," and he doesn't want to. He doesn't move.

"Do as I say!" says Father Moravec, louder. "Don't you know the Church owns you and we can do anything to you we want. The devil will do terrible things to you if you don't do it!" Scott still doesn't move. Bert puts down the camera and grabs Scott by the arm. The priest opens the door with the police officer dragging Scott behind, and Claire, left with her father, hears them go into one of the nearby rooms.

Claire has been in the room they enter. It's empty and there is a door on the side wall. Father Moravec opens the door and reveals a small, dark closet, with wet pipes running along one wall.

"You were born a sinner and you'll always be a sinner. Think about your sins in there!" shouts Father Moravec; Scott is thrown inside and the priest slams the door. He takes out his keys and locks the closet door.

They walk out of the room and slam the outside door so Scott can hear, and go back to Claire. Frightened by what she has heard, she poses by herself and the men praise her for being such a good model, and she feels a little pretty. After about twenty minutes, they hear Scott begin to scream.

Claire says she doesn't remember anything after that.

"Scott said we had to keep it secret," says Claire, "or we'd go to hell and jail." Claire's face has the open sadness of a vulnerable little girl. "Sometimes Father Moravec would come for us after school and make us watch the movies while he played with his pee pee until white stuff came out. Miles and Karl would come out when I got too scared."

"The movie you saw reminded you of this?"

"Yes, I thought I was just like the boy in the movie, but then he turned out to be faking."

I recall the plot of *Primal Fear*. "He lied to his friend, the lawyer, didn't he?"

"Yes. Do you think I'd lie to you?"

"It hadn't really occurred to me, Claire. Why would you?"

"I wouldn't, but they always said no one would believe me. I didn't want you to think we were like the boy in the movie."

"You were the one who wanted help. You wrote me that first letter."

"Yes, I know. I wanted you to help us."

"I'll do all I can, Claire." She steps back and Karen lurches forward.

"I thought the movie was great; there was blood everywhere!" says Miles.

"What about the blood?" I ask.

"I liked to see the priest cut up. I always wanted to do that stuff to that priest Moravec. But I didn't let Claire see the bloody stuff."

"Did you help Claire during these times with the priest?"

"Yeah, I never let her see any blood. Once the priest slapped her and cut her lip. Then I came out and they made me kiss Scott, and then they took his picture, because it looked like he bit me 'cause he got blood on his lip, too." I get distracted, thinking about this scene for a moment.

"What do you make of it all, Miles? What were these men about?"

"I don't know. They're pervs. I think they mostly did it for money."

"The men took the pictures for money?"

"Yeah; it makes me so mad!"

INTEGRATION

PART THREE

16

HOLDON'S SOLUTION

"The headaches are getting worse, Dr. Baer," says Holdon in Karen's deeper voice. Karen sits as tall as possible; her bearing is formal and serious, but she's urgent in her speech. "There are too many of us coming out at the same time; it's too much! The distinctiveness between Miles, Katherine, and Ann is blurring. Claire and Thea are blurring, too. But it's making them sick!"

This is a big problem. I'd been hoping that as a result of the distinct parts sharing time more and more, the barriers separating them would dissolve. But Holdon is now telling me Karen can't stand the process.

"I'm not sure what to do about this, Holdon," I say. "On the one hand, I want to encourage the sharing of time and integration of the separate parts, but I don't want to cause all of you undue distress and make you sick. Can you think of anything we might do?"

"I'll think about it, Dr. Baer."

During June and July 1996, Karen experiences more and more of the thoughts and memories of the other parts, but the increased loss of time is driving her crazy. Every day brings a pack of nuisances. She goes to a wedding and knows only a few people, but many more know her and call her by different names. She keeps losing time to accommodate whomever she meets. She leaves the house for the grocery store, but wakes to find herself at the store two hours later, unable to account for the time in between. Later that night, at the system's "meeting," she's told one of the parts had a prearranged luncheon date she wasn't aware of. She finds a pager in her purse she never bought. She wakes to find herself at a department store with the clerk waiting for her to pay for the clothes some part of her had picked out minutes before. People get irritated with her for failing to keep appointments when other parts have made conflicting plans. She's inconsistent in disciplining her children. Although she's feeling better physically and is on a medication for her high blood sugar, when she measures her glucose, she claims the number varies depending on which alter has been out.

I inform Karen I'm taking a vacation and will be gone almost two weeks. Before I leave, amid Karen's expected flurry of concern about my well-being, and hers, I receive the following letter, or should I say memo, from Holdon.

To: Dr. Baer

From: Holdon

Re: My Guidelines to Integrate

After quite a bit of thinking I came up with a plan to start our integration process. Knowing how we work, I feel this might be the only possibility. I must not talk of this out loud until you have a chance to read my idea. The others can hear what I say out loud, but they cannot know my thoughts or read my letters. If the following guideline seems to agree with you, we can talk when you return.

1. After putting Karen under hypnosis, you need to ask her if you can enter her safe place. I am confident she will let you in.

2. You need to explain to her what you will be helping her do, which is having the alters join her one at a time.

3. Choose an alter from outside the room. (One at a time.) I feel the following alters are ready to integrate: Thea 6 years, Karl 10 years, Elise 8 years, Sandy 18 years, Karen Boo

2 years, Julie 13 years, Karen 1 10 years, and Claire 7 years.
The other nine of us are not ready at this time.

4. *Dr. Baer calls the alter in and explains to Karen who this*
   alter is and this alter's purpose in her life.

5. *Dr. Baer explains to Karen that the alter is not needed to be*
   a separate part anymore.

6. *Dr. Baer asks the alter to step into Karen's form (body).*

7. *Integration complete.*

   Holdon

I read the letter over several times. Holdon has given me a step-by-step procedure for Karen's integration. I am utterly amazed. Could it work? This is similar to the fusion rituals Putnam described in his book *Diagnosis and Treatment of Multiple Personality Disorder.* I didn't really understand what he was talking about at the time; it was a bit vague. It's also a little scary. We've been gradually dissolving the separation between the alters, but this is an all-at-once, wholesale integration of an alter. I can't imagine what will happen. Fortunately, this plan shouldn't be too hard to sell to the alters since it comes from Holdon. I thank Holdon and tell him we can start when I return from vacation.

When I return, Karen is in turmoil. Her mother has made relentless demands. She finds that if she hesitates with her mother, she loses time. Sandy comes out, gives in, and placates. Ann feels guilty and in need of punishment. Miles wants to choke and kill people. He's separated again from Katherine and Ann, no longer sharing time with them, but now feeling strange and alone. Katherine can't keep things organized; the alters are lurching from one crisis to another. She complains they're coming out at all sorts of times. Holdon says he's a zombie from all the driving. I decide we need to start to integrate Karen's system fast because it's falling apart. I talk to Holdon about whom we should integrate first. He suggests Julie; she's in the most distress and her symptoms are affecting all the others.

· · ·

It's August 1, 1996, and I'm clutching Holdon's letter while I wait for Karen to arrive. I want to suggest to Karen that we try what Holdon has proposed, but worry that this won't work and we'll be where we started. I'm still wrestling with my thoughts when Karen shows up, on time as she usually is, not suspecting what's going to happen to her today.

"Holdon has suggested a procedure for integrating the alters into you," I begin. I go through the steps in his letter. "I'm hoping we can try the first one today. What do you think?"

Karen nods as I'm speaking, then asks, "How do they get inside me?"

She's got me. "I don't know exactly," I say. I don't want to let on that I've never done this before, and I have no idea whether it will work. It's important that patients have confidence in their physicians; confidence can heal. "I think it will happen through the imagery under hypnosis. You will see yourself and the alter physically come together. We'll have to see when we get there." I guess I'm not exactly a pillar of reassurance, but I'm doing the best I can. We're all trusting Holdon's wisdom. "Are you afraid?" I ask.

"No, I'm willing to try this," Karen says, "but I do have concerns about the unknown. What will I be like afterwards?"

"I think you'll be the same, but you'll grow, with some new feelings and memories. Each alter is a small part of you. Those memories and feelings belonging to the alters, that have always been a part of you, will become available to you. You shouldn't be that much changed." I'm guessing, of course. "Julie will be the first alter we'll integrate. I think you will have fewer headaches and pains in your legs after she integrates. Are you ready?"

"Ready." Karen settles into her chair, her face betraying some fear, but she's already relaxing and closing her eyes.

I take extra time putting Karen under hypnosis, wanting to make sure her trance state is deep. My heart is pounding; I try to keep it out of my voice. Although I feel this is really weird, I need to be positive about this process and trust what she herself, through Holdon, has devised to reintegrate the parts she herself has split off. So we go forward.

"Find yourself in your safe place," I say. My eyes close, too, for a moment to better feel Karen's relaxation and her plunging into herself. "You're in the little room where you have all your things that comfort you. Look around and see them vividly, the colors and textures. When you are comfortable, nod your head."

After a few seconds, Karen slowly nods her head. She looks as if she's profoundly deep in thought.

"Can you step back and let Julie talk with me?"

"Okay," Karen says slowly and then her face shifts and takes on a pained expression. She begins coughing.

"Julie?"

"Yes, it's me."

"Has Holdon spoken to you and are you ready to be integrated into Karen?"

"Yes, I think so, but I'm afraid."

"I understand. I think you'll feel better when you join Karen. You suffer so much now." She nods and looks as if she's about to cry.

"What would you like me to tell Karen about you when I introduce you?"

"Well, I'm thirteen years old," she says, her speech punctuated by coughs. "I was born in 1970." Her brows come together and she leans forward in her chair. "If I can't walk, then will Karen not be able to walk? I couldn't walk yesterday when I came out."

"Karen may feel the pain in your legs, but she'll be able to walk." I hope. "What else can I say about you?"

"I was born when Karen's grandfather molested her. I came out to spare Karen a bad relationship with her grandparents. I come out sometimes when other people hurt us, too. I'm the one who always went to the hospital, ever since Karen was eleven, when she got pneumonia when her father choked her. I took all the pain in the legs when we were beaten with the extension cords. Sometimes I give Karen these feelings of pain so I can rest. I made us go deaf in the hospital for two weeks to get some relief from hearing bad things. They thought we were in a coma, but we just shut down. I helped when Constantine hurt us. . . ."

"That was you that got hurt?"

"Well, Jensen helped, too. Actually there were four of us that helped that time. Miles took the pain from the hanger. . . ."

"What role do you take now?" I ask.

"I mostly come out during illnesses. . . ." Her voice trails off and she settles back in her chair.

"I'd like to tell Karen these things when I introduce you before the integration, okay?" She nods. "Okay, then why don't you step back and let Karen come back. Stay close; I'll call you back soon."

"Okay." Karen goes blank for a moment as Julie leaves and then returns as Karen.

"I've talked with Julie, and she's ready to integrate. Shall we proceed?"

"I'm ready," says Karen slowly. She seems to be talking from far away. She speaks slowly, almost mumbling, her head nodding slightly, as if she's struggling to come up to where I am from deep inside herself. I pause a second until she relaxes back in her chair.

"May I come into the little room with you?" I ask. "I can come through the same entrance you did. Would that be okay?"

Karen nods her head again slowly.

"Then see me come into the little room and stand off to the side." I pause while I read Karen's face and watch her mind creating these motions. "Am I there with you?"

Karen nods.

"I'd like to invite Julie to come in and join us in your special place. . . . Karen, tell me what you see."

"I see a young girl; you're extending your hand to her. She has black hair. She's coming in slowly. She's crippled and has a crutch."

"Karen, this is Julie," I begin. I'm completely winging this. I have Holdon's letter next to me so I can follow his steps exactly. But regarding what to say, I'm feeling my way along as we go.

"She's thirteen years old," I continue, "and was born to spare you from being hurt by your grandfather." I go through the details Julie just shared. As I talk, I try to maintain a mental picture of Karen's little room so I can see this process along with her. When I finish, I pause, letting it all sink in.

"Are you ready?" I ask. Karen nods and says, "Ready."

"Julie, too?" I ask.

"She's nodding," says Karen.

Okay, so now what? I don't know how to get them together, but I guess they have to act it out within their trance state in the little room. Holdon says the alter has to step into Karen's body.

"Julie, can you step toward Karen?" I wait a moment while Karen is working.

"Julie can't really walk," says Karen, "I'll lie down so it's easier."

"Then I'll help Julie lie down next to you," I suggest.

"She still has her crutch," Karen says, waiting, it seems, for me to do something about it.

"Julie can throw her crutch away, and she can throw all her illnesses away with it. Those are memories from the past." A little extra suggestion shouldn't hurt, I think. "Is Julie next to you?"

"Yes, I am," says Julie.

"I'll step to the side," I say. "Julie, you need to slide over and move into Karen's body. Can you manage that?" After a moment's pause, Julie's voice speaks softly and with a quiver.

"We're touching. It's strange. I feel changes. Everything is locking together." Karen is writhing slightly in her chair; she's experiencing something significant—I can only guess what.

"There are little explosions" says Julie. "I feel like an X-ray." Julie is struggling. Karen's face shows the strain and her body is tensed. "You won't talk to me again," she says faintly.

"You'll always be with me as a part of Karen," I assure her.

"Karen is in pain," Julie says, fading.

"She's experiencing memories of your past." I want to let her know I'm still with her. Karen is tense in her chair, fists clenched, brows knit, deep in thought. "Are you all right?"

"It's like I'm in a spaceship," Julie says from far away, "rushing past stars. I feel like I'm dying—getting weaker. Will you remember me?"

"Yes," I respond with genuine affection and tenderness, "and I'll also recognize you in Karen."

"Then I'll let go. Good-bye." I say good-bye and watch her fade from Karen's expression.

Karen looks shaken, still deep within herself. I don't want to rush her, but I want to know if she's okay. I wait a few moments until I see the integration process fading from Karen's face.

"Karen?" I ask. She stirs a little. "How are you doing?"

"Strange," she manages, as if she's struggling to speak, being so internally preoccupied. "My hands are numb. My blood feels different. My heart is beating differently." She cocks her head slightly. "Julie is not answering anymore."

"Take your time," I offer.

"I see a lot of what she went through. Family members I trusted are hurting me. It's like watching a movie. They're calling me names—it's degrading. Memories of mother. I feel like I have cuts all over me." She sighs and collapses further into her chair. "I feel weak . . . exhausted. . . ."

"You rest," I say, "I'm going to leave you now. You can see me leave your little room and go back to the office." I let Karen sit for a few minutes. Before she comes back, I suggest to her that she'll remember everything that has happened today. I go through our usual procedure for bringing her out of her trance and back to the office. As she awakes, she shrinks back, as if she's being assaulted by the light.

"Are you all right?"

"I don't know. Everything is so bright. I can hear everything: my own heart beating." She looks bewildered and disoriented.

"Do you remember what happened?" I ask.

"Yes, I remember everything." She tries to gain her equilibrium, and I sit with her for a few more minutes, but it's almost time for her to leave.

"When you go home, call me if you're worried about anything. And why don't you write down your thoughts about this experience."

"Okay." When she's ready to go, she gets up, still shaky, and walks haltingly out of the office.

I wonder about what has just happened. Will it hurt or help her? I'm on thin ice here. There's really no blueprint, except Holdon's, for what we've just done. I just hope she's okay. I'm exhausted, too.

Although I check on her by phone several times, it's two weeks until I see Karen and get the full story of how she's fared since the integration of Julie. She tells me that the feelings of the integration have resolved. She's no longer shaky and uncoordinated, and her leg pains and blurred vision are gone. The integration experience was really hard—gaining all the new feelings that were Julie's.

"At first I couldn't believe it," she says, animated, using her hands to talk, "but the new memories coincided with bits of my own. For example, I remember once going swimming when it was fifty degrees out. I didn't realize why I'd done it. But I learned Julie did this to use the cold water to help the pain in her legs. I had remembered all of it except the pain part."

"What else?"

"Well, for the first few days, I'd look in the mirror, and I'd do a double take. I wouldn't see myself right; my hair would momentarily appear black. My hand would look crippled, but then it wasn't. I felt awkward; I had to consciously think about which leg to walk with. It all got a little better every day."

This is fascinating to me. What strikes me, what I hadn't really expected, is that not only did Karen get Julie's memories, she also got Julie's way of experiencing her body, which was apparently very different from how Karen experiences her own body, and this discrepancy required the most time to accommodate and sort out. Karen gives me a letter she wrote about her first integration.

Aug. 24, 1996

To Dr. Baer

The Merging of Julie

Three and a half weeks ago I integrated with the first of my many personalities. Although hesitant at first, I soon became convinced by the others inside that it was time to start uniting with each of them. I was nervous about how this would affect me. I didn't know if I wanted to remember memories that were taken from me to protect me. I wanted to run away and hide, but at the same time, I felt I needed to be guided into this process.

Karen spends the next few paragraphs describing entering her little room and the process of integration. The letter continues:

After Julie and I integrated, I immediately started feeling very sensitive to all sounds around me. I was able to hear the sounds of your breathing and the sound of your pen writing on the

*paper: the traffic below, the air conditioner, etc. When you talked,
it sounded as though you were screaming at me, though all you
were doing was talking. When I opened my eyes, I was blinded
by the brightness of the room. My eyes ached with pain and I
wished the blinds were closed. I seemed sensitive to everything
around me. I felt shaky and uncoordinated. I didn't expect to feel
this way and I was afraid I was going to feel this way forever. I
wondered if something had gone wrong and we shouldn't have
integrated.*

The next paragraph describes Karen's getting into her car and
driving herself home with racking pain in her legs, then . . .

*This integration felt like I'd gone through major surgery and I
had doubts about ever doing it again. I pulled all the shades
down in my bedroom and turned off all the lights. As I lay in
total darkness, my mind raced as if I were watching a movie in
fast forward. As the memories poured into me I felt every pain
associated with them, and even though the pain lasted only as
long as the memory (a few seconds), I felt so drained and I just
wanted these memories to stop. Sometime late that night, I called
you when the memories coming in had slowed down. The light
sensitivity and sensitive hearing went away after the fourth day.
During the next week, I gained all the memories from Julie, the
pain stopped, and I started gradually functioning again. My
coordination came back by the end of the second week and I was
again able to hold a pen and walk straight. I was relieved that it
was over and the effects didn't last forever. I'm thankful that you
were there helping me. I could never have come through this
without you.*

I simply can't imagine how horrible it must have been for
Karen to suddenly have all of Julie's experiences. Having Julie had
always been a form of protection and now she's going to have to
deal with memories of the degradation herself. There's also no way
for me to know whether she's received all of Julie. Has Julie really
been fully integrated into Karen? Will it stick? It seems so hard to
believe. Has Holdon's prescription worked?

I'm also reminded of how very careful I'll have to be as we progress. Karen went through so much following Julie's integration that I didn't anticipate. I'll have to take greater care every step of the way. Integrating Julie has been an incredible breakthrough, but this is just the beginning. We've got sixteen personalities to go, and I'm afraid we're in for a rough ride.

17.

MERGING CLAIRE

At our next session, I discuss integrating another alter, and Karen agrees, but which one? I put her under hypnosis and, as usual, ask if someone would like to talk to me. Karen squirms in her chair charmingly.

"Claire?"

"Dr. Baer, could I join with Karen?" Claire pulls at her hair, turns her head, and looks at me coyly. Claire seems like a good choice, but I feel a tug on my heart; I will miss her.

"I think it would be fine for you to integrate, Claire," I say. "Let's plan it for next week. When I introduce you to Karen, what shall I say about you?"

"Well, you could tell her I was born on her Communion Day," she says in a little singsong voice, "when Karen was hurt in her white Communion dress. Later I came out whenever they put that white dress on her. That was the signal . . ."

"When they put the white dress on?"

"Yes, I was supposed to be married to the devil. They said God wanted me to be hurt. They'd experiment on me—put things inside of me. Then they'd laugh. I'd be out while they strapped Karen to the metal table at the funeral home. When they started to hurt me, Miles would come out. When Karen was getting married, she had a white dress on and I came out. I was afraid of all the people and went right back in. Karen fainted then." I'd never heard Claire's side of this episode before and it fills in some gaps.

Sidney comes out after Claire and says he worries if he merges with Karen, then Karen will start stealing things. Sandy wants to integrate, too. She's unhappy; she can't stop doing things for Mother. Sandy watched Julie integrate and thinks it wouldn't be so bad. I'm glad; it makes it easier for me if the alters are on board.

During the third week of August 1996, Karen is ready to integrate Claire. She's carrying a letter. It is written in pencil with large printed letters and misspellings. Claire writes:

Dear Doctor Bear,

I wanted to tell you some things before we get together. I did everything I could to not let Karen remember things and I think she's going to be scared. I know you're not going to leave her. Did I tell you about the games when I was suppose to not feel pain? When we get together are we going to forget how to not feel pain? All the times we were hurt I pretended not to feel things but I did and could not say anything cause they would zap me with a wire on my ankle. Could you please anser these questions before we get together?

What will happen when I am needed?

Who's going to take care of Karen Boo?

Will you take care of Thea and ask to talk to her sometimes cause she only came out when I told her to and I am worried that she will be forgotton.

Doctor Bear there is something else that bothers me but I am embarased to say cause Karen might get upset with me and not want me to join her. I know that I am not really going to die but there is a feeling I need to feel before I go. You see I always wished you were my daddy and hold me, sometimes I pretend your holding me when I am scared. But I know you can't hold me and that makes me feel sad. I love you and I want to know what love feels like. When you meet me inside could I pretend to hug you goodbye. If I join Karen what will she feel about you? Will you get mad at her if she gets my feelings. You made me feel good about myself and I feel that everything bad that happened to me was not my fault and I feel good about this, but I am a little scared about what Karen will think.

   Doctor Bear. Thank you for being my friend and my daddy. I know you are a good soul and I am glad you are a part of our lives. I am glad that I was the first to come out and let the others know it was okay to trust you. I will miss you and I hope that somehow I will still be abel to be with you again. Maybe you won't forget about me. I hope. You could write a story. You helped take away the pain in my heart. I feel its time for me to grow. I love you. Always take care of your children and watch them so nobody will hurt them.

Claire

God, I'm going to miss little Claire. I show Karen the first page of the letter from Claire. I feel it will be helpful if she sees Claire's willingness and also her concerns. I don't show her the rest because I don't want her to anticipate the hugging issue. Karen reads and nods her head. She turns the paper over and holds it away from her, looking at the page as a whole.

"It looks like the writing of a little girl," says Karen.

"It is; she's only seven. I think she did pretty well. Do you remember the funeral home?"

"I remember bits of it. Stainless-steel tanks, electric shocks if I expressed pain, being lowered into shallow water—just fragments."

There is a silence between us; I think Karen is waiting for me to proceed, so I do. I begin the hypnosis process and give Karen plenty of time to go deep into her trance. She's so adept at this that I suspect she's simply waiting for me to get on with it, but I just want to make sure. I ask for Claire to come out.

"Remember when Karen had a dream," says Claire, playing with the hem of her blouse, "where a little girl comes over and sits next to you? It wasn't a dream; it was my thoughts I gave to Karen." Claire pauses and bites at her lower lip. "Could I sit in your lap before I integrate?" she asks.

"Right now?"

"No, not now," she says with a bit of regret, "I know I can't do that. Inside Karen's safe room."

"Sure, I think that would be fine." Claire's smile is radiant.

"I'm ready," she says, still smiling. I thank her for her letter, and ask her if I can use some of what she told me there to introduce her to Karen. Claire agrees.

"Okay, then, why don't you step back and let me talk to Karen." I can see Claire leave Karen's body as if she's been dispossessed. "Karen?"

"Yes."

"Claire's ready. Shall we go ahead?"

"Okay."

"I'm outside your special room," I say. "If you open the door, I'll come in and sit down." I want to give Karen instructions she can visualize, but I let her decide where I will sit. "Can we invite Claire to come in?"

"Okay, I'll open the door."

"Is Claire inside?"

"No, she's standing in the doorway."

"I'll go get her," I say. "She can sit on my lap while we talk." I pause a moment while Karen visualizes the action. "Are we together?" I ask.

"Yes, she has her arms around your neck. She looks very happy."

"Good. Let me tell you a little about Claire." I recite some of the facts Claire gave me in her letter. "Claire, are you ready?"

"She's holding on to you tighter and hiding her face," says Karen.

"Let's let her sit here for a moment," I say. I pause and wait for about twenty seconds. "Claire, it's time for you to scoot onto Karen's lap." I watch Karen's face for the movement to occur.

"She's talking to me."

"Yes?"

"She says to take care of you and her favorite blanket." Karen pauses, and a look of trouble fills her face. "She's afraid."

"Don't worry, Claire," I say, "I'll be with you and Karen. You can go inside now."

Karen shows concentration in her face, as if she's working.

"She's crawled inside."

I stay still for a few minutes, letting this process unfold. Karen's face is creased hard in concentration. "I'll leave your room now," I say, and I watch Karen's face for the subtle movements that signal the operation has taken place.

Karen's face turns sad; tears drop precipitously from each eye. "I can picture every tool in the funeral home. I see the tables, the buckets at the end of the tables with tubes coming out, surgical tools, saws, hammers, cabinets—what's inside? Jars of fluids. Outside the room are coffins, some shiny and finished, some plain wooden boxes. Everything is gray, the walls and floor.

"How do you feel?"

"The shakiness is going; I'm less nervous." She gives a slight grimace. The sounds are real loud again. Telling her she'll remember everything that happened, I bring her out of her hypnotic trance. She squints her eyes against the light.

"It's not as bad as last time," she says, and drifts off, lost in thought. She looks at me with a tilt of her head.

"Before, the funeral home felt like someone else's story. I knew some of the events and images, but I didn't feel it. Now, it's beginning to feel like it happened to *me.*" She speaks more about the new images of the funeral home, and the chemical factory where her grandfather worked.

This integration doesn't seem to take such a toll on her as last time, and I'm glad we aren't as rushed as we were with Julie. Next time we meet, she says she's absorbing Claire's memories, and she gives me her writings about Claire's integration.

August 25, 1996

To Dr. Baer

The Merging of Claire

On Thursday, August 22, 1996, Claire integrated within me. This experience was quite different than the merging of Julie and I found myself feeling content. The following is what we experienced.

In the days before our scheduled session, Claire started feeding me some memories. She felt this would make the merger go more smoothly. I also felt some of Claire's fears and at night I felt afraid someone was sitting on my bed. I became a bit nervous about

coming in to see you because Claire has strong feelings for you.
After arriving in your office, I gave you Claire's letter and you
read it. I wondered what she wrote but I respected her privacy and
knew that I would know soon enough.

After describing the integration sequence in approximately the
same order I experienced it, Karen goes on to describe some of the
new memories and changes taking place inside her . . .

Claire was so happy to be near you. I felt a tinge of jealousy. I
watched her put her head on your shoulder and you wrapped
your arms around her. She looked so content. Claire was hesitant
in wanting to merge. I think she was afraid of losing you, Dr. Baer.
Claire hugged you and scooted onto my lap and started to cry. I
told her that she's helped me so much that I'd love to have her
with me all the time. This seemed to calm her and she crawled
inside. For the first time in all the years we had been together in
therapy, I felt loved and cared for by you. Claire must have really
loved you and trusted you because I feel it.
   For the first time in 23 years, I took a bath instead of a shower.
I even used scented soap.
   I gained the pleasure of playing with my children.
   I noticed pretty things.
   I feel more feminine.
   I used body lotion.
   I bought new bras with matching underwear (the girly kind—I
never bought anything pretty before).
   I cried watching a love story.
   I craved chocolate milk.
   I brushed my daughter's hair and painted her nails.
   I feel younger.
   I could go on and on about the good feelings but for each good
feeling there is a bad one, and I need to tell you those.
   Claire was born on October 29, 1967, on my Communion
Day. They were degrading me, humiliating me, touching me,
saying dirty things to me, swearing—I couldn't take it anymore.
Claire was born to help, stay pretty, and be the perfect daughter,

*granddaughter. Don't fight it, they said. You're here to do as we
say. Never say no! Obey God's orders. White dress. Always a
white dress. No colors in room, only gray. Funeral Home. Laughter. Bad men. Bad priest. No one can help. Telephone rings:
one a.m. Answer it. Go with them. God's order. Tools are ready.
Lie down. Please don't. Lie still. Needles in nipples. Pain starts.
Claire calls Miles.*

*Dr. Baer, I am unable to detail the memories. I hope the words
help you to understand. I don't want to think about it.*

*Why did they pick me? How did the men find each other? How
could Claire trust after being treated that way? How did Claire
stay sweet? I don't understand.*

"Claire had a lot of feelings for you, Dr. Baer." Karen sits
across from me and seems softer. Is it her posture, the slight tilt of
her head? With both integrations, Karen has become a fuller
human being, but this time, I can actually see it. I had feelings for
Claire, too, and it makes me think about how, with my separation
from my wife, I'm trying to get used to the visitation schedule with
my own children, and of the distress my own daughter, who's
about Claire's age, shows as a result of my no longer being at home.

"What else have you noticed?" I ask.

"I tried to play games with my kids. I had to pick and choose
among Claire's memories in order to play. Mind games were played
on Claire. Father's games would have physical consequences. When
Father played card games with his friends, the winner would get to
molest Claire. When we played Monopoly and she landed on a certain square, she'd get stuck with a pin."

"You still talk about these things as happening to Claire."

"I have the memories now, but it doesn't feel like they all happened to me."

"Maybe they will over time," I say, wondering if that's something to dread. "What else?"

"The feeling of hurting myself came back a little bit, but it
doesn't feel like it's from Claire. Some other part is mad about
what I wrote."

"Perhaps we can find out about that," I say, and I proceed to put
Karen under hypnosis to see if some other part can tell us about

these thoughts of self-harm. Karen sits in her chair, relaxed and limp. I ask if anyone wants to talk with me about Karen's thoughts about hurting herself, and she straightens up and looks at me with eyes that show fear and anger.

"I don't like everyone getting together!" Karen snaps.

"Who is this?" I ask.

"Karl."

"Karl!" I say. Who the hell is Karl? I try to think back. I vaguely recollect Karl was associated with the worst of what happened to Karen, and that he was the "evil one." "What worries you about the parts getting together?" I ask, as innocently as possible.

"What's my job going to be now? Everybody is learning everything!" Karen, as Karl, is shaking and challenging me with his stare.

"Your job?"

Karl looks at me, exasperated, like I'm an idiot.

"Yes, my job!" he snaps. "The cult stuff. We're supposed to keep it secret. Me and Elise. Only we know about it!" Karl's eyes, wide, dart around the room.

I need to calm him down; he's frightened and agitated. I'll try to distract him.

"Tell me, Karl, when were you born? What was happening?"

"I was born during the rituals," Karl says, annoyed with my question. "I know about all the details—the worst of the worst. They used different languages. I signed in my own blood that I belong to the devil. . . ." His voice begins to rise again and picks up pace.

"How old are you, Karl?" I say, interrupting him and deliberately slowing my rate of speech.

"Ten."

"And you were born to keep secrets?"

"Yeah."

"And how exactly were you born?" I'm plodding along now, speaking slowly. The questions I ask don't matter, as long as they require Karl to organize himself around forming concrete factual answers. I'm really just interested in forcing Karl to adopt my mental pace, not his hysterical one.

"They made us split. Miles stepped outside himself and made me and Elise. Miles took the pain; I took the words. When the pain got too bad for Miles, then I'd take that, too." Karl begins to calm down.

"You took the words and kept them secret?" I ask in a slow, measured pace.

"Yeah. I destroyed a lot of letters sent to you, too."

"Letters for me?" I'm surprised.

"Yeah," he says with less exasperation. "The others wanted to tell you stuff, but I stopped them. I got the letters before it was too late."

"Too late?" I ask. "Why didn't you want them to tell me stuff?"

"They'll kill you." Karl looks at me, and I see a mixture of fear and compassion in his eyes.

Because Karl is only ten, and I suspect he knows the others trust me, especially Holdon, Katherine, and Miles, I think I can overpower him by suggestion. He's been willing to be led by my tone of voice, so maybe I can use my authority to counteract some of these persisting false beliefs. I've said this to other alters, but it seems each needs to hear it for himself. I also remember I need to talk to Thea briefly before we stop today.

"Karl, I have some important things to say to you, so listen carefully." My voice is not mean or reprimanding, but interested, earnest, and firm. But I will brook no argument. "The people from the rituals; they're gone now. They can't hurt me, and they can't hurt you. Years have passed. They're all gone." Karl looks taken aback, but softens. "It's important that I understand as much as possible about all of you, so you don't need to keep any secrets from me. No harm will come from your telling me things. Do you understand?" I look directly at him, knowing, at ten, he's not strong enough to defy me.

Karl nods, uncertain.

"If you have any concerns, talk to Holdon, but you and I will talk again soon. We've had a good talk. Can you step back and let me talk to Thea?"

"Okay." I can tell he's become submissive to me. It's important that I manage him and his violent thoughts. Through my acting strong and paternal, he'll feel safe, just like a ten-year-old boy.

Karl's rigidity yields to a smaller, softer girl.

"Did I do something wrong?" asks Thea, looking up at me, and then away.

"Claire asked me to check in on you to see that you're okay." My tone is now gentle, like a mother's.

"I'm staying with the baby."

"Karen Boo?"

"Yes. If I go inside Karen, I'll take the baby with me."

"That's a fine idea." I was wondering how we were going to merge the baby. "We have some time; can you tell me a little about how you were born?"

"I'm six years old. I go to first grade. I have to keep everything okay for the teachers 'cause Karen is sick. I have to go to school for a while. Karen has been inside for about a year. The teachers like me but the other kids make fun of me; they call me Franken-stein"—I look at her, with a look that says I don't understand—"'cause of the scars on my forehead."

"When were you born?"

"When Karen died—well, she only died for a minute, then they brought her back. It was at Children's Memorial Hospital. I took the tests and treatments when Karen was a baby. We were five when I was born. Katherine, Holdon, Karen Boo, then me. We had a tumor and an aneurysm [she stumbles over this word] and I got surgery, radiation, and medicines. All my hair fell out. I was born so Karen wouldn't die."

"I see. Thank you. I hope we can talk again soon, Thea."

I ask her to step back and ask Karen to return to her safe room, tell her to remember everything, and bring her back to the office. She leaves, and we're both a little shaken over all that's just happened.

18

SANDY AND MILES

"Karen's not sleeping," says Ann. *It's 11:00 p.m.* when Ann calls and I want to go to sleep. I get calls from Karen most evenings, but this one is later than usual. "When one part sleeps, another takes over; she's getting overwhelmed and can't keep up!" says Ann. Me, too, I think.

"Thank you, Ann. I'll try to help. Is that all?" I'm really tired.

"Wait a minute." The voice on the phone changes, giving way to one that is more guttural and aggressive.

"You're going to tell them, aren't you?"

"Karl?"

"Yeah. If you tell them, they'll kill us."

"Karl, what year is this?"

"Nineteen sixty-five."

"Karl, it's 1996. September. There's no one left to tell. Besides, I wouldn't tell anyone what you've told me, anyway."

"Nineteen ninety-six? Are you sure?"

"Look at the newspaper, check it out with Holdon, and then we'll talk about it together tomorrow." I've told Karl all this before. I wonder what it will take to make it stick. I ask Karl to step back.

"Okay," he says. Since they're switching on request, I treat

Karen as if she's under hypnosis and pause to see if they have any other concerns. Another voice comes on.

"I'm back with Katherine and Ann."

"Hello, Miles, I'm glad to hear it. How are you doing?"

"We're not doing so good. Sandy is causing problems. Katherine says she should be the next to merge into Karen."

"Okay, if that will help everyone," I say. I'm surprised they've come to this decision about Sandy, but I'm going to go with it. I need to get to sleep. It's 11:40 p.m. I ask Miles to step back and ask to talk to Karen, suggesting to her that all the parts will sleep tonight. When I awaken her, she's surprised to find herself talking to me on the phone. I tell her to just get some rest.

On a subsequent evening Karen calls again late—it's 11:30 p.m.

"Karen wanted to go downtown and see Oprah," says Karl's voice on the phone, "but I stopped her. What if we were spotted? They'd come and kill us."

"You won't be hurt anymore by those people," I say with my best voice of conviction. "Did you talk to Holdon?"

"Yeah. It is 1996. Why didn't you lie to me like everybody else?" Karl speaks quickly and hushed. "I hear Sandy is going to merge. Will it hurt?"

"It won't hurt, Karl, but why don't you watch Sandy merge? Can you do that?"

"I think so."

"Good, then you can see for yourself."

There's a pause on the other end of the phone, then a new voice.

"Dr. Baer, this is Ann," she says, in her clear, silken voice. "I worry that when Sandy merges, her eating habits will become Karen's."

"Sandy's habits will become part of Karen," I say, "as they are now, in a sense. When she merges, her habits will become diluted, and won't any longer be present in pure form like when she's out by herself."

"Oh, I see; that makes sense. Thank you."

This is all still running through my head as I try to fall asleep. It's past midnight.

Karen hands me some photographs I'd not seen before. The first shows Pankratz & Sons Funeral Home, a mousy, drab little brick building, where she says she was tortured in the basement. The next few are of the house where she grew up, the yard, the accordion door to her bedroom through which she overheard her parents' sex parties, and finally pictures of her father, mother, grandfather, and uncle. I looked deep into these small, black-and-white snapshots to see if I can peer into the soul of these people. I cannot. In these pictures, her mother is a gaily dressed woman eager for the camera; her father a big, powerful man whose eyes betray a certain haughtiness and arrogance; and her grandfather, whose picture I'd seen before, a plain, apparently humorless bald-headed man. Her uncle is turned away from the camera. Somehow, after all Karen has told me, I expect these figures from the past to turn hideous on the old Kodak paper. It's difficult to imagine sadistic cruelty residing in people so ordinary looking. Her mother is the only one left alive. I tell Karen I'm glad she brought the photos, so I can better picture what she tells me.

Today is the day we are to integrate Sandy. I know some of the other parts still have urgent issues, so after I put Karen under hypnosis, I ask if anyone would like to talk to me.

"Dr. Baer, this is Thea."

"What's on your mind, Thea?"

"I don't want Sandy to disappear!"

"What's the trouble?"

"No one else takes care of the baby. It makes me sad. I don't want her to go."

"I understand it will be hard on you for a while, but it's best for everyone if Sandy integrates now. If possible, you and the baby can integrate soon, so you won't feel lonely, ever again."

"Okay, I know it's what they all want . . . but . . . okay . . . thank you."

"I'll talk with you again soon, Thea. Can you step back now?" Karen's face goes blank for a moment. Then she becomes shifty eyed.

"I listened to the other parts . . ."

"Karl?"

"Yeah . . . I understand more. I won't interfere with Sandy's merger today, but she's sick; I think she's nervous."

"Thanks . . . anything else on your mind?"

"My thoughts are beginning to change," he says, "ever since I found out what year it is. I've been looking for the people who hurt us, on the street, wherever we go, but they aren't there. I only came out before in the funeral home, or the church basement, or wherever Karen was hurt. I thought the whole world was in one room."

"This is an amazing amount of growth for you, Karl," I say, genuinely impressed at what he's assimilated. "Please let me know if you need help with it or have questions about what you're learning. I want to help you. Can you step back and we'll see who else wants to talk?" Karen goes blank again for a moment.

"I was sick last night because Mother was at the house," says Sandy. I recognize her helpless and hopeless manner and how she crumples in the chair.

"What made you sick?"

"Mother yells at me, says I don't appreciate her, tells me I don't know how to clean, and makes me do it over again."

"I understand you've had to suffer this kind of abuse all alone. But you won't have to endure this by yourself anymore when you merge with Karen." Sandy nods; how could she disagree? She can't say no to anyone.

"How would you like me to introduce you to Karen? What shall I tell her?"

Sandy shifts uneasily, embarrassed. She steadies herself and starts her story.

"I was born when Karen was eleven or twelve years old. I was born to take Claire's place. I wasn't supposed to disagree, and I would do whatever anyone asked of me. I have to listen to all the criticism and abuse, especially from Mother, Father, and Josh. But to everybody else I pretend everything is fine. I get depressed and food makes me feel better. I know our body is out of whack, but whenever I come out, I have to eat. Tell Karen I'm sorry . . ." Sandy pauses and falls deeper into her chair, signaling she's finished.

"Sandy, would you wait outside the door to Karen's room?" She nods and disappears. I call Karen back and ask that she let me in her little room, which she does. I ask Sandy to come in and join us.

"She's very, very heavy," Karen says.

I introduce Sandy to Karen with the information Sandy just gave me, and ask Karen to describe what is happening to her.

"She says she's sorry about all the inconvenience and all the food. She's also sorry she brought Mother to the house today, but she wanted Mother to see her as Sandy one last time." Karen pauses, attending to some inner business with Sandy.

"Sandy's ready," she says. "She hopes, with her memories, I'll be able to turn things around."

"You'll do it together," I say. There's a pause, so I feel it's up to me to aid the process. "Are you ready to come together now?"

"I'm taking her hand," says Karen, and then her brows knit and she recoils slightly. "She's going too fast!" Karen says, "I'm more hesitant than Sandy; she wants to get it over with." She pauses, and her face turns red, as if she's straining with a weight. "She's in."

I wait a few moments, letting Karen take some time to undergo whatever this process entails. I don't pretend to understand it all— how this merger process takes down so precipitously the barriers to the areas of her memory she'd spent so long keeping separate, or why she has the hypersensitivity to light and sound she does at the end, but it seems to accomplish what we're striving for. Since each alter was born whole, that is, all at once, I suppose it makes sense they can integrate all at once, too.

"How do you feel?" I ask.

"Very loud." Karen cringes and looks sick. "Bloated, headache is worse, nauseous."

"It will pass."

"I don't understand why she did everything for everyone. The memories are flooding in." She shivers. "I don't like the feeling of wanting to see Mother, of wanting to go to the cemetery." Karen slumps in the chair. "She never felt good about herself at all. She felt worse than I do." I'm hoping this integration won't make Karen so depressed she'll become a danger to herself. She's certainly taking on a load of humiliation.

"My eyes are hurting—it's so bright, even though my eyes are closed!"

"Your senses get heightened for a time after each one." I say to remind her it's temporary.

"I hear the traffic so loud!"

It's time to bring her out of hypnosis, so I want to say something to wrap things up on a positive note.

"I think this integration will help you both. Sandy will get the benefit of your better judgment, and you'll gain her compassion and helpfulness." I suggest to Karen she'll remember all that went on today, and bring her out of her trance and back to my office.

Sept. 16, 1996

To: Dr. Baer

   The Merging of Sandy
   On Thursday September 12, 1996, Sandy merged within. As you introduced her, I felt uncomfortable and I didn't like her very much. She rushed into me before I was ready and could change my mind. After we came together I felt very sensitive and sad. I became disgusted with her weakness in handling people. How could she be so naive? How could she let everyone take advantage of her? I felt fat and ugly. I felt as though I gained 100 pounds in a minute.
   During the next few days, many things have changed in the way I function. I was no longer able to lose time when dealing with my mother, husband, and friends Hanna and Rose. This angered me because I didn't want to deal with them. I felt as though I was being punished. Hanna kept calling me on the phone and telling me how much I've changed—for the worse according to her. Hanna has always taken advantage of me. Rose always steals things from our home. I tried to realize the important part Sandy had in my life, but feeling the way I do, I can't see it. I am sure as more memories and feelings come in, things will look different. But until then, I feel awful.

I realize integrating Sandy was no picnic for Karen. There isn't much to redeem what Sandy brought: basically a lot of pain, humiliation, and helplessness. It's been hard to decide on the order for integration. I want to leave it to Karen's system to make the choices; I think they'll be wiser about it and more motivated to cope with the consequences of the integrations if they get to choose.

Karen comes back to see me a few days later, looking tired and depressed; her back is slumped and her head is hanging. She moves slowly and heavily to her chair.

"It was hard getting here," she says, "my coordination isn't right. I'm nervous driving." Her eyes well up in tears. I wait.

"Sandy must have been telling stories to garner sympathy, to please people. She lied a lot to appear blameless. She would feign sickness to get Mother's sympathy; that's why Mother did stuff for her." Her voice trails off. Again, I wait. "I'm eating things I don't even like. I have to stop and realize I don't like it, and then I can stop eating." She shakes her head. "Josh degrades me all day. I never heard it before. I must have lost time to Sandy when he started in."

That must be why I haven't heard much about it, I think.

"No one comes out to help me," she continues. "No one cares." Karen puts her head in her hands and the tears begin to stream down her face.

"Integrating Sandy has been a burden," I say, "because she carried a lot of suffering. Perhaps we can find the best way to help you with this by discussing it with some of the others." Karen takes this as a cue to begin the hypnosis part of the session; she nods her head and we go through our usual induction process.

"Karen is getting wimpy," says Miles with bravado.

"Because she has Sandy's influence inside her?" I ask. I like Miles. He consistently shows courage.

"I guess so. She needs some help."

"Do you want to help her?" He looks at me with surprise and a hint of pride.

He thinks a moment. "I can see it would help Karen to have someone like me to help her."

We discuss what it would be like for him to merge with Karen, how he could lend strength and backbone. Miles steps back.

"Things are going fine, even though they seem chaotic," says Holdon. "I worry about Sandy's suicidal thoughts. I can't see her anymore; there are only vague images of the integrated parts."

"Like shadows?"

"Yes, hanging around Karen." He pauses for a second or two. "I think merging Miles is a good idea. I can take care of things inside with the other children."

"Okay, then we'll plan on him next."

It's one in the afternoon and Karen's appointment is at two. The phone rings and it's Karen, sounding small and shaken. She tells me she's at the planetarium, overlooking the water. She had the thought to jump into the lake, she lost time, and now finds herself there. I'm thankful I'm not sitting with another patient right now. She says she's trying hard not to lose time; she's afraid she'll do something terrible. Karen is clearly not in control of herself, and I need to find someone who can be. Over the phone, I quickly put her under hypnosis and request Holdon, who apparently isn't monitoring Karen's situation. I ask him to take over and get Karen to her appointment. He assures me he will.

Despite the call, Karen appears for her appointment on time. Once Karen is under hypnosis, Karl is the first to speak.

"I won't let you integrate Miles," says Karl, more afraid than angry. I cock my head to ask why. "Me, Miles, and Elise—we have things to do with the devil. The devil is strong in me." I need to do some therapy with Karl before we can do the integration of Miles.

"Have you ever seen the devil?" I ask.

"No, but I know what he wants me to do."

"How did you get the devil's message?"

"During the ceremonies, they made us watch movies and showed us signs. I saw the devil in the movies. He had red eyes, horns, a beard and pointy chin. If Miles and me integrate, we'll make Karen totally mean."

"Miles doesn't see himself as mean anymore," I say. Karl looks frustrated and pauses.

"I've been trying to give the others death thoughts." The planetarium, I think. "I was going to bring a knife; I was going to do something. . . . I wanted to choke you. I don't know why." Karl is clearly in turmoil. He's trying so hard to accomplish something.

"Are you scared of me?"

"I'm scared of what you're doing. I can't take over the memories of Sandy, Claire, or Julie since they got merged. When they merge, I can't stop them sharing their memories with Karen. I can't do my job!"

"Miles changed how he felt about sharing his memories. He realized the time to protect Karen from knowing her own past was over. You can change how you think about it, too. I can help."

"I don't know, I don't like it. . . . I'll think about it."

"I need you to feel okay about this, Karl. You're important to all the others. You've always been their last resort. We can't do it without you." I know I'm really laying it on.

"Really?"

"Really. Miles has looked forward to integrating today. Would it be okay with you if we go ahead?"

"Well, okay, I won't do nothin'."

"Thanks." I make a dramatic pause. "Perhaps you can step back now, Karl; I need to talk to Miles."

Karl steps back, and Karen goes blank for a moment and shifts in her chair.

"I'm causing a lot of problems, huh?" Miles says with a broad smile.

"Karl's afraid the memories of the devil will get out and he won't be able to do his job of keeping them under wraps."

"Yeah, when I couldn't handle the talk about Satan—the chanting and weird language—Karl would take it."

"Right. I'm going to try to help him with all that. But what shall I tell Karen about you when I introduce you to her before you merge?"

"Well, I'm eight. I was born six, but I grew to eight. They needed a boy to come out when Karen was being hurt." Miles grows serious and leans forward, speaking in a whisper, as if it's just for the two of us to hear. "I couldn't feel the pain of things being put inside the vagina." Miles brightens again. "She also needed someone to tell people off. I was the only one who fought back. It caused a lot of beatings, but it did get rid of some of the anger and hurt. Karen wanted to be a boy because boys don't get hurt. I'd stay out for a month or so if Karen was hurt bad." Miles sits forward in his chair. "Once Thea was out for over a year when Karen was little. When I was out, Karen's father would say I was crabby and 'on the rag.'" Miles pauses, sits back, and looks around the room.

"How do you feel about integrating?"

"Oh, I'm looking forward to it. I like being with Katherine and Ann, so I know how it will feel, because of being with them."

I say good-bye to Miles and tell him I will miss him. I will, too.

Under hypnosis, Karen lets me into her little room and locks the door. She says there are more locks than before. She was given Karl's death thoughts yesterday, and is trying to keep his thoughts away with the locks. I ask Karen if she's ready to merge with Miles; she says yes and invites him in. I introduce Miles to her and tell his story.

"Can you see him?" I ask.

"Yes," says Karen. "He has a smirk on his face." That's Miles, I think. "He says he will help with the mother lady, and won't hurt anybody. He wants to talk to you, Dr. Baer."

"Okay."

"I'd like to shake your hand before I go." There is a fearlessness and at the same time an eagerness to please about him that reminds me of my son.

"Good luck, Miles," I say as I get up and lean over to him and give Karen a good, warm handshake.

"Is it okay to go inside? Do I sit on her lap? Just do it? How?"

"Any way you can," I say.

"He's on my lap," says Karen. "He's sticking out his tongue at me and smiling." Karen looks in pain. "Oh! It's really strange! It feels like every cell in my body is exploding. I feel a lot of pressure, a little sick feeling."

"Keep going, you'll be fine." I try to be positive.

"He's all the way in. . . . I can see some of his world. It's different than the real world."

"What do you mean?"

"It's cold . . . gray rooms . . . candles."

"Miles brings strength," I say, "but he also brings a burden of painful memories."

"I feel his strength. He has opinions—no one will push us around. I felt weak before . . ." She appears to be listening inside herself. "I can still hear him, separately, but he's inside. He says we'll do this slowly so I don't get scared. I think it will be okay—my head hurts really bad." She puts her hands to the sides of her head, over her ears.

"The sounds are loud?"

"Yes . . . I think I will be able to pace the memories with Miles." Her speech is still slow and distant. ". . . no memories until safely home . . . he's inside, but separate and aware . . . when we get home, he'll fully integrate."

"You'll be getting a lot from Miles." I bring her out of her trance, again suggesting she'll remember everything that has transpired. She leaves the office, unsteady. I hope Miles sees she gets home okay.

Karen was depressed during the first few days after Miles integrated; she couldn't even write down all the details of the memories. There's a lot of distortion of reality in what he believed. Miles was fascinated by talk of Satan, but it really just revolved all around lies, child pornography, and stealing.

"Everyone says I've been bitchy," says Karen.

"I can see subtle mannerisms of Miles in you."

"I've been much more aggressive in my speech—before I even think."

All through the years, Karen explains, certain people she knew would abruptly stop calling her. Now she knows Miles told them off. She can remember these incidents. Miles would tell them off, and Karl would take the memory of this person away. Miles always wanted to do it to Mother.

"I guess it went okay," says Karl, after Karen is in her trance. "I kept some of the memories from Karen so she couldn't write them for you."

"What didn't you want me to know?"

"Miles wasn't gay!" Karl blurts out.

"What do you mean?" I ask. Karen and her alters never cease to surprise me.

"Miles wanted to have sex with a woman, but the only way he could was for Karen to have sex with another woman, you know, gay sex."

"I think I understand. Miles would be having boy/girl sex with the woman, even though it would look like two women."

"Yeah, but it didn't happen." Karl falls quiet for a moment, then blurts again, "He wanted you to hurt him."

"Why?" I ask, surprised again.

"So he'd feel loved."

I don't know what to say, so I just let Karl continue. For someone who keeps secrets, he certainly has a need to talk.

"Her hands are feeling much better. Miles had four broken fingers. They would hammer his hand if he put it up to protect himself. Then they'd tie his hands and ankles down. . . ." Karl seems to be picturing it and falls quiet again.

"How is the integration with Miles going?" I ask.

"It ended yesterday. He's gone."

I try to be positive about it, saying all that he was, is now part of Karen, and still with them all. Karl is forlorn.

I talk briefly with Ann, who says she feels guilty over her past, but she doesn't really elaborate. I ask if she's considered merging with Karen. She says she'll think about it. Holdon says things are going well overall; he hasn't been interfering. I ask if Ann would be a good choice for whom to merge next; he thinks so.

Sept. 28, 1996

The Merging of Miles

The night before Miles merged within, I had many doubts. I knew that Miles was created to handle most of the severe abuse and I didn't know if I'd be ready to handle any of those memories. There was only one alter who was in disagreement. That alter, Karl, gave me a day full of problems. As I tried to sleep the night before, Karl kept on trying to persuade the others not to integrate. I don't really know how long we slept, but when I woke up, I felt terrible. While driving to your office I lost time again, and found myself parked by the planetarium, facing the lake, with a strong urge to jump. This feeling was so strong I felt numb and was willing to obey whoever's urge this was.

Karen goes on to describe the process of getting to my office and the subsequent integration with Miles. She spends some time discussing what she received from Miles. . . .

As we merged together, I felt Miles' strength and I regained some of his good memories. After coming out of hypnosis, back to your office, my wrists, hands, and ankles hurt. My hands kept forming tight fists throughout the next few days. I kept having the urge to tell people off.

After I finally got home, the integration hit me like a ton of bricks. As Miles' memories flooded my mind, I wondered how these things could have happened to me. I felt angry. I wanted to hit someone. How much more can my mind hold?

There were feelings I am not able to explain regarding Miles' views on sexuality. I'll try to explain as best I can, so here goes. When I was 17, in 1977, I moved in with a woman named Jane who was 34 years old. Jane was a lesbian and I was unaware of this at the time. But Miles enjoyed females and he spent a lot of time with Jane, leading her to believe I was a lesbian also. Jane would make comments about starting a relationship, and I turned her down while Miles led her on. This caused some very uneasy feelings between Jane and me. Does this mean I might be gay? Now looking back I realize why I angered her so much. Miles teased her. As Miles merged within me I found myself looking at females the way he did. Talk about screwing up my sexuality!

I saved the worst of the memories for last, because I am very afraid to write them down. I feel the need to warn you because it is very upsetting. As much as I want to tell you, I feel we should protect you and talk to a priest or pastor. So I will write down some of the memories without going into much detail. I wish I didn't have to write about this. I can't believe there are people who do these things.

There were different levels to believing in Satan. The first level hooked me because I was curious and fascinated by what they told me. I wanted to know more; at least that's what Miles thought. After this they took me to the next level, which was pray- ing to Satan and giving him control over our soul. Then third, I was made to keep all of it a secret. By following these steps, they said I would become powerful.

If we did not obey the leaders, they said we would be killed. I remember white sheets with blood on them. Lots of blood. Whose blood, I don't know. But I do remember them killing animals for sacrifice.

I was encouraged to dissociate; this kept their secret safe. I was so confused; I thanked any part that could take over. The people involved were important people in our neighborhood. They wore robes and masks. Miles was tortured in an unbelievable way. We were not allowed to talk about the rituals; if we did, they'd kill us. Do you know what really bothers me most—the evil. We are still suffering from the effects of being made to feel evil and I don't feel we will ever forget what happened.

No child should ever have to endure this pain and suffering. I wondered about the other children that went through the same things. Our abusers were so good at covering up what happened. I wonder where all the films they made are. I remember chanting, "baby Jesus is dead," over and over again. I don't think I can recover quickly from these memories. I worry about you, Dr. Baer; I don't want you to burn out because of us.

Karen Overhill

19

ANN AND SIDNEY

On October 10, 1996, Karen simply looks weary. She says she lost time on the way here, woke up in a parking garage, and was lost. With no new memories from Miles today, she must have gotten them all. The worst memories, she says, are of the ceremonies. There was so much hurting of her body. Miles's way of taking the pain made him want to tear himself up inside, because he felt he was the devil. He wanted me to hurt Karen's body, too. She says it took years for them to believe I wouldn't.

The memories from Miles don't really have a time frame, a chronology. She hates most the memories of when they made her say she wanted to be hurt, and then hurt her, or when they made her believe she could only be saved if they hurt her, and then did. Karen recalls for me one of Miles's memories about the priest who participated in her abuse. He sprinkled holy water on her to see if it would burn, to demonstrate she was with the devil. She remembered seeing red marks where the water went, and she wonders if it was really holy water. She wonders if she brought the red marks on herself.

I listen as she debriefs me on Miles's integration, and I have in mind what she wrote: that I should tell her if I want the details of Miles's "ritual" abuse. I ponder over this. I'm very curious about it, in a morbid fascination kind of way, like people lining up to watch a public flogging. Sometimes I believe, or worry, that I went into psychiatry in part because I have a fascination for the bizarre. But I have to be careful. I don't want to inquire about these incidents just to be entertained. I'm not really sure what would be the benefit of Karen's sharing with me all the nauseating, gut-wrenching details of the abuse that make her want to vomit. Until I see a definite therapeutic need, I'll leave them alone. I do tell Karen she doesn't need to worry about hurting me with her memories, that she can tell me whatever she needs, but that I don't have a need to hear any particular one. We leave it at that. I then put her under hypnosis and Ann steps forward.

"I heard you suggested I integrate next." Ann sits straight in the chair, and has a charming and demure—cultivated, really—speech that I always recognize. "I'm interested, but first I'd like to know more."

"Sure; how can I help?"

"Karen needs the perverse religious thoughts straightened out." Ann is exasperated in her own way. "God is supposed to love everyone and they've ruined it for us."

"You mean from what you were told during the ceremonies?"

"Yes."

"Only some of the parts have those thoughts," I say. "Perhaps you can bring a better balance to those false beliefs."

"I don't know. We feel so undeserving in the eyes of God." Ann looks at me more directly. "Did you know, when they had the ceremonies, they played choir music? It is a powerful reminder whenever we hear it."

"There has been a lot of damage to Karen's religious feelings," I say to validate her.

"It was monstrous."

It's taken several weeks for Miles's integration to settle down. My own divorce proceedings are wearing on me, but I try to keep those emotions out of my sessions with Karen. She doesn't ask about it. I further discuss integration with Ann and get her consent. Before we begin, though, Sidney comes forward. He thinks his own integration will be okay, and he's looking forward to it.

Although sometimes it's better to do things without Karen, he says, he's been sad and lonely by himself. Miles used to be with him, and Claire, too. He doesn't have anybody to play with. It's so quiet inside. He asks, "Will the merging hurt?" I say it's like hugging. He asks to watch Ann's integration.

"It's okay for Sidney to watch," says Ann, sitting primly. She looks at me directly, and speaks calmly and clearly.

"I think it will help him and some of the others with their fears," I say.

"I hope so. Since we first discussed integrating, I've been moving back and forth between Karen and myself without integrating. I was never abused. It's hard to believe what happened to the others. When I saw Miles's memories, I became very sad realizing they were true."

"What shall I tell Karen about you when I introduce you?"

"Let me see. . . . I am sixteen years old; I was born at 11. I was born to go to church every day, and confession on Saturdays. I worked for the priest; I would go away when the priest came to hurt us. I was to be the perfect girl. I made sure James and Sara were christened and celebrated Communion. I tried to give them religious beliefs and a positive outlook as they grew up. I calmed the children down after Karen was abused by her husband. I tried to teach them right and wrong."

Ann pauses and settles a little in her chair. I tell her what the steps for the integration procedure are and ask if she's ready; she says yes. I ask her to step back a moment and I bring Karen to her little room. I join her there and ask her to let Ann and Sidney join us. Sidney is there to watch.

"Tell me what you see," I say to Karen.

"Ann and Sidney are in the room," says Karen, painting the scene. "Sidney is a little boy with blond hair. He has a smile that makes him look like a rascal. Ann is plain, with short hair; she seems very calm. There's no frightened or nervous feeling coming from her. . . ."

I take Karen's pause as an opportunity to introduce Ann, and suggest when they're ready, they can go ahead and merge.

"She's hugging me, brushing my hair out of my face. She says everything will be okay. She says if I hug her, too, she'll go right in—the quicker the better. I'm a little nervous." Karen pauses and listens. "Ann is talking to Sidney. She says this integration is a good and exciting thing." Karen pauses again, changes, and Ann speaks.

"I want to thank you for everything, Dr. Baer. It's been an honor to work with you; I hope you didn't get upset with me." I thank her for being with Miles and Katherine, and for providing such a good model for merging for the others.

"Ann is going inside," says Karen. "I feel uneasy . . . she's all the way in . . . Sidney can't see her anymore . . . Ann's calmness . . . getting some of her thoughts . . . I can feel her looking forward to her niece's christening." Karen falls quiet and I let her process Ann for a moment. Then suddenly she sits forward.

"That's it?" asks Sidney. "That's no big thing! I thought it was like getting sucked up into a vacuum cleaner, or something."

"What did you see?" I ask.

"Ann looked real, then all distorted, like a ghost, then poof! Gone."

"What do you think?"

"What if I want to talk to her? How do I do it? We used to go from room to room inside to talk to each other. Now some rooms are empty. How do I call her?"

"Ann's a part of Karen now; she's still there, but you can't see her anymore," I say, trying to explain the unexplainable. "You can always talk to Karen. Ann will be there. Why don't you tell Karl what you've seen?"

Sidney steps back, and Karen says she feels calm, but again the lights are bright and the sounds are loud. She leaves the office with less difficulty than with the other integrations.

Oct. 20, 1996

The Merging of Ann

On Thursday, October 17, 1996, Ann merged within. Integrating Ann was not an upsetting experience, but it seemed very intense. Ann's memories will affect my whole being.

On my way to your office, I wasn't sure I would be able to merge with Ann. I was afraid because with Miles, the memories were about Satan and evil. I felt I was again in for trouble. But as soon as Ann merged, I realized her memories were the opposite of the others. Ann never handled stressful situations, abuse, or any of my physical functions (like walking, finding things, or getting places, etc.).

My mind races with memories, thoughts, and views on life; maybe at another time I can elaborate.

- *People loved Ann. She was bright, sensitive, and helpful. She felt it was a miracle that we found you, Dr. Baer, and you believed in us.*

- *Ann felt that we were gifted. God gave us the gift of dissociating to help us cope with what He could not stop.*

- *Ann felt that we did not choose to be abused, and she prayed for us all the time.*

- *Ann would have loved to have told our story to the world, hoping that it will help someone.*

- *Ann hid the evidence of the abuse. No one would have believed us, and we were not in the position to expose our abusers.*

- *Ann did the emergency work. When something dramatic happened, Ann would put Karen to sleep and confer with the others on who to take over.*

- *Ann believes once we are whole and reconcile with God, we will be free.*

On Halloween 1996, Karen comes in shaking and tearful. The most recent memory she's recalled involves a police officer, Bert, who committed suicide. He was one of the men who regularly abused her. She recalled Bert apologizing to her, saying he never thought it would go that far, and that he couldn't live this way. He said he knew he'd burn in hell, and he was sorry. He stood in front of the mantel and put his gun to his head and fired. She remembers his hand made a mark in blood on the mirror. It's his apology that keeps going through her head.

Under hypnosis Karl comes out, adamant that there's no reason for Karen to remember these memories. He's already having trouble keeping the uncomfortable feelings from her. The memories, he says, are poison, evil—she can't know these things! He is urgent. Holdon has been holding Karl back, because he doesn't want Karl to hurt anyone and doesn't think there's any need for Karl to be out in public. Holdon wants to integrate him, but he's too angry. He needs to be calmed down, like Miles was. I acknowledge to Holdon I'll have to spend more time with Karl.

I detect an undercurrent of real sadness in Karl; it's either his or mine, because my divorce had become final the day before, but I assume at least some of it is Karl's, so I ignore the content of Karl's rant and address the sadness. If I'm correct, he'll respond to an act of empathy by allying more strongly with me. That will help bring him along like Miles.

"What makes you so sad, Karl?" He looks at me with surprise, but is still guarded.

"I don't like my job getting tampered with." He's still defiant, but the resistance slips a hair.

"I agree you've had an important job, and that you may be upset to see things changing inside. Perhaps you can still keep your job if we change it a little."

"What do you mean?" He's still guarded, but interested.

"Karen needs to get these new memories in smaller doses, not all at once. She gets overwhelmed during the integrations. Perhaps if you first tell the memories to me, give me the doses first, we can decide together what Karen should know."

"Hmm . . . well, okay." He's still suspicious, but a part of him wants to cooperate and shed his burden.

"Where should we start?" I ask, giving Karl the power and autonomy to run this show.

"The men in masks," says Karl, grim and solemn.

"Go ahead."

It's Halloween. Karen is thirteen years old. Her mother is at work. It's after school, and her father comes home with four or five friends. They've been drinking, and all are wearing Halloween masks. They've been here before. Her father grabs Karen and brings her back to her parents' bedroom, and throws her on the bed. The others follow. She recognizes Bert, a police officer, who's wearing an Al Capone mask. The others wear clown masks. At the foot of the bed, her father says her body belongs to Satan now. Halloween is Satan's day. This is the night for it.

Being pushed onto the bed and having her mouth taped is the last Karen remembers. Karl comes out and refuses to remove his clothes. One of the clowns punches Karen in the mouth. Bert puts his gun to her head. Karl takes the clothes off. The men are laughing and mocking her behind their masks, calling her cocksucker, cunt, whore.

The doorbell rings and her father goes to the door. The pleas of the trick-or-treaters come back to the bedroom. Karen's father gives them candy from the bowl by the door, says happy Halloween, and comes back to Karen.

"Open your legs!" someone says. Karl opens them and feels them poking her with something sharp and hard. Her father is laughing, and then he speaks.

"Take her soul today, Satan," he says, looking up, and then points his finger down at Karen. "You belong to Satan now. Nothing in this world can change this. Pronounce your love for Satan." Karen is screaming. "Louder! Louder!" The men are laughing and putting their masked faces close to Karen, poking their tongues through the hole in the mouth and putting them in Karen's mouth and ears, and slapping her face. Three of the men rape her. In the end, they spread Halloween candy over her body and pour beer on her.

For weeks afterward, Karen punches herself in the stomach and puts hangers inside her because she's afraid she became pregnant that night.

"What is it about this memory, Karl, that makes you select it from all the times Karen was hurt? Did you have special trouble with it?" I want to understand more about the "why" of this memory, rather than the "what."

"It was unexpected," says Karl. "It screwed up the order for who would take the pain. We all went in and out so quickly." Karl looks lost and really frightened for the first time. "I tried to take all these memories, but I couldn't. They leaked out. It was the one time all seventeen of us had a part in the day. It's not the worst memory, but it's the one that makes us the sickest."

"Because it was sudden and unexpected?"

"Yeah. The other times it was more . . . routine; we could see it coming. Karen keeps waking up with the nightmare of being on the bed with the gun pointing at her. That's all."

"You've had a tough job, Karl," I say, hoping to pull him in tighter to me. "Since Karen is gaining the memories of the others, why don't you do what Miles did—dose her with partial memories, so she doesn't have to remember these episodes all at once?"

"I never did that before." Karl pauses, waiting for me to say something, but I don't. "Okay, I'll try."

"Where am I?" asks Thea. Thea puts her hand to her face, palm toward me, in a charming gesture of surprise and amazement.

"My office," I say.

"I was just in the hospital with lots of bright lights. I've been there lots of times—Children's Memorial, St. Anthony's, Mercy, Holy Cross . . ." Thea drops off into her own thoughts.

"What happened to you in the hospital?"

"Oh, I remember lying on a table with hundreds of doctors looking at a film of the thing on my head. Dad used to examine me with bright lights, too, down there," she says, looking at her lap. "He'd put things inside of me to see how far I'd stretch."

"Did the colonoscopy Karen just had remind you of that?"

"Yes, except the doctor wasn't laughing. I'm afraid I must be damaged down there. The doctors must be able to tell. I keep thinking the doctor will find a hammer or something left in there from before."

"It sounds like you have suffered terribly," I say, taken aback at these quick revelations.

"Oh, I didn't feel the pain, but I was always in the hospital. I was born to undergo the tests."

"So you've been to a lot of doctors?"

"Yes. Doctors are mean. One doctor gave me a shot every Saturday morning. It made me tired and groggy. I'd go there after we were hurt on Friday night. The doctor would check me and give me a shot for pain." Thea paused and gazed out the window. "I'm lonely. There's no one left inside."

"Would you like to merge with Karen and join the others?" I ask, introducing her to the idea.

"I still have to take care of the baby." Thea seems very well informed, so I think I'll use this opportunity to get answers to some of the questions I've been wondering about.

"Oh, how old is the baby?" I ask.

"Less than two; she barely talks."

"Why was the baby born?"

"She was born at the same time Holdon and Katherine were born. They split from one into three. When Karen would cry, her parents would shake her, and that shaking would go to Karen Boo. There is no 'real' Karen."

"No?"

"No, there's no one main part that is Karen."

"When you all merge, you will be one big person," I say. "How do you spend your time?"

"Inside, I float from one room to another, and in and out of hospitals. I don't sleep."

I wish I could spend more time just talking with Thea, but our time is running short today. I ask her to step back and then ask if someone else would like to talk to me. Karen changes abruptly.

"If I merge, will Karen start to steal?" asks Sidney.

"I don't think so, Sidney; there will be a lot of Karen that wouldn't want to steal, to balance your feelings." I'm guessing, of course. "What worries you, Sidney?"

"My feelings aren't too good. I'm afraid I'll hurt the others if I merge."

"If you don't merge, the others will miss out on the good parts of you—your sense of humor." He smiles and we agree he'll be the next to merge.

Holdon comes out briefly to tell me Karl tried to interfere with Karen's writing about Ann's memories. Karen changes abruptly again.

"How does Holdon know it was me?" challenges Karl. Karl is angry, and we discuss again how he feels unable to control everybody's memories. I listen and sympathize with him before I send Karen home.

·   ·   ·

It's the beginning of December 1996 and the weather has turned cold and windy. From my window, the sky is overcast, with sunlight peeking far out on the Indiana shore of Lake Michigan. Karen has fallen $5,000 behind on her bill. She can't keep up with paying for our sessions and has no hope of bringing her bill current. I bring this up to her, and as always when we discuss money, she's devastated. I suggest to her that there's only one solution; I'll have to simply stop charging her and see her for free. I know as a psychiatrist I'm not supposed to do this, that all sorts of parameters are introduced into the therapy when you see someone for free. It sets up the fantasy that the patient has a special, exclusive relationship with the therapist, which in Karen's case, I have to admit, is true. But I don't know what else in good conscience to do. We've been working together for eight years, many of them spent simply building up a sense of trust. How can I turn her out now? I tell her if there comes a time when she can repay the bill, then she can, but in the meantime, we're just going to forget about it and continue our work together. She's grateful, and I think we're both kind of glad the burden of worrying about payment has been lifted.

We turn our attention back to the integrations. Sidney's turn has come.

"I was born when I was four years old and Karen was three," says Sidney. "I'm five now. I came because Dad wanted a boy. I liked the things Dad wanted me to like. Baseball, playing with the dog, chasing chickens at the farm—I didn't mind getting dirty even though Karen hated it. I hid the things Father stole: a cassette recorder, a watch, things like that. He'd say I was good at it, and that made me feel good. Father always stole silverware in restaurants. He said you paid for it with the tip. If Father said he liked something, I had to steal it—or he'd hurt us. But then he'd hurt me for stealing, but that punishment wasn't as bad if I didn't do it." Sidney talks on a bit about Father's different methods of punishment.

"I like to play tricks on people. Sometimes I play them on Josh."

"Karen's husband?"

"Yeah. Father did pranks, too, but his were mean."

"Are you ready to merge with Karen?" I ask.

"Yeah, let's do it!"

I put Karen under hypnosis, direct us through the steps to Karen's little room, and introduce Sidney.

"Sidney looks comical," says Karen, "he wants to do this; he wants to jump right on top of me!" Karen's smile shows both amusement and a little dread. She's leaning back in the chair. "He's standing in front of me, staring, like 'What do we do now?' "

"Hug him?" I suggest.

"He's telling me where some things are. The clarinet I thought the cleaning lady stole: Sidney hid it so I'd fire her. It's under the camping equipment." Karen pauses.

"It's all right," I say.

"He's taking a running start . . . he's on his way . . . oooff . . . he's in me!" She jumps in her chair as Sidney lands. "I can feel him moving around. . . . Oh, my! I hear all the sounds of my body, my heart pounding, my blood flowing, a pressure in my head, it hurts, it's so bright!" She pauses to catch her breath. "I don't feel sick or stressed, though. I can picture things like a movie: taking a ride in the car, talking with Father." Karen relaxes a little. "I think it will be okay."

"You'll be getting memories of your father that we can talk about."

"Yes, they're all childlike, like when I was a kid. Sidney played jokes in the neighborhood; he didn't understand the conse- quences . . . he lived in a boy's world."

I bring Karen back to my office. Just then a fire engine goes by and Karen holds her hands to her ears in pain. I let Karen rest a moment until she collects herself enough to go down the elevator to the coffee shop, where she can sit until she's ready to drive home.

Dec. 10, 1996

Merging Sidney
On Thursday, Dec. 5, 1996, Sidney merged within.
As I arrived at the office, I could already hear Sidney's ideas of how he wanted to integrate.

This is how I remember it. I found myself in my special place quicker than usual. I also found Sidney walking in, just behind you. I was startled because the door was already open. It is usually bolted with many locks.

Sidney was ready to unite and he looked at you for approval. He then moved back to the door and started running towards me and with one final leap, we became one.

I can't remember which memory came first, but here are some listed below:

After leaving your office, I began to want things I never paid attention to before, like toys and Christmas ornaments. The urge to steal things was strong, but I was able to control it.

Sidney had to side with Father when Mother and Father would fight. When Father beat Mother, Sidney always watched. Father always justified his actions so Sidney believed she deserved it.

When Father needed money, Sidney had to go and ask Grandmother for it, and if she said no, he would steal it from her purse.

Sidney would save the first report card of the year and say he lost it. Then he put A's and B's for the other semesters in school. This was to avoid the whippings: one lash for a B, two for a C, three for a D, and ten for Fs.

There are more memories, but I'm having a hard time writing because of the pain in my hand. I'll try to write more later.

As Christmas approaches, the effects of Sidney's integration are fading. It has gone quickly. Karen no longer hears his voice. She says she's picked up some new bad habits. She drank out of someone else's glass and didn't wash her hands after she went to the bathroom. In stores, she's fascinated with items in a new way. She has the urge to steal Christmas ornaments. She has a craving for Sloppy Joes.

I ask about her plans for Christmas. She checks her appointment book. I ask to look at it; all the entries are in the same handwriting (Katherine's?). Karen says she checks it every morning to see what she's supposed to do. She says her mother has invited her for Christmas Eve. I caution her on the possible consequences of her going; Karen agrees, but says she'd like to see her brothers.

I speak with Holdon. He says since Julie and Sandy have

integrated, their blood sugar has been normal. He wants to know how he should explain this to Dr. Loeshen. I suggest Karen get retested and let Dr. Loeschen explain it to himself.

I ask Holdon who should be the next to integrate. He says it's going well integrating the younger ones. He and Katherine will be the last to go. Thea is a good one to go in next, he says. She'll have the baby with her. Jensen has expressed some interest, too. They're all waiting to be told when it's their turn. Karl is still hesitating.

I ask Karl how his wrist feels; Karen has been complaining of pain.

"Pain hurts me," says Karl, his lips pressed tight against his teeth, "but it doesn't bother me like it does everybody else."

"If you were to merge with Karen," I say, "she'd have your ability to tolerate pain."

"If I merge with Karen, I'll be dead," he says, gravely.

"You won't be dead," I say, "you won't be gone; you'll merge and be with the others." I need to sell Karl on this; he's the most resistant of all. "All that you are, all your strengths, will become part of Karen."

"I couldn't take the pain away after Sara was born," Karl protests. "I don't feel mean anymore; I'm worried." Karl looks lost, and little. His attitude has changed, softened. "For the first time I understand the giving of a gift. I'm coming out with Karen more. I even sent you a Christmas card, Dr. Baer."

"You're changing, Karl, growing up. You'll be a big help to Karen again when you merge. You have a happy Christmas."

"Thanks."

20

THEA AND KAREN BOO

"What do I say to the friends of alters who no longer exist?" asks Karen. It's early January, and Chicago is frigid and blanketed in snow. Karen has been absorbing the effects of all the integrations she's endured so far. How do I counsel her?

"When I see these people, I have a memory of them, but no feeling," she continues. "They make me uncomfortable. I don't know how I maintained so many relationships."

"You didn't sleep," I suggest.

"You're right. I usually slept two to four hours a night; lately it's four to six."

"Now you'll be able to form your own opinions about your friends."

"I've lost a lot of time the past few weeks. I painted my daughter's room while I lost time. Actually, it doesn't look bad. . . ." Karen rubs her forehead and smiles.

"I'm really ticked off at everybody inside. There's no unity, no getting along." Katherine is venting like a piqued schoolteacher. "The integrated parts are doing fine—it's the ones who are left behind who think they can take control. Jensen was never unpredictable; the other day he decided to paint a room! Karl has been

angry. Holdon just sits in the house and doesn't do a damn thing. Thea and the baby are getting distraught; they need to be integrated next."

"Who's causing the most trouble?" I ask.

"Jensen, Karl, Karen 2, and Elise." Katherine goes back inside, and Karen's body take a familiar forward, assertive posture.

"Should I give Karen some memories?" asks Karl. "She has a headache; I'll take the headache pain. I can give her some memories, but I won't give them all at once. I'll give her a flash of memory, and see how it goes."

"Go for it," I encourage.

Karl goes back inside, and Karen looks away, with her eyes down, and drops one shoulder.

"I felt like painting," says Jensen. "I like to decorate." I need to try to make Jensen's canvases smaller.

"I understand you did a nice job with Sara's room, but how about drawing some pictures for me instead?"

As Karen comes out of hypnosis, I suggest to her that her headache pain is much better, and when she wakes, it is. Was it me or Karl?

"*I couldn't let us go to the courthouse or they'd throw us in jail!*" says Karl.

"Jail?"

"They'll ask questions, make her lose time." Karl has desperation in his voice. "We can't take chances." Karen has been summoned for jury duty.

"Did you think you committed some crime?"

"I don't trust policemen. They'll think we're guilty of something. I'm afraid we'll end up in jail someday."

"Because you're bad?" I ask, making an interpretation to Karl about why he's so paranoid, that he feels deserving of punishment because he feels evil.

"Yes," he says, looking down. "They can tell."

"Karl, I don't understand why you view yourself as bad when you're always sacrificing yourself for the others." I'm trying to create chinks in his wall of defenses against his soft emotional underbelly.

"We were always told we were bad."

"I know you were. You were told that by bad people who wanted you to be like them. But you're not." Karl mulls this over a bit.

It's interesting doing psychotherapy with a part of a personality. A part's issues are really two dimensional; a part doesn't have the layers of complexity that a fully integrated personality would have, and it seems to have a dependency and readiness to cooperate that makes my job easier. I've been surprised how quickly the parts, especially the little boys, take in my comments and incorporate them into their view of themselves.

"I'll write Karen a doctor's note to excuse her from jury duty," I say.

"You can do that?" Karl is impressed that I can so easily protect him from something he so feared. Karl says he's been leaking bits of memories to Karen, but he worries because he's always taken the pain. He asks me if I think he'd hurt anyone. I say no, I don't think so, he's always wanted to protect, and he should be proud of that. We've done a good bit of bond building.

Thea comes out next. She's been sharing time with Karen, although Karen hasn't known about it.

"What has been your role for Karen?" I ask, as part of my standard routine to help the alters relax. "Why were you born?"

"When Karen was six months old, she was always very sick," says Thea, who is girlish, open, matter-of-fact, and cute. She is a very pleasant little girl. "She had the tumor on her forehead. Karen Boo, the baby, was out, but she couldn't handle the medicine and the doctors, so I was born. When Karen was five, she had another operation and radiation treatments. It was me in the hospital all that time." Thea smiles and turns her head, looking at me from the corners of her eyes. "Actually, it was nicer to be with the doctors and the nurses." She pauses a moment. "There were things that weren't nice, shots and things. Sometimes when things got bad at home, I would wish us to get sick."

"Wish yourself sick?"

"Yes, I could make us have a fever and rashes."

"How could you do that?" I've heard of this sort of thing, but I've never seen it.

"I just thought I should have a fever. If I was really mad, I'd just stand there and my temperature would just go up and up and up. Once it went to 104 degrees. That was too high. They put ice water on us."

"You can do this anytime?"

"Only if I'm upset." Thea smiles in her girlish way, as if embarrassed, yet pleased. "Once I put us in a coma for a month. We just stopped participating in life for a while. Father would come in and sit by our hospital bed and switch the channels. We acted as if we couldn't hear. Then they wanted to operate, so I decided we could hear again." Thea tells this story as if she's talking about an incident at recess. I'm not sure I buy any of this, but to Thea's child's mind, this is the way it happened.

"I was out when you put us in the hospital," says Thea, her voice rising and back stiffening, "and I was mad at you. They gave us medicine; the medicine doesn't work the same on all of us. Claire and I knew you needed to learn about us, but I didn't think you'd believe it. She betrayed us by sending you the letter."

"She was reaching out."

"Yes, but I was afraid. No one ever bothered with us before who didn't hurt us."

"Can you tell me about Karen Boo?"

"She's the perfect little baby that the mother could love; she understands some Hungarian. But Karen was always in pain, and she just kept splitting and splitting. Karen Boo first split, then Holdon and Katherine—we needed them to be internal parents. We never really had an outside mom and dad."

"How did Holdon and Katherine know how they should act?"

"There were some good people we liked. We read storybooks. They kept changing over the years. We'd see a mom treating her child a certain way, then Katherine and Holdon would be that way."

"They could do it so quickly? Make it a part of themselves?"

"Oh, yes, we got ideas from everywhere. TV shows. *Dick Van Dyke, Father Knows Best, The Partridge Family.* We wanted Holdon to be understanding."

I'm amazed at the facility she's describing. She is saying the alters have an almost immediate capacity for identification. This is borne out in how quickly they adopt the suggestions and interpretations I give them. They seem to make me a part of them at the moment we interact. What usually takes months with other patients, takes only days for the part personalities of Karen. Perhaps this has something to do with how she can split apart and integrate her parts together. It seems as if reintegrating would take an enormous amount of plasticity in Karen's ability to reorganize her self-images, and indeed she seems to possess this plasticity in abundance.

A few weeks later, I ask Thea if she and Karen Boo are ready to integrate, and she says yes. I begin what has become our routine. She and Thea enter Karen's little room. I discuss their role based on what Thea has told me, and Thea sits on Karen's lap with the baby.

"Thea has pigtails and freckles," says Karen slowly from her trance. "The baby is small next to Thea; she's about eighteen months old and thin for a baby. The baby is hugging her around the neck real tight. Thea is happy about this; she won't be so lonely. Should we merge together or one at a time?"

"One at a time or together. You should feel your way through it." How should I know how they should do it?

"I feel strange; there's a pull . . ." Karen pauses, shifts, her face is working; she seems to be really absorbed in her task. "Thea wants them both to lean on my shoulder and blend in—will it work?"

"Sure," I say confidently, hoping for the best.

Karen is silent for about thirty seconds. Her face is full of concentration.

"They're in, I think."

"Let it happen completely," I say. I don't want to rush her. We haven't done two at once before.

"I'm getting memories from Karen Boo. *Nagymama* [grandmother] wrote poems in Hungarian; she wants to hear them. Lots of lights, a hospital room. A man in a beard . . ."

After several minutes, I bring her back to the office. The lights are bright for her and her head hurts.

"There's a movie going on in my head," she says as she leaves my office. We agree to talk by telephone the next day.

Jan. 26, 1997

The Merging of Thea and Karen Boo

On Wednesday January 22, 1997, Thea and Karen Boo merged within. This merger was very draining because it is very hard to separate which memories came from whom. Karen Boo was so tiny, like a doll, and she had blond hair. I remember Thea holding Karen Boo on her lap and them hugging each other tightly. Then we merged together. As they merged inside me, I immediately became light and sound sensitive, and I heard Hungarian songs sung, like nursery rhymes. Following that, I felt and heard hospital sounds. I was lightheaded and off-balance leaving your office. But somehow I knew I'd be okay until I got home.

I'm trying to use "I" meaning "me," Karen. It is very hard to do this because I want to write and say "we". The first day after integrating I recalled all the memories of the hospital stays. Thea spent most of the time befriending doctors and nurses and other patients. Thea spent hours and hours reading medical books, and was able to bring on symptoms by just thinking of it. Thea thought she was able to alter her immune system and believed this should be taught to people so they can cure themselves.

During the next few days I regained more memories of being in hospitals and memories of words and phrases from Karen Boo. Karen Boo had a habit of chewing the sides of the skin on her fingers. I found myself repeating this behavior for about a week after integrating.

It took about two weeks for this integration to be complete, and I feel I'm learning more everyday.

I don't really believe the part about Thea being able to "alter her immune system" at will, but it would be interesting to study. Anyway, that's not part of Karen's therapy, so I let the thought go.

Karl had decided to withhold giving Karen any more memories until Thea and Karen Boo were fully integrated. I ask him if he is ready to integrate, and he says he still feels angry. I say that won't go away, but will be diluted when he joins the other parts. He sees in Karen feelings of Miles and the tempering of Ann. If he integrates and Karen gets the rest of his memories, he says, that will be the worst of the worst. He has all the pain and sadness. He's tired of it; he doesn't know what it feels like to feel good.

I ask him if he ever feels like hurting himself now. Sometimes he feels he should be brave and end his life so the others will never feel his pain, but he's come to realize that if he kills himself, he'll kill all the others, too, since they share a body. He hadn't known that.

21

KARL

Karen comes in carrying a bulging manila envelope and several sheets of paper. The envelope is an obvious object of curiosity.

"These are things the parts that integrated left for you." Karen hands me a piece of paper entitled "Contents of Envelope for Dr. Baer." The paper enumerates the items, but I turn my attention to the items themselves. I dump them on the ottoman to the side of my chair and sift through the pile. There's a heavy pair of pliers and a well-used 1½-inch paint scraper; the note says these are tools that Grandfather used to hurt "us." Miles sent them and asked me to throw them away. Also from Miles is a candle, about 10 inches long, oddly bent in the middle at ninety degrees. Miles said this was the type of candle used during the ceremonies. It's surprising how common these items are. The pliers and scraper look so ordinary— like tools from the bottom of an old man's tool box.

There's a plastic crucifix, a small gold metal cross for a necklace, and a cross-stitch with the saying: *Ask for God's blessings on your work but don't ask Him to do it.* It's surrounded by a border of flowers. These were from Ann. Sandy left report cards for grades one through four, showing Karen to be an average student, with check marks for inattention during class and some disruptive behavior.

Julie left a cotton hankie with a crocheted border that she carried with her for more than twenty years, and a picture of a schoolteacher who Karen says tried to sexually attack her. The picture shows a fat, middle-aged man with black-frame glasses looking startled by the picture being taken.

There's a small metal charm from a fishing lure that is painted decoratively and a leather bracelet, fastened by a snap, with the name Karen carved in it. The bracelet belonged to Thea, and Karen's name was carved by Miles. There's a diaper pin from Karen Boo, a large marble from Sidney, a button, a zodiac medallion, and other pieces of summer-camp arts-and-crafts jewelry. I look at these things and they seem so common—like the bits of trash that end up in the bottom of a closet before it's been cleaned. But to Karen and the parts that integrated, they have a solemn meaning and importance. I put them carefully back in the envelope and turn toward Karen.

"I understand how meaningful these things were to the parts that have integrated, and I'll keep them with the other things I have from you." I look at Karen for a sign that I have accepted these items consonant with her expectations. I detect a slight sense of satisfaction.

"Next Tuesday we plan to integrate Karl," I remind. Karen nods, but her face shows dread. As she hands me the paper she brought, she looks at me with sorrow.

The paper is entitled "Karl's Memories." Karen has been writing down the memories Karl has been leaking to her for the past several weeks. She says they're extensions of the abuse she's already told me about. Here is a sampling of the five pages she wrote.

I was put into a coffin at the funeral home. I couldn't breathe. At first Claire, then Miles took over for me. When they could no longer deal with it, Karl came out until we were released and then took the mocking and degrading.

Karl took the pain from the radiation treatments and the surgeries we had as children. This pain was what Julie and Thea could not handle. Karl was the one who took the pain during our C-section with Sara. I was given a spinal anesthetic, but Thea came out and then Julie. Julie moved our legs when we could feel the doctors cutting our abdomen. I was anesthetized, but Julie was not. Karl took the pain from the lung surgery.

Karl took the pain during the ceremony when they stuck our breasts and privates with long needles with pearl balls on the heads. He then took the pain when our father struck our hands with a hammer for trying to protect our breasts.

Karl took the pain from Miles and Julie from the beatings with extension cords, the electric shocks, the punching and the candle wax dripped on our sensitive areas. He took the pain from the gang rapes by our father and his friends after they watched porno movies.

I put the paper down. There was much more, some too horrible to describe, but that's representative. I think about Karen being dosed with these memories over the past several weeks, living with these images and feelings every day. I understand her look of sorrow, and Karl's panic at the thought of sharing them after spending years trying to protect everyone from knowing.

"Do you think it's wise to integrate Karl?" asks Karen, with resignation.

"If you're not ready, we can always postpone," I say. "There's no timetable but yours." Karen is afraid of Karl and what he's suffered; I don't blame her. But since I put the decision back onto her and don't rescue her in the face of her own fears, she's left to decide whether to go forward or shrink back. She never shrinks.

"It's a lot to go through," she says, looking weary. "I've felt different since Thea and Boo merged. I'm feeling some old memories for the first time, and sometimes just old feelings. With each integration, I feel like I didn't exist before, like I'm starting all over again." Karen pauses and stares at the rug. I just wait.

"When a part integrates, it feels like I've been given a new past life"—she looks at me, lost and pained—"someone else's life. Who am I?" She pauses and looks out the window. "It's not easy learning to be . . . 'me.' " She half smiles at her joke, but she isn't joking. It isn't only the merging parts that are giving up their individual identities, but Karen, too, the part that comes to see me, experiences each integration as an assault on her own person-hood. For her, each integration isn't an addition, but a diminishment of her own self. The whole is really quite different than the sum of the parts. I let her sit a moment.

"I appreciate the difficulty of what you're going through." I pause. "Are you ready to integrate Karl?" I ask.

She bows her head and nods. She doesn't speak. I ask her to sit back and relax in her chair, the usual prelude to her hypnotic trance. She relaxes and closes her eyes.

Karl comes out. Karen looks at me, eyes wide, breathing sharper. "Karen has worries," says Karl. "She expects to feel pain. She's not going to believe the rest of my memories." Karl's look implores me to somehow make the task ahead bearable, survivable, but I'm not sure how much protection is possible.

"The memories will be more believable if you give her the feelings that go along with the memories," I suggest.

"How do I give her the pain?" Karl looks at me with desperation. He's in a real dilemma. His whole purpose was to keep the pain away from Karen and make her forget. Now he's faced with dumping it all on her all at once. "How do I give her the feelings?" I'm quiet, hoping Karl will come up with an answer to his own question.

"Should I let her know about the time they put fishhooks in us, all over Karen's chest? They pulled on them and laughed and said they'd tear her skin off. They finally cut the tips off the hooks and took them out and then poured alcohol over her. I always came out when it was really bad."

He has a point, so to speak. How can we minimize the trauma to Karen when these memories become a part of her? Or can we? This would really change her "past life." As Karl has told me about these events, he acted as if he were experiencing them. But I don't think Karen needs to gain these experiences in their Technicolor reality.

"I can think of two things that might help," I tell Karl. "First, do you think, when you integrate, you can unfold your memories to Karen over the next two to three weeks, rather than over a few days?" This might help Karen absorb Karl's feelings more gradually, thereby avoiding overwhelming devastation.

"I can try," he says, with a bit less panic.

"Second, as you give Karen your pain, can you also give her your strength for handling that pain?" Karl thinks a bit longer about this. It seems integrating this part of himself hadn't occurred to him.

"I will do that, too."

I asked Karl to step back for a moment while I talked to Holdon. Holdon already knows that Karen may be in for a rough time, and promises to remain alert for Karen's distress. He reminds me there are seven inside who can help. He says he thinks Karen will be stronger for Karl's integration. But he asks me to be available by telephone over the next several days, just in case. He says Karl will wait until Karen gets home before she gets any of his thoughts. I call Karl back and ask him to wait outside Karen's room.

Karen opens the door and says, "Karl is coming in."

"Can you describe him?" I ask.

"His face is full of pain." Karen winces. "He has dark hair, a chain around his neck. He's shaking my hand, introducing himself. He says everything will be okay."

I hope he's right, I think. I need to do a little introduction, even though Karen is aware of Karl's role.

"Karl's role has been to hold the pain no other part could hold. He holds the pain of the memories, but also has the strength to tolerate them."

"He's awkward," says Karen as she watches him in her mind. "He's not a person who likes contact. He has lots of scars on him, on his arms and hands; he's been hurt." Karen squirms in her chair. "He's beginning to come in . . . not touching. He wants to thank you for listening . . . he's coming toward me, he's coming inside, he's fading, like a spirit, walking into me . . . he's in." Karen winces and once again tells me the sounds are loud and the lights, bright. Also, this time she feels cold. "He's in, but I'm not getting any thoughts," she says.

"You probably won't get any until you get home," I say. I bring Karen out of hypnosis, and I chat with her a bit, just to make sure she's calm enough to go home. We both fear what will come in the next few weeks.

Feb. 12, 1997

The Merging of Karl

On Tuesday, Feb. 11, 1997, Karl merged within. It's been less than 24 hours since we integrated Karl and there's so much to absorb I need to start writing earlier than usual. First I'll begin with what I remember from your office.

Although Karl's been feeding me memories for weeks, I was extremely nervous about integrating him. I knew in my heart it would be another step towards becoming whole, and I knew that you would be there for me. I've heard the others talk, and the part that is Karl seems to be the worst. I guess part of me admires his strength and courage. How could he possibly live through this nightmare? I hope I can gain his tolerance for pain.

I remember being in our safe room and unlocking the door to let Karl in. Karl walked over to me immediately. He did not look scared, but he did seem angry and in pain. I could see many bruises on his forearms and face. He said goodbye to you and stepped into me. He did not reach out. I don't think he wanted to touch before merging. I understand he never felt a good touch and I was sad for him. I did not feel anything when Karl stepped inside. I had this empty, lonely feeling.

I finally made it home and fell asleep. When I woke up, the integration hit me. The first feeling I gained was feeling ice cold, like I was in a cold damp dark place. My body was racked with pain. I could not bend my arms and legs. I never felt so much pain before.

Two days after integrating, I awoke at the sound of the alarm, but as I tried to move, I couldn't. I was in pain from head to toe. I couldn't move fast enough to turn off the alarm. This slowness caused my husband to punch me and call me a lazy fat ass. As hard as I tried, I felt paralyzed. Throughout the day, I felt pain and remembered the events that caused it. I didn't think I could survive this. I'm still freezing and shivering and I believe this feeling is coming from being locked in the cold dark shandy and the attic. My mouth seems deformed and my speech is slurred. The following are the memories I gained today. Although unpleasant, I've accepted them and can go on. I pray that no one else had to endure this from the same people.

I remember the torture these men did to me. I can feel the needles and fishhooks piercing my body. I hear the laughter and the degrading remarks. I feel the presence of evil.

I remember being strapped down on a table with one of the straps anchored under my chin and pulled above my head. My jaw hurt so bad. I know I suffered a broken jaw at some time in my life, but I am unsure if it happened at this time. I remember them making small paper cuts on tender areas of my body and pouring the alcohol on the wounds. It stung so bad, but I did not flinch.

Three days after integrating I woke still in pain, mostly in my joints. My jaw pain is gone and my speech is back to normal. The pain from the needles and fishhooks is gone, but now new pain and memories are starting. I have severe cramping pains in my sides and lower abdomen. This pain comes with my memory of tools being pushed into me. I spent all of the day recalling the many different times these awful things were done to me. I feel so disgusted with myself I don't think I can ever have sex again. I can't believe that I was capable of having two children. I feel like everyone who looks at me knows what happened.

Four days after integrating Karl, I woke still having joint pain, but the cramping was gone. My hearing sensitivity was gone and my vision was back to normal. As I lay next to my husband in bed I recalled the verbal abuse he gave me. Karl took on the hurtful words and rejection. I recalled how every time I would accidentally touch him while I slept, he would kick and punch me. I realize he has not touched me nicely in the last ten years. How I slept next to him, I'll never know! Thank God we have a king size bed. Somehow, looking at him this morning, I realize he just extended the abuse from my childhood. I wonder what it would be like to feel loved. I feel Karl's anger as my own.

I remember every single satanic ritual, every single detail. This makes me so sick. I don't want to accept these memories and I don't feel like writing about them. I feel Karl's fears that we will be *killed if we spill any information. I hear his thoughts that we were evil and the cult members were our only family. I realize Karl was only 10 years old and these thoughts may have been distorted. I know the "cult" people were family and friends in their own stupid made up cult, with my grandfather as their leader. I keep living these memories through flashbacks. I feel paralyzed. I feel Karl's hatred for holidays, especially when the holidays are celebrated in church.*

I'm having horrible visions of abuse happening in the funeral home and shandy. I hear and feel Karl's pain in keeping memories always from me. The only problem is I can never forget again. I believe we lived through hell on earth.

A week after integrating Karl, Karen walks into my office slowly, almost hobbled, with lines showing strain on her face. My condolences show on my face. She moves to the chair and sits with a grimace.

"Most of the pain is gone," she says with a sigh, "but my joints are still stiff and sore."

"How do you feel about what you've remembered?" I ask.

"Really bad. I think when people see me they know what happened and they despise me."

"Do you despise yourself?"

"Yes," she says and begins to cry. "I see every detail of everything! I can't write it all down. I feel I should have stopped it, it's my fault, somehow my choosing . . ." Karen pauses and thinks for a moment; some sadness recedes from her face. She continues.

"Remembering makes me realize I haven't even lived half my life; other parts did. Who am I really? What will I be like when I am all integrated?" The sadness returns in her. "I wish these memories were just some stories I made up. I think these men just made up the rituals; they weren't a real cult. There were only about eight of them. I never read anything about cults, but I would expect them to have more people."

"This group was headed by your grandfather and father?"

"Yes. Most of the men were employees of my father or grandfather." She thinks for a minute. "They made everything gray, so I couldn't focus on anything else. I remember being locked in little rooms, needles and cuts, laughing and humiliation, my husband's degrading and punching . . . lots of pain." She sighs and relaxes a little. "Enclosed places still bother me; in the car I've had to drive with the windows open, and it's February!"

"You're going through so much," I say, "but as you've said, this is the worst of the worst, and you're through most of it. I know you'll be able to persevere through the rest. Let's see what's going on with the others."

Under hypnosis, Holdon comes out, reaches into Karen's purse, and hands me an envelope. Before I open it, I ask him how Karen is managing day to day. He says it's going well; they haven't had to come out to help. The problem is she doesn't want to believe what she's remembering, so she has to have the feelings, too, for the memories to be real to her. I read his letter and we discuss it. He says these are his opinions, but I can do what I think is best.

Feb. 13, 1997

Dr. Baer,

We passed the halfway mark and I feel all is well. I am sure that Juliann is the next one we should integrate, but you really need to talk to Katherine soon. She is not well; I've never seen her so despondent. Please wait until Karl is integrated more.

The most troubled alters are now integrated. The rest of us, besides Elise, are functioning for Karen. May I suggest the following order for integrating the rest of us?

1. *Juliann—she will be a great help in further journaling. She has so much inside her to write and I feel she will benefit from the others.*

2. *Elise—she will complete all the memories from the ritual abuse. She helped in the back and forth of trying to be normal.*

3. *Jensen—he will give a new view on how to apply ourselves.*

4. *Karen 2—she will help us enjoy life.*

5. *Karen 1—she needs more counseling before integrating.*

6. *Karen 3–she needs work on self-esteem before integrating.*

7. *Katherine–she needs more therapy. She needs to be brought back to her original purpose.*

8. *Me, Holdon–I'll be the last to integrate for final closure.*

Holdon

It amazes me that I have the help of this part, Holdon, to guide me in structuring this process of putting Karen back together again. What would I have done without him? I'm glad I don't have to try to figure this all out by myself. I haven't seen anything in the writings about this disorder that discusses this type of process for reintegration, where one of the alters directs the procedure. Karen has really developed her cure for herself, and it seems to be working. I intend to follow Holdon's guidance for the order and try to deal with the individual issues that come up for each part to prepare them for their turn.

Before I bring Karen out of hypnosis, I ask to talk with Katherine. She's depressed over not feeling needed without the children. There's no one to listen to her, need her, and respect her. I try to support her by saying how helpful her strengths have been, and remind her that when she integrates, all that she is will be needed once again. She feels a little better.

22.

ELISE AND KAREN 1

Because of my vacation, it's been three weeks since I saw Karen last. She's early as usual, and comes into the office looking somehow altered—not in her outward appearance, but in her movement and posture.

"How have you been?" I ask.

"The other parts are still keeping my schedule for me. Yesterday I woke and found myself getting physical therapy. . . . It seems like a year since I saw you."

"I know, the separations are always hard."

"For the first time I had all the feelings of the other parts about you leaving on vacation. Claire's feelings . . . even though they're integrated, I can still tell who they're from." She pauses. "I find I have all this information I didn't know I had. I don't know it until I'm asked, and then there it is. My son asked me, When did Wrigley Field open, and what are the heights of the three tallest buildings in Chicago, and I knew the answers! I didn't realize before how much I've gained from the integrations."

"How else have you changed?" I ask.

"I never had personal tastes before. I just existed. Now I have to figure out what kind of person I am. What do I like? What am I going to do about my abusive marriage?"

"You really have integrated the other parts. You never asked such questions before."

"Yes. For instance, I find I have a lot of medical knowledge, especially about childhood diseases. I love to watch medical shows on the Learning Channel; I never cared before. I'm interested in people and events. Now when I lose time, I get upset because I think I've lost out on something. I've gone from wanting to die, to hoping I don't die."

As I look at Karen and hear about these changes, I feel I'm looking at a more complete person. There are nuances to her feelings and a depth to her thoughts that are quite new. I'm amazed; this all seems to be working. It reminds me of when I was a medical student and I delivered my first baby. The woman was depending on me to help her, but really, she was the miracle and did all the work; I was just there to catch.

"I have a confession to make, Dr. Baer," says Katherine, adjusting the hem of her skirt down. "I'm the one causing the headaches."

"Oh?"

"Yes, I've been coming out more. I'm afraid I've been a little greedy for time. Now that the children are gone, I don't have anything to do anymore. After the bills are paid and the house is clean, I'm at a loss." Katherine looks at me as if I should comprehend her plight. She speaks in an even, measured tone, without much emotion, and sits primly.

"It sounds like you need to integrate with the others, too," I say.

"Holdon said I should wait"—she straightens her posture—"and Karen 2 wants to integrate."

"What can you tell me about that?"

"Well, she wants to change things. She wants to get us in shape physically. She can't tolerate Karen's weight." Katherine shifts herself in her chair sideways, as if to appear leaner and lighter. Then she leans forward and speaks softly. "She's also the one attracted to men."

"How do you feel about that?"

"I don't like it; it frightens me."

"Frightens you?"

"Getting close to people scares me." I know she has a thousand reasons for this, so I don't pursue it at this time.

"Do you have any thoughts on who might be ready to integrate next?" I ask.

"Elise and Karen 1." Katherine becomes more animated, now that she has something to contribute. "They're both ten years old. Elise's role was to go from being abused to going to school and acting normal. Karen 1 played with the other neighborhood children in a normal way. If we integrate these two, I could follow." She looks at me for my consent. I hesitate, not sure whose agenda to follow. Katherine sees my indecision and continues.

"Karen 2 doesn't really need me, and I've never had much to do with Jensen. Elise is ready to integrate."

"What you say makes good sense, and I will try to do as you suggest, but I have been confused by something. Holdon talked about integrating Karen 1, 2, and 3. So who has been coming to see me?"

"We've all been coming to see you at some point, but Karen 3 is the one closest to who you'd recognize as the one you see. She's the one the others are integrated into. And with the changes in her and her enjoying things so much more, it's harder for me to come out when I'm needed, although I'm not needed much now. It makes me jealous."

"So there are three Karens, Holdon and Katherine, Elise and Jensen, and Juliann to integrate?" I summarize where we are for my clarification more than hers.

"Right," she says. I'm still confused how we are going to integrate Karen 3 into herself, but I let it go for now.

"Elise is ready," says Juliann. *"She's not afraid. I'm ready, too; I can integrate anytime. When I do, I'll start journaling again."*

"Thanks," I say. "Can you step back and let Elise talk to me?" Karen's face goes blank, then she squirms and plays with her fingers.

"At Catholic school," Elise begins, "when we did something bad, the sisters would say we had the devil in us. If I was bad, Sister Frances would pull our hair and throw holy water on us, but I would never cry or show any feelings, and that would scare her."

Elise starts to go on, but then pauses and looks down, picking at something invisible on her slacks.

"Why were you born, Elise?" I ask. "What was your job?" I know there must be more to her than episodes at school.

"Well," she starts and stops, "I was born to fill in the gap in the morning." I open my palm to motion her to continue. "When we were hurt at night, afterwards, I mean, they put us in a dark room. That's when I would come out." Elise pauses. I think she's never spoken to anyone like this before.

"What else?" I ask. Elise shifts in her chair, unable to get comfortable.

"There wouldn't be much time until we had to go to school. I would take a shower or a bath and put on my school uniform and go to mass. I'd pretend nothing happened. Ann would come out in church."

"When did this happen? How old were you?"

"Karen was ten, but I was eight. I was supposed to look younger. That's when most of the hurting happened, when Karen was between ten and twelve." Elise slumps a little and looks at me for the first time. "Do you think I'm evil?"

"No, I don't, Elise. Karl told me the same story—how you were told you were evil, made to believe it, so you would think you deserved to be hurt. But none of it is true." Elise nods and chews her lower lip.

"That's what Ann said, too. We spent a lot of time together, but she's gone."

"I think it's a good time for you to join Ann, Karen, and the others," I say. "Are you ready?" She nods three times, quickly. Poor Elise seems so sad.

Under hypnosis I introduce Elise to Karen and summarize her role. Elise approaches Karen and says she wants to go with the others. I ask Karen to describe her.

"She's small, with black hair and blue eyes," Karen says. "She looks about eight or nine. Her face is round, cute, with dark eyebrows. . . . Elise is holding back, but I'm taking her hand and sitting her on my lap." Karen pauses; I can see her struggle. "I'm bringing Elise inside of myself. I feel cold."

I bring Karen back to my office. She feels light-headed, as if she will faint, and nauseous; the sounds are loud and the lights are bright. I let her sit for a minute before she goes home.

March 27, 1997

The Merging of Elise

On Monday, March 24, Elise merged within. This integration went quickly, and much more smoothly than the others. I did feel light and sound sensitive and off balance, but this seems to be normal when we merge. By the end of the day I had a terrible headache and was exhausted.

From Elise, I remember going from being hurt and then acting perfectly normal within seconds. I would always appear like a well-adjusted child to all those around me at home and at school.

I remember hearing conflicting stories and adjusting to each one. I had to be on everyone's side no matter what I believed. I had to be the keeper of the lie of innocence. I had to say I was okay, happy, and didn't know what happened. I did everything I could to cover up the truth about the men involved.

I see Karen a week later. She tells me the merging of Elise went fine—she had expected worse. Under hypnosis, Katherine tells me Karen 1 has been causing problems, trying to take over everything. She knows it's her turn to integrate. Katherine's mourning the loss of the children: especially Miles, Elise, Thea, and Karl. She feels lost and empty.

"Do you look forward to your own integration?" I ask Katherine.

"Oh! Well, yes and no. I would like to stay and keep things under control. Holdon and I have been around the longest. I make a lot of the decisions and keep things organized."

"That's hard for you to do now."

"Yes. I hear Karen's thoughts, and I don't like her very much now."

"Why not?" I'm surprised at this.

"I don't like her having opinions and being stronger."

"Are you afraid you'll lose your old role?"

"I've lost most of it already." She leans back in her chair a little. "Karen is a different person."

I nod and sympathize, and say we'll talk more later. I ask for Karen 1 to come forward. Katherine retreats and Karen seems to melt. Her erect back becomes soft, and a look of uncertainty comes over her.

"Are you ready?" I ask Karen 1.

"I'm scared." Her eyes dart around the room, and finally rest on me.

"I understand," I say. "Why don't you tell me about yourself, how were you born?"

"I was born to help out, to start things. I was two when I was born; I'm ten now. I didn't want to grow up anymore, so I didn't. I did some of the schoolwork and I helped out babysitting my brothers. I learned to walk for us."

"You have courage," I say.

Karen 1 smiles, and adds quickly, "But I was quiet, and I didn't want to grow up and be a girl. Girls get hurt. I'm the one that put the bandage around my chest so the men couldn't see I was a girl."

I explain the integration procedure to Karen 1, and under hypnosis we find ourselves in Karen's small room.

I start to introduce Karen 1 to Karen as the part that takes initiative and has courage, but Karen 1 is already merging.

"Her arms are around my waist," says Karen, "and her head is on my shoulder."

"Is she going inside?"

"Yes. I feel strange, shaky."

"Memories?"

"I'm sitting on a football field, watching the marching band practice. The bandleader looks familiar. . . ."

Afterward, Karen is assaulted by the light and noise and she complains of a new headache.

April 2, 1997

The Merging of Karen 1
On Tuesday, April 1, 1997, Karen 1 merged within. Karen 1 is ten years old, with blonde hair and brown eyes. I originally thought she appeared withdrawn, but I soon realized she was very

sensitive and shy. Although shy, she was our initiator; she had the courage to start things. Karen 1 wanted to stay small; she did not want to develop into a woman.

Although this merger appeared to go smoothly, I did not realize the effects left over from Elise's integration. Somehow I arrived at your office and found myself waiting on the bench in your lobby. I wasn't too concerned how I got there, but I was glad to see I wasn't late. This just "showing up" somewhere is totally normal for me. When you arrived in the lobby too and opened the door for us to go in, I had one of Elise's memories hit me. As I stepped into the elevator with you, I remembered the service elevator at the chemical factory. The ride became the route I traveled, or Elise traveled, on the way to the room where the ceremonial rituals were played out.

I remember looking over at you wishing you could read my mind. The silence in the elevator was so much like the silence with my abusers. I tried not to let you see the fear I was feeling. Elise was very good at pretending nothing is wrong. When we exited the elevator, it took all my energy to follow you to your door. Thank God you asked me to wait a few minutes in the waiting area. This gave me enough time for this memory to pass.

I don't remember what you and Karen 1 talked about before we merged, but I do remember the light and the sound; everything was so bright and every sound so loud.

There was a difference with this merging. Karen 1 started being absorbed as soon as she approached me; she merged quickly. The first thing I remember was getting off a high school bus after a night of abuse. We exited the bus at a funeral home across from the school and Karen 1's first thought was "just what we need, another funeral home." Karen 1 then heard band music and wandered over to the field and sat down. Karen 1 enjoyed the marching band playing. I recall many memories from Karen 1 and I know she was a big part in starting things for me. She was also the one who wanted us to start therapy with you.

There was a girl that lived down the block from where we lived—Gail Jones. I was friends with her brother. She always aggravated me and humiliated me. Gail was about five years older than us and knew just how to pick on us. One day she was bragging about riding a two wheel bike, and Karen 1 said she *could ride a bike too, although she never had. Karen 1 got on that bike and rode it like she had ridden a thousand times. This is how we started riding a two wheel bike.*

I continued to have more memories over the next week. All Karen 1's memories were pretty much added to Elise's. Whenever Elise took us somewhere, Karen 1 would come out to initiate something, and then the others would take over from there.

"Karen 1's memories were mostly between Elise and Miles," says Karen when I see her the following week. "They filled in a lot of gaps."

"So how are you feeling now?" Karen looks out the window, her chin resting on her hand.

"This last one was different. I haven't adjusted as quickly. I'm feeling a little depressed, but I feel more like a person now. Karen 1 felt closer to being me."

"Maybe that's why she was a 'Karen'?" There is a difference in the Karen I see. She's more of a person. She speaks more thoughtfully, as if she has more thoughts and associations to sift through before she talks or answers. Her personality is deeper and richer, as if her soul is being added to.

"I recalled lots of memories from childhood—friends, games we played; I had no memories of those things. Karen 1 had likes and dislikes. She's still integrating."

"We won't integrate anyone today," I say, to give her time for the previous integrations to complete. "Let's put you under and see if someone else needs to talk to me." For the first time, Karen thinks a moment and then nods her consent, instead of just being obedient.

"I'm the one who's depressed," says Katherine.

"That's not like you," I say.

"There's no need for me anymore. I feel so alone without the children."

"I understand. Karen seems to be benefiting from the integrations."

"You don't understand. I have been Karen's mother and the mother to all the children inside. She *created* her own mother and father. If I integrate, who will be her mother then?"

"How do other adults manage when they lose their mother?" I ask. Katherine only glares at me. "Their mothers are kept inside them as part of themselves," I say.

"You haven't seen all Karen's changes. I've been holding her back. Karen wanted to play an April Fools' joke on you, but I prevented it. She's become more lighthearted, she's developed a sense of humor, and she's more involved with life. Where do I fit in? I don't like these changes. I wish things were like they were before. I know they weren't good, but I don't know what to do."

"We need to integrate you," I say, and gently stare her down.

"There's so much I want to do first," she says. "I need to organize everything."

"That's a pretty long-term task," I say.

We discuss what she might and might not do. She's afraid she will leave duties undone, and she's been nothing if not dutiful. I finally suggest that her sense of duty and organization will reside in Karen and be carried on. We agree that she'll integrate next week.

23

KATHERINE

"*I'm a little nervous,*" *says Katherine, sitting erect and lean-*ing earnestly toward me as she speaks. "I haven't interrupted Karen all week. She doesn't really need me. I wanted to get some things done, but I've let them go. I'm uneasy about leaving. It's like dying . . . but not really, I suppose. . . . I'm worried Karen won't be able to handle the changes with my integration."

"It will be a joining, rather than a leaving," I say.

"I'd like to feel that way. Originally, I wanted everyone to inte-grate with me, not me with another part. I wanted to integrate last, you know, to see how it all turns out. But Karen will benefit more now than later. She really needs to be more organized."

"You will bring those qualities to her. Can you tell me anything more about Karen's system that I don't already know?"

"You know, Dr. Baer, Karen was not out for most of her life. We started splitting when Karen was just a baby. The abuse started even before she was born, during her mother's pregnancy. I under-stand her father used to punch her mother when she was preg-nant. The alters have built a life for her. Most of the other parts were born for special reasons. They would come out only when they were needed. Usually Holdon or I would decide who would go out."

"Why was Karen 3 chosen to be the one that the others are merged into? Is she the core person?"

"She was the most compliant; she had no opinions of her own. She was the most accepting."

"Ah, I see, she was the best vessel." I recall she is the alter that "carries" the rest.

"Yes, that's it. Karen 3 is the part you see most. Karen 1 and Karen 3 are almost the same person. They're mirror-image twins, although they're not the same age; it's hard to explain . . . but there's no core. There's a childhood part of Karen 3 that needs to be integrated. Karen has always been, as she says, a passenger in her own life."

"What were the circumstances of your birth, Katherine?"

"I was born to be Karen's mother. She was only about a year old, but I was born a couple years older. My jobs were to bring in information and to keep things organized and intact. While we were growing up, I read the encyclopedia, dictionary, and Bible from front to back. I kept us updated. I'd complete things Karen or the others left unfinished. I'd know how best to take care of problems, and who to send out to take care of specific tasks. After high school, I did most of the secretarial work for Karen at her job. When Sara was born, our system got kind of crumbly. We had trouble holding things together. That's when Karen 1 decided we needed help." Katherine falls silent and looks at me with the slightest cock of her head.

"Shall we proceed?" I ask.

"Yes, please."

"Then step back and I will prepare Karen." I'm not sure it's possible for a baby's personality to split up at four months, since at that age a baby hasn't developed a cohesive personality, but this is the way Katherine tells it.

I follow our usual procedure, and place myself in Karen's special room and summarize Katherine's role for her. She opens the door to let Katherine in. Karen describes Katherine. She's a tall, thin, pale woman, taller than Karen. She has a soft smile—maternal— and she's holding Karen's hand and looking at her.

"You can merge any way you like," I suggest.

"I'm not going to get all teary eyed," says Katherine.

"She wants to hug me quickly," mumbles Karen, "right at the doorway, and go inside me. She wants to say something to you first . . . she says she'll miss her chats with you, and wants to thank you for your patience with her."

"I'll miss her, too, but I'll see her in a new form."

"I'm hugging her, she's crying, I'm feeling her already. She's on her way in . . . I can hear the sounds real loud now. I feel a little anxiety, my chest hurts. I feel her nervousness. She's in. I feel strange. My neck is stiff. I'm not remembering much now; maybe she's waiting."

"Why don't you step back from the door and close it," I say.

"I forgot to mention," Karen says, "there were a few people at the door, watching."

"I'll leave your room now."

"Don't go, not yet; I'm nervous."

"Okay, I'll stay."

"Just for a minute . . . she used to take care of me. . . ." Karen pauses; I don't know for what. I wait. "I'm okay now."

I bring Karen out of her trance. She's trembling and says it feels as if there's a vise on her head. She's light and sound sensitive. This may be different, I suggest to her, because Katherine was such a big part.

"My eyesight is changing, everything is blurred. . . . Oh, I forgot!" She hands me a letter from her purse.

"Did you drive yourself?" I ask.

"A friend drove. Katherine prearranged it."

April 15, 1997

Dearest Karen,

It's 4:00 a.m. and today we integrate. There are so many things to tell you, but since I'm pressed for time, I hope you will receive my knowledge. Here's what's most important for me to tell you before integration. I will list them so it will be easy for you to understand.

1. Regarding Dr. Baer: I've always felt him to be truly honest and helpful. He has taken on our whole system and has accepted us all, each and every one of us. I hope that the feelings you are

*experiencing regarding him abandoning us will subside as I inte-
grate. If they should not, please give him a chance. He is very dear
to me. Can you possibly imagine what we have put him through?
I hope together we continue to appreciate all he's done for us.*

*2. Regarding Pastor Jeremy: we've been seeing him once every
two weeks to receive religious support. This is not because of any
lack of trust of Dr. Baer, but we needed to know more about what
we are in God's eyes. Our doubt in God was tested and Jeremy is
helping us.*

*3. Please do not loan out money to the following people: Harriet,
Mother, brothers, any relatives and friends. They'll never pay you
back. I have left you a file of necessary papers. It is in the top
drawer of your dresser. Please familiarize yourself with its contents.*

*4. I have left a list of things that I wanted to purchase. My
intention was to purchase one item a month. I know you'll like
these items, so if possible, please keep up with it.*

*Please try to leave the past behind and start anew. Please have
faith and remember the people who really care for you. You need
to get on with your life without me. Always remember I'm in your
heart. I enjoyed being a part of you.*

I love you,
Katherine

Attached to this letter from Katherine is a list of items she left
for Karen, neatly arranged and labeled. The package included certificates for birth, Baptism, Communion, Confirmation, and Marriage for Karen; high school sweater and letters for band and
drama; high school diploma and yearbooks; husband's birth certifi-
cate; death certificates for her grandfather, grandmother, and
father; children's birth, Baptism, and Communion records, etc. The
list is exhaustive and ends with a complete list of dates of every
visit Karen has made to see me.

"I can't keep up with all the new thoughts! All my usual
ways of thinking have changed!" I remain quiet.

"I look at everything I need to do differently. I know all types of
things I didn't know before. But I haven't received all the memories

yet. For example, I went to buy one of the items on Katherine's list, and I knew right where in the store to find it, but I didn't know what it looked like. In the closet, I found clothes in plastic with the label 'Katherine.' Mostly, I never dressed myself in the morning. I can't stand to look at myself in the mirror. I don't look like I should. Katherine was not heavy. Now I feel really fat. Katherine also had all the bills organized, like she was going to die."

"She put her affairs in order."

"Yes. You know, I'm getting a little depressed about integrating the others."

"How come?"

"I'm disappearing. With each integration, I'm becoming less of who I was. I really noticed it this time."

"I see your point. You're becoming more, but different. Not you."

"Yes, it's so strange."

"I haven't been out much," says Holdon.

"What do you do when you're inside?"

"I keep things going, I talk to the other parts, make sure they're okay. Jensen is hesitant to integrate; he wants to be his own person. Jensen wants to do some artwork for you, but there hasn't been time with all the energy being spent integrating Katherine. Since Katherine's integration, there are big changes inside. Karen is stressed—this is the longest integration so far. But she's handling things pretty well. Juliann should be the next to integrate, when Katherine is finished. Karen's self-esteem is better since Katherine integrated."

"I'm glad to hear it," I say. "When Jensen finds time to start drawing and things have quieted down with Katherine, then it should be time to integrate Juliann."

"That sounds good," says Holdon.

It's the beginning of May 1997. The park is green again, and the spring air is cool and brisk as it blows in from across the lake. Karen comes in carrying a light jacket and sits with her back erect, slightly forward and to the side: hints of Katherine's posture.

"I'm not sure Katherine regarded me as capable," says Karen. "I worry about living up to her expectations."

"Tell me about it."

"Her phone book has so many addresses! What am I supposed to do, call up each one and say, *Hello! How do I know you?* I went to see a friend of Katherine's, Christina, that Katherine helped out, giving respite care for the woman's dying mother. I knew how to get to the house, I went inside and recognized the dying woman, but I couldn't remember any of the conversations we'd had. I visited Pastor Jeremy for Katherine's appointment. That was strange. I knew him, but I'd had a completely different relationship with him. I recognize the faces of Katherine's friends, but not their names or the interactions or conversations we've had. I've gotten her emotional and visual memories, but the words are just starting to come. This week I used the phrase 'quite frankly'; it's Katherine's phrase. I never used it before. I hear words and phrases in my head, but I'm not comfortable using them."

"You haven't quite taken ownership of who Katherine was yet."

"No, just the opposite."

"It sounds like you're going to be working on this for a couple more weeks."

Under hypnosis, Juliann, soft-spoken and girlish, comes out to tell me she's annoyed with Karen for not writing more about Katherine's integration. She reaches into Karen's purse and pulls out several handwritten pages and hands them to me. She also says she's supposed to tell me Jensen got his drawing materials.

The Merging of Katherine
On Tuesday, April 15th, 1997, Katherine merged within. This integration is the most exhausting yet. The problems started after I arrived home. I found schedules, notes, and instructions everywhere. As I glanced over these things, I started feeling depressed, probably because I started to feel I couldn't fill Katherine's shoes. This first day totally exhausted me, and the next day I stayed home because Katherine wisely left that day unscheduled. That day I absorbed more of Katherine; she was obsessed with organizing things. I, myself, like to be on time and have things planned, but in the past, I always lost time if I felt rushed.

Katherine had her integration planned. She had a pile of papers and other items neatly stacked, wrapped in plastic. Besides all the paper work, I'm finding it quite difficult to keep up with my new "friends". These friends were Katherine's and I don't feel right about keeping these relationships. I feel as though I'm worming my way into another person's life, and betraying them, because I really don't know these people. Where was I all this time? When were these friendships established? As I continue to adjust, I have been adhering to Katherine's schedule. She has committed herself for the next four months. I will try to keep these commitments as long as possible. I find myself actually liking some of her friends and preferences.

"Hello! I haven't talked to you in a long time!" Whoever this is in Karen is certainly in a good mood, I think. She's squirming in her chair, talking fast, and taking in the room as she speaks.

"Well," I say, stalling, "how have you been?" I'm acting like Karen when she meets somebody who knows her but she's at a loss about who it is.

"I've been fine! I've got no problems. But I must say I'm disappointed in the rest of the group. They're all so sad. I'm never sad myself. There was this fire on an airplane at the airport. Everybody got so upset, but I said 'What's all the fuss? They'll be fine, and if not, it won't bother us!' They're all so glum, I'm the only one left to do fun things with Sara."

"You have a wonderful, cheerful spirit," I say to stroke her a bit. "It's a quality that will be greatly appreciated and helpful to the whole when you integrate."

"Well, I certainly could help Karen in the men department. When I married Josh, we got along fine." Ah, it's Karen 2, I think. "I loved him for a while. But he just couldn't get used to our system. I can't blame him, really. If I integrate, I could help Karen have a healthy romantic relationship."

"You're not sure about integrating?" I ask.

"Are you kidding? What a downer! Still, there's hardly anybody left for me to talk to. I'll tell you one thing that's better, Karen doesn't look forward to death like she used to. Now she hopes she doesn't die. That's a hundred-percent improvement!"

"I started working a couple days ago," says Jensen, "but I won't be finished for a couple weeks. I'd like to show you what our rooms looked like. The brick walls have come down. I made all the walls out of brick. We used to live in separate rooms, but now we're all in the same big room, but we each keep to our own corners. I've been thinking about integration."

"That's fine, Jensen. I'd like to know more about you. How old are you."

"I'm eleven, but I feel older. Nobody really considers me a kid. Katherine didn't treat me like one of her kids. Maybe it's because I'm black. Sometimes I worry the others are prejudiced. I miss the other kids."

"I'll look forward to seeing your drawings."

"Here's some more about Katherine," says Karen, handing me four handwritten pages. "It's amazing how much Katherine did; I keep finding things." She hands me a business card, but it's really a calling card. It has Karen's middle name spelled out. That's a Katherine touch. It has her address and phone number—something to give friends or new acquaintances so they can contact her.

"I found the clothes she bought for my son's graduation; I don't remember doing any of these things."

"What else has happened?"

"People say I'm turning into a bitch."

"Congratulations!" I respond. Karen manages a half smile but shakes her head.

"Is it a good thing?" Karen wonders. "My sister-in-law used to order me around on the phone; get her this or that, without even saying hello. I'm not even taking these calls now. I told my brother to leave his attitude behind when he wanted to come over and was acting mean on the phone. My whole family is dysfunctional. I don't know how the other parts could handle it. How did they keep it all straight?"

"Mostly they didn't," I say, "they just tolerated it." I see Karen is worn down from her new assertiveness. "Sandy just let your mother have her way," I continue, "and was sick, in pain, and ate all the time. Some parts wanted to hurt you because of the anger and frustration at being abused. Now that you're coming together, you can use the experience and strengths of the other parts to start making changes in the way you respond to all the dysfunctional people around you. Your family will resist these changes, because they liked it better when you would do whatever they asked, no matter how much it hurt you. As the others integrate, you'll get stronger yet. You've come so far already."

"I am stronger. I even refused to run out and get my husband cigarettes. I'm not taking the blame and feeling guilty as much."

"It's interesting, even though Katherine was the last one to integrate, I'm seeing a lot of Miles in you."

"With Katherine integrating, I've felt the other parts stronger. I don't know why."

24

JULIANN AND KAREN 3

"*I was out all day Sunday, but don't tell Karen; she'd just die!*" I can tell Karen 2's manner now. "I went to a sex demonstration—sex toys, vibrators, and videos. It was fun! One of these days I'd like to do these things. A bunch of my friends from high school had a party. We had a male stripper, who was a cop, come. Also, a person from one of these sex stores to show all her stuff to the 'ladies.' We laughed a lot! I stayed for the Bulls game. The policeman would have really bothered Karen, but I can't really see it her way because I was never abused. When I integrate, I'd like to give Karen just some of my memories, but I don't know how to do that. Well, Karen will be much less boring when I'm in her!"

At least now it's when, and not if, I think.

"*I'm ready to integrate next,*" says Juliann in her soft way. "I'm pretty calm, and I think Karen could use that. Karen's too nervous about her schedule to put her feelings into words. I'll be able to help with that. I'm the one who kept the diary."

"*I miss switching,*" says Karen, frowning, her chin in her hand. "Sometimes I wish I could lose time more. I get tired being out all the time."

"Are you losing time at all?" I ask.

"At night mostly; I just accept it. I'll be watching TV at eleven p.m., and the next thing I know it's five a.m. There will be papers out, a movie on. . . . Then I start my day."

"We're scheduled to integrate Juliann today."

"I know; I'm ready." Karen doesn't brighten any. I can't imagine what a personal burden going through all these internal changes is for her, but I don't know what else to do but proceed. I put her under hypnosis, taking care to put her deeply under, and it's Jensen who comes out first.

"I've been drawing. All the drawings we've done have been mine." I think back to the drawing of the house. "Will Karen be able to draw when I'm integrated?"

"I guess so, but it might be changed, because it won't be just you drawing. The drawings won't just rely on your skills, but will integrate ideas from *all* the parts."

"There are some drawings I want to do before then."

"I understand. You should go ahead with them. Is Juliann there?" Jensen steps back and Juliann comes forward.

"Juliann, what shall I tell Karen about you and your purpose?"

"Well, I was born in 1970, and I was thirteen years old. Karen was eleven; she needed somebody a little older. I grew to age fifteen, which is how old I am now. I haven't aged much. Karen started writing about her abuse when she was eleven; I was born to be the journalist of the group. I wrote so much about what the father did. Grandmother had an old chest, and I'd put my tablets of paper I'd written on in there to hide them. Several years ago, the mother found them and threw them all away."

"I see. That's quite a loss. Do you have any concern about integrating?"

"The only thing that bothers me is I haven't really accomplished what I wanted to. I wanted to write it down so I could prove it all really happened."

"Perhaps after you've integrated and your memories become available to Karen, you can reconstruct some of it. Why don't you step back now and wait outside Karen's special room. We'll come get you in a moment."

"Okay."

Karen describes Juliann as having long brown hair, with a little red in it, and green, very green eyes. She's young and has a teenager's energy. I tell Karen about Juliann and her wish to write about her story.

"Juliann is sitting on my right, and is a little teary eyed," says Karen. "She's holding my hand. She's hesitant. I feel her presence— very strong. She's telling me she has everything in her memory about what has happened to them." Karen pauses. "She doesn't know what to do."

"Maybe you can help her."

"I'm putting my arms around her. She's kissing me on the cheek . . . hugging me. She's saying good-bye to you, thanking you; she says you'll know she's still around; she's not going far."

"I feel her whole body, her heart," she continues. "I hear you writing on your pad of paper; the sounds are really loud. It's bright inside. She's all the way in; she's no longer in the room. I feel her inside."

I bring Karen back to the office. She's shaken and everything looks blurred to her. She seems surprised by how much integrating Juliann is affecting her.

"Maybe you should write about it," I suggest.

July 11, 1997

The Merging of Juliann

On June 17, 1997 Juliann merged within. This integration seems the most complex. Juliann had such impact it has taken me almost a month to begin writing. After Juliann merged within I began feeling truly whole; I finally accepted the others already integrated.

The first day after integrating Juliann, I started recalling pages and pages of journal entries. I'd write them down as fast as I could remember them. But there was no way I can write years of journals all over again, so I wrote only a few. In writing these pages, reality hit me. I know that mine is no fabricated life. Although Juliann is 15 years old, and her main purpose in my system was to keep an internal journal, she managed to organize all the memories until I was ready to fill in all the blanks of the others' experiences. It's an amazing feeling of relief to put the puzzle pieces of my life together.

The last few weeks I've been mourning the loss of my childhood. As all the past memories get put together, I'm forgetting the alters individuality—at least those who have already integrated. I feel terrible about this because I feel since they helped me so much, they should each be remembered. Somehow, once Juliann integrated and I started remembering her journal writings, the other alters' purposes began to fade. I became so sad; I started wishing I never integrated them. I do remember all they went through; I just can't remember which alter did what. How can I forget about 38 years of the inside help?

This feeling of loss is overwhelming. I am struggling to find out who I am. Once I'm fully integrated, I might be able to start to become me. In the meantime, I'm trying hard not to change on the outside, although I am not the same on the inside. I thought once I was fully integrated, I'd snap into some type of person all at once. Why don't I allow the change after each integration to become "me"? Who am I, really?

Juliann's integration left me with hundreds of questions. I feel a need to prove everything so I can accept what happened to me. But realistically, there probably is no proof, because it all happened so long ago. I know Juliann would not write a lie, but I really need to let go of the urge to find the people and places.

Karen hands me a few handwritten pages of her reconstructed daily journal from Juliann's memories. She says she had tablets and tablets of these diaries that were destroyed. I look at the first one.

Midnight: Asleep at grandparent's house.

1:05 a.m.: The security company calls, there's a problem. Karen doesn't sleep tonight; grandfather awakens her. He asks, "Do you want to take a ride?" Karen has no choice and goes. Protectors summoned (Elise, Miles, and Karl).

1:40 a.m.: Arrive at the chemical factory. Ride down elevator, stop for ice cream bar. Abusers await.

1:55 a.m.: Rituals begin. Claire out.

2:16 a.m.: Claire in, Miles out.

3:20 a.m.: Miles in, Karl out.

3:50 a.m.: Karl in. Karl erases memory.

3:55 a.m.: Elise out and cleans up in the dark room. Prepare for ride home.

4:15 a.m.: Elise in, Karen out.

4:20 a.m.: Karen home.

4:35 a.m.: Karen sleeps.

6:45 a.m.: Karen wakes, Elise out, eats breakfast.

7:15 a.m.: Elise in, Sidney out, watches morning cartoons.

9:00 a.m.: Sidney in, Karen out.

1:00 p.m.: Karen gets severe headache, Katherine summons for help. Claire volunteers and is accepted.

2:20 p.m.: Claire in, Karen's mother leaves for work.

2:30 p.m.: Katherine out and cleans house, watches Karen's two brothers, and starts dinner.

4:30 p.m.: Father home. Katherine serves dinner and cleans up.

6:00 p.m.: Katherine in, Holdon out to read newspaper, watch news, and update system.

6:55 p.m.: Updates by Holdon finished. Holdon in, Sandy out.

7:00 p.m.: Sandy watches TV with father; puts up with constant channel switching.

8:00 p.m.: Father asleep on front room floor. Sandy in, Karen out to visit with neighbors, Henry and Edith, sitting on front porch.

8:50 p.m.: Karen in, Karen 1 out to take bath and Miles is briefly out to put broom stick in position so father can't open bathroom door.

9:30 p.m.: Karen 1 in, Karen sleeps.

There are other, similar entries for several other days. Each involves between six and ten alternate personalities.

"Karen doesn't really have any parts left in her to help her," says Holdon. "She wants to keep one alter in reserve, just in case . . ."

"Just in case she wants to run and hide again," I say, to finish his sentence.

"Yes," continues Holdon. "Karen 3 just has a 'poor me' attitude. She acts like a victim and is the most depressed of all of them. Karen 2 is popping out more and more; she'll add some joy to the group. Just to keep you up to date, there is Jensen, Karen 2 and 3 and, of course, myself yet to integrate."

"Have you thought more about integrating?" I ask Karen 2.

"Yes, I've been thinking about it a lot. I'm not sure I want to join that depressing group. I don't want to take on their pain . . . and lose my pleasure."

"I think you could share your pleasure with the others; you were spared for a purpose. Can you tell me more what your role has been, when you were born?"

"I was born in 1969. We were in high school, meeting boys and dating. That's what I did; it's quite normal for me. I usually dated older men. When I went back in, Karen 3 would come out and that would usually be the end of the relationship. She was frigid, and I was, well, more experienced."

"Karen's husband has been really mean," says young Karen 3, under hypnosis. "Yesterday, Karen 2 told him off, and then she went back in. When I came out, he had his fist in my face."

"That must have been frightening."

"Frightening, yes, unusual, no." I can feel Karen 3 pulling my mood down. It's almost as if there's a death ray emanating from her that kills good spirits. This is what I felt from her when she first came to see me. This is the split-off, childhood part of Karen 3 that still needs to be integrated into the whole. "I don't have anyone to talk to," she says, "I used to talk to Katherine and Ann, but they're gone. I'm angry at Karen 2. She yells at me and tells me not to come out and 'spoil everything.' When Josh gets mad at her, she goes back inside and I have to take it. I feel like I'm stuck in a mirror, and my reflection is sad and ugly."

"You sound very unhappy. The only solution I can think of is for you to share this burden with the others and integrate."

"I don't want to make everyone miserable; it's been my burden to take on the depression."

"I understand, but I don't think there's anything else to do. The depression really belongs to everybody."

"Well, okay, if you think so."

"I think it's best. We'll integrate you next."

"Okay, but sometimes I wish I had the alters back," says Karen, despondent. "They were always there for me. I feel like I've lost them; I forget they're inside me. I'd like to know everything about every part; I know it's in me, but there aren't enough hours in the day to remember everything. I know I took care of my brothers for years, but I don't remember actually doing it. I never cooked, washed a dish, cleaned my clothes, dusted—Katherine did this. Now I'm doing it. It's not so bad; why didn't I do it before? I feel a loss, a void. I can't really remember the alters individually anymore, not since Juliann integrated. There are funny moments, though. I'll be eating something and my daughter will say, 'Mom, you hate asparagus!' And I'll say something like 'I forgot' or 'It doesn't taste so bad today,' because I don't dislike it anymore."

"It's scary, Karen is thinking on her own," says Holdon. *"She's* understanding the purpose of everyone. The parts that have integrated are blended. We can't distinguish which part now is responsible for doing what. I'm sorry Karen has to listen to all the insults from her husband. I even had thoughts of killing him, and that's not like me. Karen can't understand how she could have been married to him all these years." I thank Holdon and ask him to step back.

"If you're going to integrate Karen 3, you're headed for disaster," says Karen 2. "Karen will get depressed! What if she wants to kill herself? I may have to come out and have some fun." She gives me a wink.

"Karen 3 is integrating into a much larger whole," I say. "It may be tough for a while, but I think it will turn out okay."

"When I integrate, I hope I dominate Karen for a long time."

I'm still struck that Karen 3 is somehow distinct from the "Karen" the other parts are integrating into. Maybe I shouldn't think of it so concretely. Karen 3, her childhood part, had a role in the system, to take on the depression, and perhaps that needs to get released into the whole. I try to picture what goes on inside Karen's head. It is as if we're pouring personalities into a bucket. But really, segments of information or mental structure that have been disassociated from the rest of Karen's awareness are being allowed to become un-disassociated, or re-associated. Certainly, there could be in Karen 3 walled-off feelings of depression that need to become unrepressed and available to the rest of her.

"Now when I lose time," says Karen, *"it feels abnormal. I* never used to mind. I lost time all of yesterday and half of the day before. I have so much to do; now when I lose time, I get behind."

"Are you ready to integrate the young Karen 3?" I ask.

"I guess so. She's the depressed part, isn't she?" Karen doesn't ask this as a question. She already knows the answer and shares her dread with me.

"You may be depressed for a bit," I say, "but I suspect like the other integrations, this feeling will fade and will become a smaller, more integral part of you."

"Too bad we can't just let this part stay inside."

"If Karen 3 stayed inside, I'd worry about this depression with which you'd be out of touch. It could manifest unexpectedly, and you might act on it. If it's integrated into you, we will be able to treat it if we need to." Karen seems satisfied with this. "Why don't you settle yourself into a comfortable position," I say, to start the hypnosis session and the merger of Karen 3.

"I worry about bringing the depression to the others," says Karen 3.

"You've kept it all these years?" I ask.

"Yes," she says, "I've taken all the emotional pain and low self-esteem. I take the pain of the husband's insults. Karen only hears the words. I take the feelings."

"How were you born?" I ask.

"Soon after Karen was born, Katherine and Holdon and Karen Boo formed. Then Karen 1 came to act like a girl. Karen 2 was born to be unaffected. I was born when Karen was two or three years old. I went inside for a long time, but I came back out after Sara was born. All three of us Karens were originally born about the same time, but we had different functions. That's why we all have the same name.

"When Karen was sad, I would take the sadness. When Father called her a slut, cunt, or whore, I'd take the feelings of the words from Karen. When Father would humiliate her, like when Karen was thirteen and her father took her to buy a negligee, telling the saleswoman she was his sister, I took the feelings." Karen sounds weary and forlorn as she recounts her role. "Karen couldn't really cry; I did her crying for her. Sometimes when Karen came to see you and would start crying, it's because I came out. I hope I didn't confuse you." I was confused all the time, I think.

"Are you ready?" I ask.

"Yes."

"Then wait outside the door to Karen's special room, and we'll come for you in a moment."

Karen and I go through our familiar steps. I explain Karen 3's role and how she was born. She lets Karen 3 into the room. Karen describes her as teary and trembling; she's a younger image of her-self and she can hear her thoughts. They reassure each other.

Karen 3 doesn't move, so Karen goes to her.

"She's standing next to me now and is moving into me quickly." There's a pause; I can see Karen struggling with the work of it.

"I can feel her. Everything is bright and loud . . . she's all the way in. I don't see her anymore."

"I'll leave your room now," I say. "You'll be getting a lot of feel-ings from her, but you'll be able to manage them."

I bring Karen out of her trance and back to my office. She shields her eyes from the light.

"What do you remember?" I ask.

"The picture I see is of a young black man. I'm in the car and I hear Father say, 'The only good nigger is a dead nigger.' "

July 21, 1997

The Merging of Karen 3

On Thursday, July 17, Karen 3 merged within. Before integrat-ing Karen 3, I had some doubts. I knew little about this part of me. I knew she was depressed and sad most of the time, so I worried if this would hurt me. The first memory I recalled from Karen 3 was my father driving by Lincoln school. He drove into the school yard through the opening in the iron fence and towards some black teenagers who were playing basketball and tried to run them over. I was in the back seat of the car as he flashed a police badge that he stole from Bert and threatened the teenagers to leave the neighborhood and never return. He laughed as they ran. He then turned to me and said, "The only good nigger is a dead nigger." This statement hurt me because he always called me nigger, nigger lips or nigger nose.

As I drove home I started learning who Karen 3 was. I learned she was 30 years old, born shortly after my birth (at about two years old). She was the one who started therapy with you. She always felt suicidal and suffered severe headaches. She slept quite a bit while she was out.

Karen 3, I feel, played an important role in our system and as I recall all she's done, I feel extremely lucky to have had her on my side. During the past few days I learned she suffered most of my husband's verbal abuse. I knew he called me names and degraded me, I just never knew how much until now, or how it felt.

I'm not sure what I can do about my husband. There are times when I understand his anger towards me. How can he possibly put up with all my changes since the integrations started, when he has no idea why I'm changing? I can't stay as I was for him because I can't remember which alter he liked. I honestly don't know this stranger I've lived with for the past 17 years. I see his hatred towards me every time I look at him. Now that Karen 3 is integrated, I feel anger back at him. I hate him for treating us with such cruelty. I find myself wishing he'd leave, or even sadder, wishing him dead.

Karen 3 felt there was no reason to go on and wanted to die. I feel this integration closing and I'm relieved. I don't feel ready for another integration soon. I'll spend the next month adjusting to my changes. It's been a whole new experience seeing the world through the others' eyes and I want to take some time to appreciate all they've done. I don't want to forget them.

25

KAREN 2 AND JENSEN

"What is it?" I ask.

Karen shakes her head, as if to brush aside the question. "I just feel the despair of all these years of criticism." There's not much I can do about this, I think. It will just have to all percolate down and become a part of Karen over time. It must be terrible to get such a concentrated dose of humiliation all at once.

Under hypnosis, Jensen says he's afraid to bring the pictures he's working on; he doesn't know why. I question him and he admits that he knows when he brings them, it will be time for him to integrate. I try to reassure him that we'll separate the looking at the pictures from his readiness to integrate, but we both know that's a little bit of a lie. I think he feels better just knowing I understand his apprehension.

"Karen 2 says I have to integrate next whether I like it or not!" says Jensen. He has a gentleness and thoughtfulness the other little boys in Karen lacked. "She's trying to boss me. I came out to draw, but she pushed me back in so she could watch TV." I say I will try to talk to Karen 2 and make sure he gets his share of time.

"I heard that little weasel!" Ah, Karen 2, I think.

"It sounds like you're giving him a little bit of a hard time," I say, cajoling and trying to hide my annoyance.

"He's so slow!" she says, oblivious to me and my tone of voice. "He goes over and over those stupid pictures."

"Perhaps you can give him some time this week so he can finish the pictures. He can't integrate until he does."

"Hmmm . . . well, okay. I haven't really been out all that much myself. I've been letting Karen 3 integrate without interfering. But it's been hard to hold my tongue. I hate Karen's mother. I want to tell her to just shut up. Holdon is trying to get me to tone down."

"Isn't she your mother, too?" I ask.

"I've never considered Karen's parents to be my mother and father. I've built a vision of a mother and father that I keep inside by picking the traits of different people to make a perfect mom and dad."

"Where did you pick them up from?"

"From bits of TV programs, movies, whatever. My parents aren't dysfunctional or abusive, but they're not real, either. The other parts mostly used Katherine and Holdon for their parents. Sandy used to pretend she was adopted, and that her real, loving parents were out there somewhere."

"How do you spend your time when you're out?" I ask.

"I like to enjoy people; I like to spend time with Sara and try to build up her self-confidence. I don't want to lose the ability to do things. I wish everybody would have integrated into me."

"What difference would it make?" I ask. "You into them, them into you: You're all swimming around in the same bucket. No advantage either way, it would seem."

Karen 2 ponders that for a bit. I caught her by surprise. I think she assumes whoever is the recipient of the alters would maintain a measure of control and autonomy. It's not turning out that way; Karen is changing each time in ways she can't control.

"I'm afraid if I integrate, I'll be a tiny part of the whole."

"Not so tiny!" I say and laugh.

"No, maybe not." She smiles. "I'm pretty strong. Holdon can't force me back in if I don't want." This may be an opportunity for me to get more of a feeling of what switching is like.

"What's it like for you to go back when you've been out?"

"When a part is out and starts to come back," Karen 2 says, as if she's explaining to a child, "noises sound muffled and your vision

gets blurred; then you get sucked back. If I'm not active and con-
centrating on something, that's when Holdon will pull me back.
Once I'm back, I'm not strong enough to bump Holdon out.
Katherine could get me to come back sometimes, too, but she'd
trick me, and say someone inside needed me."

"You have so much self-assurance," I flatter. "Karen would really
benefit from what you have to bring her."

"Maybe we could leave things at two alters, Karen and me!" She
is bright and enthusiastic, as if she'd just thought of how she can
afford a new dress. "You could go ahead and integrate Jensen and
Holdon. I like being separate; I feel like a whole person. I have my
own mind. Nothing bad happened to me. If I integrate, I'll have
been abused, too. I like who I am!"

"When do you think you'll be ready?" I ask. I recognize her
pleadings, but we both know they can't stand.

"I know it's the best thing for Karen for me to integrate." Her
enthusiasm is gone. "But what about the people I know, my
friends? I used to sneak out at night after Karen was asleep to see
them." I just look at her.

"I know my time is coming," she says, dejected.

"When would you like to do it?" I press.

"The year 2000?" she says, brighter. "Do I have to put a date
on it?"

"We can discuss that next time," I say. "Now please step back
so I can bring Karen back to the office."

"Do I have to? I wanted to stay out so I could run some
errands."

The following week, on September 9, 1997, under hypnosis,
Karen 2 comes out first and talks animatedly about getting the pictures back from her Tupperware party and posting them all around
the house. She describes shoes she's purchased for Sara and the
details of outings with some of her friends. She goes from one
inconsequential topic to another until I interrupt her.

"Have you been thinking about integrating?" I ask.

Karen 2 stops abruptly and her animation melts into a sober
concern. "Yes, I have. I'm not one hundred percent keen on the
idea," she says with a glare, "but I know it would help Karen. I've

been reading a little bit about child abuse, to familiarize myself with it."

"I think it would be wonderful for Karen to be able to imagine the world as a fine and safe place to live," I say, to bolster what she can do for Karen.

"I thought I was going to be a problem for you," she says, "that you were afraid I was going to take over and control everything. Now I'm afraid I will disappear altogether."

"When would you like to do it?"

"Next week is okay." She pauses and looks out the window, pensively. "I've enjoyed all the time out, but maybe I can still enjoy it in a different way. I've been watching Karen; I see aspects of all the old parts going about their day. At least her relationship with Josh will improve. But I don't want to integrate into her body. Ugh!"

"Maybe you can provide her with some motivation to take better care of herself."

"I hope so."

"So we'll plan on next week."

"Okay."

When Karen comes in the next week, she reaches into her purse and gives me an envelope addressed to "Doc Baer." It is Karen 2's list of pros and cons about integrating. This is the top portion.

The list takes up a whole page and she has twenty pros and fourteen cons in all. Interestingly, her pros all center around what Karen will gain by her integration, that is, what Karen 2 can contribute to the whole, while the cons all focus on what she herself will personally lose. The note is signed: *by Karen II, a unique woman.*

"Karen 2 has been out in full force for the last couple days," says Holdon, "running around, doing all kinds of things—mostly attending social gatherings and making arrangements for some upcoming events at school. She's been giving Karen some of her feelings. Yesterday Karen went to a parents' meeting at the high school and she felt a new confidence when talking to the teachers."

"She did much better feeling my feelings yesterday," says Karen 2 with a hint of smugness. "I think it will be good for her to have me on board."

"How would you like me to introduce you?" I ask. I'm still a little nervous that the "cons" will reassert themselves and she'll change her mind. I don't want to be pushy, but neither do I want to encourage indecision. I want her to feel gently swept along by the mechanics of the integration procedure.

"I was born to be the normal part; nothing bad ever happened to me. Frankly, I don't really understand it. I stayed dormant most of the time. I'd come out if we met someone important and we had to be a normal, healthy child. In high school, I wanted my own identity and to do things I liked. I joined clubs—debate, drama, band. In my senior year, I didn't need any credits to graduate, so I spent my time in art and theater."

"Anyway, since then I've come out to have fun with the children; we go to games, school functions, and social things." Karen 2 falls silent and I think she's done.

"If you step back and wait just outside Karen's small room, I'll join her and we'll invite you in." I see Karen's face relax and the spark leave her eyes. I call on Karen to come back to the foreground and I ask to join her. Karen opens the door and invites Karen 2 into the room.

"I feel nervous," says Karen. "I'm a little threatened by her. She looks different somehow. She's thin, with short blond hair. She has energy and a little bounce." I briefly recount Karen 2's history and purpose, and ask Karen to describe to me what's happening. "She's sitting next to me, smiling, and patting my hand. She says, 'Are you ready for me?' How will she react to our having been hurt?"

"That will be the work of this integration," I say.

"She's stroking my hair and telling me everything will be okay. She says no hurtful or embarrassing memories will come. She wants to know what we should do now."

"Get closer, look at each other, and embrace," I say, as if I know what to do.

"I feel strange," she says, with a small twist of her body. "She's one part I was never really aware of. She says to tell you 'thanks for everything, and she'll see you on the other side.' She's asking if I'm ready. She'll hug me and just blend in. She says 'bye.' She's hugging me; her head is close to mine . . . I'm feeling it already. I can hear all the sounds inside myself, my heart, my breathing. I feel sick."

"Take some deep breaths; let her go inside," I urge. Karen writhes and grimaces. It's as if there's more resistance with Karen 2.

"She's all the way in. I don't see her anymore."

"You did a good job." I bring her out of her trance and back to my office.

"I'm all shaky; the lights are so bright, the noises . . ." Karen is cringing. I turn off the desk lamp next to my chair, and let her collect herself. After a few minutes she sits up.

"My headache is gone," she says as if it's just disappeared. "I feel better." She stares ahead for a moment, focused inward.

"What is it?" I ask. She shakes her head to fend off the question. I ask again.

"Nothing really," she says. "I just had the memory of going to Dominick's and picking up lunch trays."

"I'm very curious about how you'll change with this integration. It's different from the others." Karen smiles weakly at me, but she gets up from the chair smartly and leaves with a little bounce in her step.

The Merging of Karen 2
On Wednesday, September 17, 1997, Karen 2 merged within. I was apprehensive approaching this integration because I always seemed to be threatened by this alter. I knew very little about her, but at the same time she played a major part in my life. As we

started integrating I remember she was hugging me. Then I felt like I was in a tunnel and my ears popped. Once again I was sensitive to light and sound. As I came back to your office, the first memory I had was picking up trays of appetizers from Dominick's. What a strange first memory.

These are some of the memories I've gained:

- *I remember high school and all the activities I joined. I see the faces of all the friends I had.*
- *I have memories of dating different men before I was married.*
- *I have memories of loving my husband.*
- *I remember getting married.*
- *I remember being a secretary and receiving promotions before Sara was born. I did a great job and people really liked me.*
- *I remember being pregnant and giving birth to my children. I love my children and I remember buying baby items and decorating their rooms.*
- *I really like being around people.*

As the day continued, I remembered things about Karen 2 I did not like. For example, I learned she made a mess of my finances by spending money on herself instead of what was best for the family. She would rather spend $30 going to a movie than pay an electric bill. She was very clever at covering herself. Now I need to go back and request copies of all my bills to figure out how much of a mess she made. This totally depresses me since I thought all the money manipulators were already integrated and Katherine had straightened everything out. I feel like such a fool. I guess Karen 2 was not so perfect after all.

I did something totally unpredictable today. I called my daughter's school and told them I needed to pick her up for an appointment. When I picked her up, she was totally confused and kept asking questions. When I got her outside and told her we were going to see the movie Excess Baggage *she jumped for joy, and said she loved me. Sara couldn't believe I would actually take her out of school early to see a movie. But did we have fun! After-*

wards, I had mixed feelings about this as I thought about it. I realized I finally have my daughter, a daughter that I never felt was fully my own, and she loves me and I can feel it.

Throughout the weeks leading up to the integration of Karen 2, from midsummer to early fall 1997, the previous integrations continued to consolidate. The memories and emotions that belonged to the integrated alters are becoming more an automatic part of Karen's everyday functioning. Now when she goes to the store, she will be out for the entire time, making her own decisions about what to buy, and there will be no surprises in the shopping bag when she gets home. She also makes her own decisions about which appointments to keep, clothes to wear, and friends to see. At first she regarded these new capabilities as foreign. She thought she shouldn't "act like that" and felt fraudulent doing so. But gradually, these new parts of her have *become* her, and she's subtly transforming into a true, integrated amalgam of all her separate parts. To me, she's becoming a whole person, not just a depressed shell—a person with a richness to her that is complex and interesting. I expect this synthesis of her selves will be an ongoing process over the next several months, or even years.

Jensen continues to procrastinate bringing in his pictures. In addition to wanting to delay his own integration, Holdon says he may also be reluctant to reveal the emotions that the pictures show. Karl told Jensen their thoughts and feelings are evil, and Jensen may be afraid of that. When I talk to Jensen, he confirms this. He knows I went to school and that I can "read into things." He says the pictures are "not normal"; he'll "be judged"; and they'll "be locked up or something." When they were in the psychiatric ward, he drew pictures, but he only drew grass and trees and wouldn't let them see what was going on inside.

"Is there more to it?" I ask him.

"What do you mean?" asks Jensen.

"You feel because you draw the evil . . . that makes you bad? Do you feel like a criminal locked up inside Karen?"

Jensen looks down and nods. He starts to cry.

I encourage Jensen to draw the good parts, too. I suggest he's just like all of us, and has both good and bad parts. He seems relieved. I ask him to tell me a little more about himself.

"I'm eleven, I'm black, and I draw," he says. He acts like a teenager. He has a child's innocence about him, but he acts more capable. "I was born around the time President Kennedy was shot," he continues. "Karen always wanted to draw things; she did tracings and sketches, but Karen was not really there. She was empty. Other parts always did things for her. I was born to have this talent."

I nod to Jensen to encourage him to continue.

"In school, sometimes, I'd doodle weird things—devils with angel's wings, candles burning blood, stuff like that. It wasn't so good in Catholic school. Father would burn my drawings if they weren't normal. I'm afraid of fire. One day at school I drew a picture of Jesus crying with a dead child hanging from each arm."

"Maybe if you had someone to understand that picture, you could have gotten some help."

"What do you think it meant?" asks Jensen.

"The children are a part of Karen. Jesus is mourning his hurt children."

"That's what I wanted to draw." Jensen's eyes moisten and he looks from side to side and wrings his hands. "The nun poured holy water on the picture and cracked my hands with a yardstick. They hurt for a week. I don't want to be hurt!"

"Do you worry I might hurt you if I judge your pictures harshly?" I ask. I'm trying to get at the underlying fears that prevent him from bringing in his pictures.

"I don't know," he says. "I feel pressured. I'm afraid I'll do something wrong. When the father burned the pictures, it felt like I was being burned."

"It's like the pictures were a part of you," I say, empathizing with his feeling. Jensen nods again, more relieved yet.

"Do you get to be out much?"

"No, not much. I haven't been out much this past year since Karen has been integrating. The last time was when we went to the natural history museum. That was cool! I wasn't out all the time; Miles came out when we saw the scary animals and Sidney came out for the dinosaurs. I saw all the paintings, the mummies, the crafts, and the relics. I'm the only one that notices all the details: the carving on the tables, the shape of the pottery. Karen was there for hours and only remembered a little bit of it—that depressed her. If you were with us for twenty-four hours, you'd get exhausted. We just keep going, switching from one to another all day. But I never got to come out much; I always wished I was Miles or Sidney; they got to come out a lot. I used to sit in a room with no windows, just a desk with a lamp so I could draw."

Jensen looks about the room. I notice he has an odd, continuous fidgetiness about him. He never settles in. Talking to me must be very different territory for him. Perhaps being outside Karen's mind is unusual for him.

"I'm looking forward to any pictures you might bring in," I say. "The self-portrait you did of all the alters was wonderful. You may be the best one to show the emotions of the others through your drawings. Now that Karen 2 is integrated, you should have more time to work on them." I'm trying to enhance Jensen's confidence so he can show his work to me with less fear of being judged harshly.

"I wanted to bring you one big painting with all my memories on it, but I couldn't do it."

"That would be a lot to talk about," I say. "Maybe we should take it in smaller pieces."

"Yeah." I nod to Jensen to step back.

"Jensen and I now reside in separate corners of the living room," says Holdon. "The rest of the house is closed down. We can see each other now. Jensen used to have no windows. Now his windows are open, and he's seeing more of life. I think that's partly why he's reluctant to integrate. It's really interesting how the house has changed inside. As each part integrates, a room is closed. They say their good-byes beforehand, and then seal off their room."

"I'm afraid you won't like them," says Jensen. "It's not the way I see them in my head." I look through the yellow folder of drawings Jensen has brought. "I don't know why I can't draw as good as before. I could work better when I was alone in my room. Now I'm learning what it's like to be outside."

"Maybe you're integrating a little bit."

"Maybe—it doesn't feel right."

I hold up to Jensen the picture of the circle of blue bricks.

"This is my room," he says. "There are no windows. The others would reach in to get my attention, but I didn't come out much. There are a few rocks and a small desk; that's where I sit and draw. There's not much light. I sleep on a dirt floor. It's like I'm at the bottom of a big well. There's light way up at the top, but down where I am, it's dark, cold, and damp. But I have a candle; you can't see it. It's held by an angel."

My room   Jensen

I hold up the picture of the figures before the eye.

"This is how we see when someone else is out. When we watch it's like we're going through an eye."

"It looks like these got crumpled up," I say.

"I got mad," says Jensen, his face in a scowl. I motion to him to explain. "You said on the phone that I was trying to postpone integrating. I do want to integrate. It's been so lonely; I didn't realize how lonely I was until I started talking to you. And I thought you wouldn't like the pictures because I couldn't do them good enough."

"I'm sorry; I misunderstood." My alliance with Jensen is fragile and I guess I blundered with my interpretation of why he wasn't bringing in the pictures before now. I'll have to be more careful. "I'm glad you decided to bring in the pictures," I say as I smooth them out over the folder. "You won't be lonely after you integrate. Can you tell me about these?"

Jensen sits up a little. He seems proud to be able to talk about his work and is reassured by my interest.

"The head on a head: that's what it's like to have an alter inside." These pictures are all done in gray crayon. Jensen says Karen's world was all gray before he brought color to it.

I hold up the next.

"That's the gray room in the funeral home. Karen is tied down. On the table are some of the things that hurt Karen: a candle, a knife, pins, and a hammer."

"That's a picture of Miles," says Jensen, pointing to the one I show him next. "When he got hurt, I covered up his wounds with Band-Aids or makeup. He wasn't very happy."

"This one's pretty dramatic," I say, holding up the screaming one.

"That's Karl. He's trying to keep the evil outside, but he can't do it."

"There seems to be a lot going on here," I say, holding up the picture with Jesus seated, extending his hand, and with the stars descending from an angel.

Jensen smiles and talks rapidly. "Jesus is reaching to the heavens, calling to the angels. The seventeen of them are floating down, coming into Karen's body. We're there to protect Karen; each star is an alter." This is Jensen's view of Creation. It certainly is a hopeful notion, I think.

Jesus summoned enough angels
to fill Karen's heart and soul to
take over until she became whole
again. Each star is an alter and below
is what each of us gave Karen and took away.
Holden - Common sense
Katherine - Organization
Sandy - Perfect daughter to dysfunction
Miles - Strength and anger
Karl - Pain control
Claire - Feminity
Thea - Medical knowledge
Sidney - Humor
Elise - Travel front
Karen 1 - Normal Child
Karen 2 - Normal Adult - Enjoyment
Karen 3 - Depression
Jensen - Art Appreciation
Ann - Religion - Faith
Juliann - Journalism
Karen Boo - Infancy
Julie - Health problems

I look at this next one for a while before I turn it toward Jensen. There's more detail and skill here. The devil dominates, and Karen is in the background, reaching toward the light but tethered in hell.

"I wanted to put the devil on a rocket that said *To Hell or Bust*, and send him where he belongs. We're not evil; I'm not afraid of the devil anymore. Miles and Karl used to say they were the devil."

"That's what they were told, over and over again," I say to Jensen. "The only way to get along with the abusers was to take up that role. But it was all a lie."

"Yeah . . . it stinks."

During the ensuing weeks I talk to Jensen, encourage him to work on his pictures, and prepare him to integrate. Karen labors with the continued integration of Karen 2 and the rest of the alters. She describes all the little changes in her. She used to be able to concentrate only if she had both the TV and the radio on while she was reading. When there was silence, she could hear the voices of the others. Now she's very sensitive to distractions, and for the first time, she can really hear silence.

She says she used to sleep only two to four hours per night. Now it's at least four, but she still loses time at night. She'll make a note of her car's odometer mileage in the evening before bed, and then look at it again the next morning. Sometimes there will be an additional hundred miles on it. Holdon likes to drive at night.

Holdon worries about what will happen when Karen can no longer disassociate. What if she's stressed? Will she create new alters? Will she "re-create" the old alters again and go back to the way she's always functioned? "Can we begin life again?" he asks. I don't know the answers to these questions. I'm worried she'll split apart again, too, but I tell him I have faith in what we've accomplished so far, just as I have faith in Karen's will to survive and heal.

Karen 2 has brought a different challenge. Karen says she's been anxious with Karen 2's memories and she doesn't like what she's finding out. She's dated before, had relationships, had sex she never remembered. I asked if these experiences were pleasant or unpleasant. They were pleasant experiences, she says, but she doesn't feel as if they were hers. She doesn't like the things she did.

A continual frustration surrounds Karen 2's friends. People she doesn't know will call and she feels obliged to make small talk until she can figure out who they are and how she knows them. I suggest as all the memories come to her, who these people are will come, too. She says she has the reflex to hug certain people in greeting, and has to stop and think whether it's a good idea.

She didn't realize how much she hugged her children. At bedtime, Karen 2 took over and put them to bed. I remind her how she was afraid if she touched her children, she'd end up abusing them. It turns out she's been showing affection to them appropriately all along. This integration has taken so much of her energy, there's little left for anything else. There's so much to write about, she says, but so little time. She hands me the second installment on Karen 2.

October, 1997

The Merging of Karen 2, continued
As I continue on with Karen 2's integration, I find myself amazed at all she did. My days are complicated, yet fulfilling at the same time. I am disturbed by the memories about the different relationships "I've" had with different men in my past. Although these memories are normal and healthy, I feel threatened by them. I cannot imagine my body having any kind of normal sexual feelings. I feel guilty and ashamed of my new thoughts. Although I've longed to feel this way for years, I am having a hard time accepting these memories as mine.

I remember the details of every sexual experience as though it happened yesterday. I've gained feelings I never imagined I could feel. I've gained a new respect for my body. The urges I have to get to know my body are strong, but I am so embarrassed by these thoughts that I cannot write them down. This whole process will take some time. I wonder if I will ever feel like a woman.

This integration is harder than any of the others because I can't

*accept the many wonderful experiences I've had without guilt. I
find myself in tears at times for no reason. But still, I feel excited
as I continue to fill my life with positive feelings. I've been dealt so
many hurts in my past, I feel I want to start looking forward. I
just don't know how to start. I need to let go and enjoy.*

*Karen 2 had a way of appearing she had the perfect life. She
dealt with people in a fun but firm way; she never let anyone mistreat her or my children. She was always happy and had a great
sense of humor. I often wonder if I can live up to her. I realize she
is now within me, but I can't help thinking that compared to her, I
am a disappointment.*

"I used to get depressed because I kept losing time," says Karen,
with a wry half smile. "Now I'm upset because I can't lose time." I
look at Karen and feel sympathy for her. It must be scary.

"And I have these urges to do things; I want to be impulsive.
But I shut them down."

"Karen 2 was never hurt," I observe, "but she was never appropriately punished, either. She never developed any self-discipline."

"No, I guess not," Karen says; she looks confused by this. "I still
feel awkward with Karen 2's friends. Sometimes I feel social and
appropriate, but it comes and goes. This week I got memories of
Karen 2 that made me feel she was wearing a mask all the time,"
she continues. "Everyone liked her; she had the perfect childhood,
what she experienced of it, but I can't fit in with the women who
sit around and talk about their nails. I have the sense of what
clothes Karen 2 would want to wear, but when I put them on, I
don't feel like myself."

"It sounds like Karen 2 *was* the mask," I say.

"Yes, I suppose, but now everyone is asking what's wrong
with *me.*"

"This is complicated," I say. "You feel Karen 2 was perfect, but
I see a lot of immaturity and selfishness in her. I think she was like
your parents in this regard, that they maintained the illusion everything was okay, and were impulsive and disregarded consequences.
I don't think you need to live up to her so much as you have to

take in her good parts, and rein in her impulsiveness, with the greater maturity within the rest of you." Karen is surprised by this, but she thinks about it.

Over the next several weeks, the integration process quiets down, and Karen continues to notice changes in herself. She's able to choose more easily what she wants to do without feeling impulsive urges. She went to church for the first time to hear her daughter sing. Karen 2 always went. She heard the priest and saw him for the first time simply as another human being. She even decided to resume regular gynecological care without fear. She hadn't had a Pap smear for fourteen years because of her panic at the thought of a pelvic exam.

It's been over a year since we started integrating the alters into Karen. The changes I see are subtle but significant. As she talks to me, I'll see a moment of coquettishness from Claire, despair from Julie, laughter from Karen 2, or empathy from Ann. Outside the office, Karen describes episodes of confronting her husband like Miles or of giving in to her mother like Sandy. These are now all her.

On November 12, 1997, Jensen is scheduled to integrate. He brings me his prized possessions: three fake gold coins, a Civil War penny, a marble, a serrated disk with a skull sticker, two small black stone animal figures—an elephant and a bear—and a beige stone with a black spider carved on it. He brings a six-inch plastic bust of Michael Jordan, "because he's black, like me"; Karen's high school yearbook, which shows she participated in Computer Club, Drama, German Club, Student Council, Concert Band, Thespian Society, and several other organizations whose acronyms I don't recognize; her Communion picture; a scrap of needlepoint; and a scrapbook of all her husband's love letters from when they were dating. In looking over the letters, I find they're surprisingly passionate and sincere. They profess primarily his gratitude at having Karen to love or his apologies for their having a fight. Jensen says the pictures he's been promising me for weeks are in the closet at home; he asks me to tell Karen where they are so she can bring them. Jensen is too embarrassed to bring them himself.

"I'm ready to integrate," says Jensen, "but I don't feel so good." He's trembling and chewing his lip; his hands are in constant purposeless movement. I can see he's trying to be brave.

"Don't worry, Jensen, things will go fine. Karen and I have done this a number of times before." I'm not sure he's reassured. Perhaps I can distract him from his anxiety. "Tell me again how you were born; what would you like me to say about you to Karen to introduce you to her?" Jensen thinks and begins to organize his thoughts around my question.

"I was born because Karen liked to look at things, but she wasn't supposed to enjoy anything. The room in the funeral home where we were hurt was gray, and the shandy was gray. I was born to bring color to our lives, to teach Karen to enjoy things that are pretty. I did her artwork, entered contests, and taught kids at a youth program in the summers. I did stagecraft in high school, painting scenery." Jensen stops, censoring himself.

"What is it?" I ask. "Is there something else?"

"Yes . . ." Jensen is hesitant.

"It's all right."

"Well, it started when Karen's mother burned her with a curling iron. She had a burn mark on her neck, and her father said she had a hickey. I don't know what that is, but he beat her for it. So after that whenever she had a bruise, I'd cover it up, with her clothes or with makeup. I thought I was protecting her." Jensen was trembling at this. Clearly he senses there was something wrong in this.

"Since you covered up her wounds, no one who might have helped could see them," I say, to bring it out in the open.

"I know that now." Jensen is near tears. "I was trying to help!"

"Of course you were, Jensen. I really don't think it made any difference. I think her father would have hurt her either way. It was easy for him to find an excuse to beat her."

"You think so?" I nod without ambivalence, and he sighs and relaxes. "I was so worried I caused her to be hurt."

"Your caring and your talents will be a big help to Karen when you integrate."

Jensen thinks a moment and asks, "Will Karen mind that I'm black?"

I'm surprised at this but say, "No, I'm sure she won't." And then I wonder and ask, "Why are you black?"

"Her father was prejudiced; he didn't like the color brown. Like I said, I was born to teach her about color." Of course. Sometimes I'm such a blockhead.

We proceed with the integration routine. When Jensen comes into Karen's safe room, he sticks his tongue out at Karen and grins, just to break the ice. Karen describes him as black, with kinky hair, and about four feet five inches tall. He's smaller than she expected. He talks to Karen and tells her he's sorry for covering up the bruises. He says for her to tell me he'll miss me, but that I'll know he's around. And I shouldn't forget to tell Karen where the drawings are.

He's trembling, she says, and has both hands on her arm. He asks if she's ready. He gets on her lap and he's ready to go. Karen pauses for several seconds and, surprised, says it went a lot quicker than she thought. He's already in; she can feel it. Her face turns red with a deep blush. She says she feels his anxiety and complains about the sound and the light. She feels some sadness.

"He was alone a lot," I say, once Karen is out of her trance. I tell her about the pictures in her closet.

November 16, 1997

The Merging of Jensen

On Wednesday, November 12, 1997, Jensen merged within. This was different from the other integrations and I wondered if he was really integrated. I did not feel much different immediately after he integrated, then all of a sudden, late in the evening, I felt overwhelmed by the thoughts and feelings.

While I was being punished or abused in the gray rooms, he came out and changed the gray into beautiful colors of the

rainbow to keep my mind occupied. Now, two day's after
Jensen's merger, I see colors on the grayest days. I was totally
unaware of the power Jensen had. I did not know exactly what
his purpose was except to draw and bring art into my world.
I now realize Jensen's existence was much more than I ever
imagined.

Jensen was the only black alter I had. He was born black
because my father was very prejudiced against blacks. He was
born into me so that I would develop an appreciation of all different types of people. He gave me perspective so that I would not
become prejudiced like my father. Jensen read about his race and
he named himself with a slave name from the 1700s. With the
knowledge Jensen gave me, I have an understanding of racial history and struggle. I especially seem to be interested in Egyptians,
and the way they created their art.

Jensen was right and left handed. He was able to write with
both hands at the same time. Jensen also brought art into my
children's lives by sitting for hours with them cutting, pasting, and
drawing. He would make up projects on a daily basis. When my
son was less than one year old, Jensen plopped some chocolate
pudding on construction paper and started my son's artistic
career.

Jensen loved to doodle and this got us into trouble many times.
One picture he drew during a religion class scared me for years. I
now see he's re-created this picture for you, and this disturbs me
so much. I can't understand it. Is it some kind of premonition of
what's to come? What does it mean? I cannot understand why he
redrew this scene. I fear the evil in it. I want to tear it up and
throw it away, but something stops me.

I remember vividly the day the original picture was drawn. I
was in the sixth grade and sat in the second row. The nun was
preaching to us that we are all sinners. I could not see myself as a
sinner, so Jensen came out and started drawing this picture of
Jesus on the cross with his hand ripped from the nail, and a girl
(I assume it is me) was feeding upon his dripping blood, while
these evil shadows are lurking behind me, waiting to take my
soul. I guess Jensen was so consumed in his art work that he

didn't see the sister approaching. She snatched the picture from him and was horrified by it. Jensen didn't understand what he'd done. He became so afraid, Miles came out to help. She poured holy water over our head and shook us so hard we thought we'd pass out and be brain dead. We clutched the pencil that drew the picture and the boy behind us, who was trying to get our attention, kicked our hand not knowing the pencil point was in our palm. The tip of the pencil went into my palm causing a small pool of blood to gather in the middle. I asked the sister to be excused to go to the lavatory and when she saw my hand, she started screaming that I was Lucifer's child. My parents were called, and I received even more punishment that night because "I shamed the family so much."

As each day passes, I see so much more beauty than I ever realized existed. Since integrating Jensen, I notice every detail of every item. But the worst part of integrating Jensen is the loneliness I feel. I miss the inner conferences held between the others. Although I never really heard all they talked about, it was a comfort to me to know that they were there. I'm also saddened that I'm not disassociating. It's so strange for me not to lose time, especially at times I really need help. It's so hard on me to have to deal with so much. How does anyone live without at least one?

I don't know what's happened to Holdon, but I really don't know him. I just can't understand that if he's still here, why can't I lose time to him? Is he refusing to help me anymore?

"Are you ready to finish the integration process?" I ask. Jensen has been integrated and Karen is working on assimilating the memories and feelings he brings.

"I'm scared," says Karen. She looks at me, hoping I might bail her out. "I still have one other part to lose time to. It's a safety net. It doesn't seem natural not to lose time." I remain quiet and let her struggle with this.

"I don't remember everything from the parts we integrated earlier. I still see things around the house that I know I didn't do."

"Although the integration process is almost complete," I say, "with respect to all the memories and feelings, there's a process of synthesis that I think will take several months."

"But what if something really bad happens?" she asks, her voice rising. I'm seeing a little of the real panic she has at the prospect of finally being on her own. "Even though I'm mostly integrated," she continues, "I'm still missing pieces. I used to work as a secretary. I did typing and shorthand—I don't remember it. I had a whole family inside; I didn't need anyone else." She crosses her arms and looks grim. "Holdon has been dormant—he makes me deal with everything!" She pouts awhile in her chair. "I didn't really realize until yesterday he's the only one left."

"May I talk with him?" She looks at me, disgusted, but closes her eyes and begins the trance process anyway.

"She's never had to catch up with herself before," says Holdon. "I've been holding this group together for years." I've always thought that had something to do with the choice of his name.

"How are you feeling about integrating?" I ask.

"I need to integrate, I know, but I feel it's my duty to watch over her for a while. I've closed up the inner house."

"What do you mean?"

"All the rooms are boarded up; there's no going back to them anymore. I've never really been a part of that, I'm always outside, protecting. But I haven't closed Karen's safe room."

"Do you need her safe room to integrate?"

"I don't think so. I think we can do it outside of the house. But I do need to close it up, too."

"How come?"

"I'm afraid it could be a place Karen could develop more alters."

After the stress of the Christmas holidays, which Karen handles better than ever, she finally brings in Jensen's last picture. She's procrastinated bringing this in, I think, because of Jensen's fear of being punished for it. The picture is of Christ on the cross, a re-creation of the picture for which the nun punished him many years ago. But to Jensen, who had no sense of the passage of time, the punishment was still fresh.

Karen remembers the more frightening version, in which the

shadows behind her are large and grabbing, pulling her away from Jesus. In this rendition, they're less vivid and farther away. I think that's progress.

Her Christmas present to me this year is a paperweight with a quote from Jonathan Swift, "Vision is the art of seeing things invisible."

26

HOLDON

It's January 7, 1998, and another winter is upon us. I can hear the wind whipping around the windows, and all the buildings have a thick plume of white smoke rising from their roofs, their heating systems trying to keep up with the freezing lakefront temperature. Karen comes to see me and brings four letters from Holdon that she confesses she's been withholding, dated from November 24 through December 4, 1997.

"I realized tonight that I was angry with this alter," she complains. "Maybe I was jealous; I'm not sure. It just seemed after Jensen integrated, I expected a lot of help from Holdon, and when I didn't get any, I blamed him." She worries that Holdon and I had a special, personal, confidential relationship, better than the one she has. Although she admits she doesn't really know much about Holdon, she does know he was the one alter who held everyone else together.

The letters mostly update the integration process. Holdon speaks of the early alters that integrated as being "blended," where Karen can no longer tell what thoughts, feelings, and memories belonged to which alter. They now just belong to her. By the end of December, about half the alters were blended. He tells me this will be a longer-term, ongoing process. In his last letter, in preparation for integrating, he writes, in memo form, a short autobiography.

12-04-97

To: Dr. Baer

From: Holdon

Re: My Story

I, Holdon, was born into this beautiful child, Karen, on February 8, 1961. Karen's age at this time was 20 months. I, along with Katherine, joined Karen Boo in what was the beginning of our much-needed complex system of survival. Karen started crying every time her father came near and desperately needed a father figure to protect her, and in her mind, she created me. I became the protector of all. Although Karen believes I grew and aged as she did, it wasn't quite like that. I was born two years old, and aged rapidly. By the time Karen was five, I was 20. At the time Karen was 12, I was 30, and at the time she started therapy with you she was 29, and I was 34. Since then I've only aged until 36, my present age. I aged according to the needs and changes in our inner world. There was never a schedule as to how or if we needed to age.

I was to be the man in Karen's life. During Karen's early years (before age 5) we (I) learned to read. We read everything we could. Karen's parents would yell at her for always reading. Of course, they didn't know it was me, Holdon. I learned quickly as I aged, despite the unbearable abuse which I could not change. I was the father she dreamed of, only I was inside of her. When she started therapy with you, I was able to direct my attention to her inner world. I made it my purpose to know every detail of each alter so that I could monitor their behavior. Regretfully I could not intervene when they were out. I put together a conference room (the inside chat room) and that was one of my best accomplishments. It was the only time we all came together and worked as a unit. The meetings were held nightly, with an open invitation to any alter wishing to attend. When adult discussion was needed, child alters were asked to leave. During this time, I kept track of how we, as a unit, were doing, and made changes, if possible.

I took pride in this job. I've done my best to keep us alive until this time of integration. There is only the need for me to integrate so we can begin our new life as one. My job is done. I'm ready to integrate.

"We used to integrate the alters when they were ready," I say to Karen. "With Holdon, we'll integrate him when *you* are ready." Karen smiles, then shrugs.

"I'm getting used to not being rescued," she says with her mixed smile, which is part irony, part resignation, and part chagrin.

" 'Rescued' is a good word," I say. "They did rescue you; they helped you survive. But you don't need their rescuing anymore."

"The other day I fell and hurt my shoulder. I couldn't make the pain go away, so I said out loud, 'Can you come out now?' But nobody did."

Karen is constantly, subtly changing. When she looks at me, there's no longer apology in her eyes and defeat in her spine. Her voice has more emotional range, and she pays more attention to her dress and grooming. She's wearing some eye makeup and she's bought some new clothes. She's evolving at a rapid pace. She says her decision-making process is speeding up. She's no longer hesitant over choosing what she wants or knowing what to do. It's all becoming more automatic now. But her husband doesn't like her new assertiveness.

"You're standing up for yourself?"

"I'm more opinionated," she says, "and getting into arguments. I even made some wisecracks. Where does that come from?"

"It may be from the blending Holdon was describing," I suggest. "It sounds like something Miles would do."

"Maybe so. I made a comment to my husband that shut him up."

"What have you been remembering?" I ask. Karen turns to the window, rests her chin in her hand, gets a faraway look in her eyes.

"It's like watching a movie," she says, and I can see her watching it. "All the memories are familiar, but now they're so vivid and detailed. Every conversation, every surrounding . . . these things happened years ago, but the memories seem so fresh. I remember high school. I had seventh-period lunch and I tutored algebra in sixth. Once, one part took off and went bowling, and when I returned, I couldn't remember the math I was teaching. I took a speed-reading test and got the highest score in the class, but that part never participated again and I got a D because I couldn't keep up. This happened all through high school; it all depended on which part liked a class. It must have been confusing for the teachers."

"It must have been confusing for you, too," I say. "The same thing has happened to your social life."

"It still happens. I went to the store and it seemed everybody knew me, but I didn't know a soul. It's so hard to act like I know what's going on and let them talk long enough until I can piece it together. I hope that won't happen anymore when I get all the memories. But I'm getting better. My brother tried to tell me he did something for me, insisting I must not remember. But I do remember, and I said so. He's used to me accepting his version of things." Karen pauses, then continues.

"I recently remembered how much you talked to all the other parts. I've recalled each session you had with them in detail, but I don't dwell on them, and they're not flashing through my mind anymore."

"I had a relationship with each one," I say, "and I guided each one through the integration process."

"I can still recall a few things about each one. Claire liked to brush my daughter's hair . . . but it's confusing to the kids, since the alters don't come out anymore. My kids complain I haven't made a real meal in a long time, which was Katherine's role, and that I haven't taken them anyplace fun, like Karen 2 did. At least I don't have to see a movie ten times for me to have seen the whole thing!" Karen and I laugh at this, but our thoughts are mixed with regret for the lost parts and the turmoil she's gone through.

"I don't want to forget all that I'm remembering," she contin-ues. "I want to write it all down, but I can't, because the memories just keep coming. It's like a faucet I can't turn off."

But Karen does write some of it down. She gives me pages of writing, and she makes two booklets for me, using family snap-shots. One describes her wedding; one describes her bedrooms dur-

ing childhood, where much of her abuse took place. She hadn't
been sure she wanted to write about the bedrooms. She says she
didn't really want to deal with the impact of the memories, but
they rush through her head. Each room holds a lifetime of pain.

"Are you getting ready?" I ask Holdon. *I'm nervous about*
getting the last alter done. I'm afraid it could all come undone if
the last one doesn't go smoothly.

"I'll be ready soon," Holdon says. "Do you have any questions
for me before I integrate? I know a lot of things the others didn't."

"Really? I'll try to think of some." Boy, this is my last chance, I
think. There must be some gaps I need to fill in. "Who came to see
me first?" I ask.

"Sandy came to see you first. It was Katherine's idea. Sandy wore
pink. She felt the pain from the operation following the C-section.
Then Sandy started missing appointments. Katherine would drive
her, but Sandy wouldn't show up. Then alters came out who
wouldn't talk. You talked to one of them and then you put another
in the hospital. That's why they were angry at you. You remember it
was Miles that called from the nurses' station. Then the medicines
came. During the hospitalization, Ann and Juliann were out most of
the time socializing, and Katherine organized the refrigerator. The
nursing staff never caught on."

I guess I could ask him to explain the mechanics of everything
that happened in the last ten years, but I'd just be satisfying my
own curiosity, and not serving Karen, so I decide I won't burden
Holdon with lots of questions. But I have a couple that I'd really
like answered.

"Why a house?" I ask. Holdon looks at me with a cock of his
head. "Why did you organize your internal world into a house?"

"Oh!" he says, surprised at the obviousness of my question.
"Every alter needed their own space. There needed to be walls
between the alters so they could have their privacy. There were no
kitchen or bathrooms. There were lots of bedrooms connected to
a conference room. The house got more detailed and developed
when we started talking to you. We created a room for you—
Karen's safe room, so we could come and talk to you without leav-

ing the house. Six locks were on the inside door, so the alters could have privacy when they talked to you."

"Okay, why six?" I ask.

"Miles and Sidney insisted on double, triple, quadruple locks. Claire wanted her own lock. We ended up with six."

"The conference room?"

"That came into being in Karen's early twenties, just before she got married. She wasn't functioning normally. It was a way to catch up, just before she fell asleep, just when she lost consciousness. When she awoke the next morning, she'd know what she'd done the previous day. It worked pretty well until Sara's birth."

"What happened?"

"Things fell apart. Karen 2 was supposed to be the one to give birth, but when she was strapped down and felt the pain of the incision, she panicked and went back in. Our whole system became a problem at that time. Each alter reacted differently to the painkillers. The depression came, spread, and progressed."

"That's when you came to me."

"Right, through a roundabout series of referrals."

"I could sit here and ask you question after question," I say, "but I'll indulge one more. How was a new alter formed?"

"Well, that's a little hard to explain, to put into words." Holdon sits back and thinks for a moment. "When a new experience came up that no alter could handle, a new alter was born. Each had their own role and purpose."

"But how were they born?" I ask. I push for a more specific answer. I want to be able to imagine it.

"Well . . . what happens is"—Holdon is trying the best he can to pick his way through this explanation—"we would all get together when Karen had this terrible *need*. The need grew into a *wish*, and the wish was transformed into an alter. I came from Karen's wish for a father. Claire came from Karen's wish to be a perfect little girl, pure as can be, to be liked by everyone. Her father said Communion was the day when God gave Karen to the father to do God's will. That meant to be abused. Sidney came because Karen wanted to be the little boy the father wanted. Sidney needed to steal for the father without guilt, and Karen couldn't do it."

"Each was wished into existence," I say, trying to understand. I'm trying to picture it.

"Because of a *need*," Holdon stresses. "When Karen got depressed, she started to make new alters, but Katherine and I put a stop to it. Karen started to realize not everybody loses time and hears voices. She was afraid if she told anyone, they'd think she was schizophrenic and she'd be locked up."

"I see. I'd like to know more, but we're out of time today."

"Since Karen is getting close to being ready for me to integrate, I'll make a tape for you and tell you some more. When you get the tape, then I'll be ready."

It's the end of February and Karen comes in tearful and weary. She complains that every day is hard. She gets no "vacations" during the day. She's always *there*. She feels pressure to get everything done. She used to be able to just go away. She wishes she could do all the things she did six months ago.

"When you didn't sleep," I add.

"Yes," she says and looks at me sheepishly. She says she's interested in integrating Holdon. She wants his capabilities. . . .

"I'll put the tape in the mail," says Holdon, when Karen is under hypnosis. "Karen was curious and listened to some of it. She didn't like how I sounded. I hear my voice as masculine. Karen assumed it would be, too, but it was really her own voice a little deeper. I think she was disappointed. She expected more." I recall how the alters' voices sounded; they were all different, but since they all came from Karen, they were simply variations of her own.

"Any updates?" I ask.

"Well, she's tolerating pain better now that Karl is blended. She got some of his coping ability, too."

"I look forward to getting the tape."

Karen continues to work on blending the alters that have integrated. She still has a jumble of thoughts about what to do about things; not everything is automatic. Each day is like a month for her, with all the thoughts rushing through her mind.

She loses time only occasionally, but she notices it. She watches the clock to try to keep track of any time she's lost. Holdon is coming out briefly now and then to take care of some bit of business. He's closed up her inner house, including Karen's safe room, and has made a place for her in front of the house, in a hollowed-out tree in the front yard. That's where she goes when she loses time. He says it's very clean and comfortable.

For three sessions now, Karen has forgotten to bring the envelope with Holdon's tapes that he's left for me. It's the end of March 1998 and I feel she's resisting the step that brings her closer to fully integrating. She says she remembers the tapes when she's at home, but forgets them when she leaves to come here. There are no accidents, I think. This is unconscious forgetting because she's afraid to let go of her last alter. She admits she's afraid Holdon might disparage her on the tape or discuss her in a bad light. She segues into talking about her husband's demeaning. She says he threatens to call me and tell me she's no good, etc., and that I'm wasting my time with her.

"He's never called me," I say, "and when I've talked to him on the phone when I've called you, he's always very polite and respectful. I think he's afraid of me. He's a bully and will only confront someone he thinks is weaker."

"I think I've made my husband out to be worse than he is," she says.

"What do you mean?" I'm surprised at this. Has she been exaggerating her abuse by him?

"It's just that"—Karen looks so sad at this—"he's put up with me for years. I'd take off and be gone for hours and he wouldn't know where I was, and when I came home, I couldn't tell him. It would drive anyone crazy. I'd be out and 'come to' and I'd be on a date. I'd have to feign illness so I could go home. My husband never understood. He never checked into things. He never read my writings or looked in my purse. I had all kinds of things in there— things the other parts needed. He just put up with it all and got angry."

"You couldn't talk to each other, ever?"

"We never . . . I never did. I couldn't. Anything I'd say to him, well, he'd always use it against me later to put me down. No one can imagine what it's like to have a husband and children and be pretending all the time. I remember having sex with my husband now, but I still don't know how it felt. I don't have those memories yet. Who can blame him?"

"It's understandable he was confused and angry," I say, remembering the bruises she's shown me, "but to deal with it he had a range of choices. Beating you was not the choice he should have made." Her low self-esteem makes her want to make excuses for her abuser, I think: Who could blame him—I deserve it.

She cries at this. She's feeling very sad about what her illness has cost her family life. There's not much I can say that can diminish this; I only say that I understand how sad this is for her. Before she leaves, I ask her to try to remember Holdon's envelope next time; she nods through her tears.

The next time Karen comes in, she brings a drawing. It shows herself in her new place: the tree in front of her internal house. The sky is blue, the sun is shining, and each branch of the tree has the name of an alter written on it.

She also gives me a letter, which I read there with her.

March 22, 1998

Dear Dr. Baer,

Now that we are near integrating my last alter, I find myself fearing I cannot live without multiplicity. I feel it is important for you to know what I'm thinking before Holdon integrates within. That way you'll know how I might feel afterwards.

What will I be like after integration? What will I be called? "Integrated Recovering Multiple Personality Disorder" or something like that?

My mind has kept me alive for many years and has always worked hard to protect and heal me. I would rather not have had this illness, but since I do, I am determined to survive. Even though I've integrated 16 of the 17 alters, I'm so afraid of everyday experiences without dissociating. Is it okay to feel afraid?

When Holdon merges within, how do we do it? I don't feel comfortable going back to my safe room. Do you know why I feel this way? Is something wrong inside my inner world? Will I start acting like a man? Who will drive us home?

Karen

"It's interesting," I say after skimming the letter. "You still think in terms of 'us' instead of 'me.' When you go home that day after integrating Holdon, you will be a 'me,' not an 'us.' Maybe that's what you're worried about. Just being a 'me.' "

"I'm afraid of the future," she says, "I've never looked ahead. It's all I've ever been able to do to get through each day." I tell her I understand her fear of the unknown, but that I think she's capable of managing it. Under hypnosis, I speak to Holdon.

"I thought Karen might bring your tape today?" I say to Holdon. I'm getting annoyed at the stalling.

"Excuse me," Holdon says as he bends down and opens Karen's purse. He handles it as if he's not used to carrying it and is a little embarrassed to be going through it. He retrieves two micro-cassettes and hands them to me. "I hope they're helpful."

Later at home, I listen to Holdon's tapes, dictated on February 12 and 18, 1998. On the first he didn't speak long, perhaps fifteen minutes, and ended abruptly. He said he wasn't used to talking into a microphone and felt awkward. He gave me his update, saying the integrations were not yet fully blended and that he felt Karen was trying to rush the blending before he integrated. He assured me this wasn't necessary, that the blending would take place over the months to come. But Karen is stressed by the rapidity of the thoughts that are coming to her. I think, weren't they the faucet she couldn't turn off?

As I listen to the tape, I wonder about something, and perhaps I'll never be quite clear on this, but Katherine talked of there being no core "Karen," just a collection of the seventeen parts. At other times, such as on this tape, there's a "Karen" that the other parts attended to and helped. Perhaps the distinction is not important, and perhaps Holdon and the others don't really have a good, objective understanding of how they're organized. But sometimes I wonder exactly who they were referring to when they said "Karen." Perhaps it was the physical Karen in whom they all lived.

At the end of the tape Holdon emphasized that he'd try to let Karen handle situations and would only come out when needed. He said the alters came from Karen's pain. If she'd had a normal child's pain, she could have handled it by herself. But her pain wasn't normal, and so they did the best they could.

The second tape, from the eighteenth, was longer, about fifty minutes, and emphasized the plans he recommends for the period after his integration. He talked of Karen going to a motel after he integrates, and said, interestingly, that he'd wait until he talked to me to "put the idea into her mind." Apparently Holdon can suppress and unsuppress certain ideas at will. He doesn't want Karen to be harassed by her husband when she's trying to cope immediately after his integration. He feels her husband is the main problem now and she'll eventually get divorced.

He wants me to keep a close eye on her because he fears she'll get depressed without alters, and could be at risk for suicide. On the tape he said he was weary from all he has tried to do, but had a sense of peace, because he felt he could now rely on me.

He said I should ask Karen about the memories she'll be getting directly after he integrates, that she'll need the memories triggered by my asking about them—that is how she'll remember. He knows that isn't my usual style, and he reassured me this won't be putting thoughts into her mind. We'll see, I think.

Letting go is hard for him, he said on the tape, but he's ready. In a way, it's like a parent letting go of a child who's growing up. He thinks the work between Karen and me will continue to be draining and exhausting, but that in the end, it will be worth it. He sees their system as God's gift, a coping mechanism beyond anyone's imagination. He feels privileged to have been the head of the group of alters and honored to be chosen to protect them.

He's been thinking about how he'll integrate. He's closed off all the rooms in the house. He'll close up his area outside the house just before he integrates. I can invite him into my office and we can do it there. I wonder how that might work.

Toward the end of the tape, Holdon said he enjoyed our talks. I'm the only adult male figure he's ever met who's worth a damn. He'll always be a part of Karen, but he's not needed anymore. It's been a miserable life. Now it's time to start over.

"I've always had another part to lose time to," Karen says, frowning. "I feel like I'll have a heart attack when the last one integrates. What if I'm changed? What if I don't know who I am?"

"You won't lose anything when Holdon integrates," I reassure. "He'll be added to you, like the others. Perhaps I could talk with Holdon now." Karen stares past me for a moment and sits up slightly straighter in her chair.

"I'm here, Dr. Baer," says Holdon.

"And without hypnosis!" I say.

"Yes, I'm out with her all the time now, but she doesn't like sharing—she fights it, though she doesn't realize she's doing it. So I don't think I can integrate without hypnosis. She prefers her special room, but I've closed it up."

"I see." We both think a minute. "We could do it in the yard, under her tree," I suggest.

Holdon ponders this for a moment. "That should work," he says.

"Fine," I say, "then that's our plan. By the way, is it because you're out that Karen wants to be left-handed?"

"Yes, she's feeling awkward. She'll pick up her fork with her left hand and start eating with it. It's been a drain on her having me out. I didn't realize it would be so hard."

"Do you think it's still necessary for you to be out with her?" I ask.

"No, perhaps not," Holdon says, and sighs. "To be truthful, it's stressful for me, too. I'll stop influencing her until I integrate."

"Okay," I say, "and we'll follow the usual integration procedure with you, except that we'll do it under the tree."

"Okay."

April 15, 1998

Dear Dr. Baer,

I was feeling very disappointed in myself because I assumed by now I would be functioning better than ever. I thought I would know everything, that I would feel great. But I don't.

As I thought about what is upsetting me, it dawns on me that fear is taking over, covering me like a blanket. This fear is the fear of life, and the future of who I am. I don't know exactly what becoming whole is. You see, when Holdon integrates, I assumed I would be whole, and therefore I should be at my best. I should be perfect. But I'm not feeling that way. I think there are two different kinds of becoming whole. Most people go on one journey to fully become the person they can be in a lifetime. I must go on two journeys—one journey to integrate all my selves, and a second, like everyone else, to discover who I am. The second journey can't start until I complete the first. I will then be no different than everyone else trying to make the best of my own life. This I fear. Do I have the strength to begin again? At this moment, I feel used up, weak, and lost.

I believe God is giving me a second chance, a new beginning, and I'm afraid I may mess it up. But I'm not giving up. I've been a victim of someone else long enough, and I will fight before someone ever victimizes me again.

Karen

On April 29, 1998, Karen arrives looking shaky and tired, yet happy. She brings me an "Album of Selves" constructed by Holdon. This album is a kind of scrapbook, filled with pictures of Karen during childhood, and Holdon wrote next to each one which alter was out when the picture was taken.

There is a letter from Holdon, and it describes for Karen all the tasks and errands he did this morning before she drove to my office, and the arrangements he made for her stay in the motel room tonight. His last actions were "registering at the motel, taking his last hot shower, writing this letter, and setting up the food and drinks" in the motel room. He closes the letter writing "I chose a motel room on the second floor right off the elevator and ice machine. Room 218. Easy for her. It's now 3:59 p.m. and I'm going back in so Karen can get ready to drive to your office for the integration. See you soon."

"It would be nice to be married to someone so organized," says Karen.

"He's made a lot of preparations for his integration," I observe. "It's clear he's trying to take care of you to the very last." Karen doesn't pay attention to what I'm saying, but stares out the window.

"This will be the first time I'll ever have been alone," she says, more to herself, and then turns to me. "I'm scared, but happy at the same time. I'm ready."

I begin our usual hypnosis routine, but rather than guiding Karen to her special room, I guide her to the lawn in front of her "house," underneath the large tree, as I'd discussed with Holdon, and invite her to see all her surroundings with vividness and color. Once she's deeply there, I invite Holdon to come out and talk with me.

"How do you feel about integrating?" I ask.

"I'm ready," he says, shaking his head with a sigh, "I'm wearing out."

"Karen has been tired, too." Holdon nods.

"I've tried to come out only when she's in a light sleep," he explains, "not when she's in a deep sleep. If I wait until she's in a deep sleep, then I'm locked in sleep, too."

"How do you do it?" I ask.

"I try not to interrupt her sleep," he continues. I can see he's struggling to put this process into words. "I wait until she's been asleep ten or fifteen minutes, or just after a dream. I try to wait for the right moment. . . . We all know dreaming is important. Then I come out and when I'm done, I just go back and lie down, go back inside, and Karen wakes up thinking she's been asleep the whole time."

"Until she finds out two hundred miles have been put on the car that night," I say. Holdon smiles, shakes his head, and then nods.

"That's when I do my best thinking."

"I want to tell you how helpful you've been throughout this whole integration process," I say. "Without your instructions on the steps to take, I'm not sure how we would have managed."

"Dr. Baer, it's been a pleasure working with you. I couldn't do it alone. I needed your help. My job always was to protect. I was the one who originally decided to tell you about the others."

"You mean Claire's letter?"

"Yes; she was out watching a lot. She was infatuated with you. She asked me when you'd know about us. She wanted to write you a letter, and I said okay, and I mailed it for her. We were always there, watching, during the therapy." Holdon smiles at me with a nod of his head, and I realize how important a guiding force he's been all these years.

"Are you ready?"

"Yes."

I ask Holdon to step back and say I will call him. I confirm that Karen is still under the tree and reinforce the depth of her trance. I tell Karen I will join her on the lawn, and when she sees me, I call on Holdon to join us.

"Can you describe Holdon?" I ask. I'm excited by this moment, but I try to keep my voice level and reassuring. Karen, in her chair, squints and concentrates on the scene inside her.

"He's tall," she says, as if far away. "He has a white shirt and tie and a black suit. His hair is brown. . . ."

"Is he saying anything?" I ask.

"He says he's happy to meet me at last." She pauses and leans forward in her chair. "He wants me to stand."

"Go ahead any way you like," I say. She doesn't stand, but keeps leaning forward in her chair. I guess she's standing inside her mind.

"He seems so tall," Karen says as she describes what she experiences. "He says he's tried to do his best for me all these years. He's always tried to protect me." Karen pauses and cocks her head, listening. "He says he's become great friends with you, and he'll miss that, but for me to be well, it's best that he merge and make me complete." She listens again. "He says not to be afraid and not to worry. I tell him I'm ready for this. He's smiling and nodding. He says when he integrates, I'll remember everything; I'll feel all the others like I should have all along. He says I needed this final integration to be complete."

"Are you ready?" I ask.

"He's asking the same thing," she replies. "He'll step into me, and that's it. He's putting his hand on my shoulder. He says he's used his arm a lot this week; he knows it hurts me. There's an ice pack in the suitcase. He's asking if it's okay to go ahead."

"Go right ahead," I say, trying to keep my voice calm and positive.

"He says he knows he'll see me on the 'other side.' " Karen falls silent, and she moves subtly in her chair.

"Everything's starting to change . . . I can feel it happening." Karen pauses; I watch her face contort with effort as she absorbs Holdon. It takes a long time, or it seems long, as the minutes slip slowly by.

"He's all in," she says at last. She covers her ears, bends forward, and rocks back and forth a little. She starts to cry. Tears are streaming down her cheeks.

"What is it?" I ask. She doesn't answer but continues to cry.

"Are you sorry to see him go?" Karen nods and continues to cry. I just sit with her for several minutes as she absorbs Holdon, along with all she's gone through and all that remains.

"Are you ready to come back?" I ask, as Karen's sobs lessen. She nods. I need to prepare her for the next step. "Holdon's integration won't begin until after you get to the motel," I say. "You'll feel alert driving there, and you'll arrive safely." I bring her out of her trance, and she shields her eyes from the light. She wipes the tears from her face.

"It's strange . . . ," she says.

"Congratulations," I say. "There will be lots of work during the next several weeks." Karen nods and begins to cry again.

"There was a whole family inside of me," she says, "and they're all gone. They've done so much for me all their life; I feel like they've all died. All these years, there's always been someone there." Karen sobs for a minute, and then says, "My hearing is real sensitive, but it feels quiet at the same time."

"It's quiet in your head?"

"Yes . . . it's just normal noises." She looks around the room. She seems to be looking through new eyes.

"You shouldn't have any problem driving," I say. "You know how to get to the motel?" She nods. "Call me tomorrow, and let me know how you're doing." She nods again.

I watch her leave the room, and I feel a deep sense of loss. I think about all the time and turmoil she's caused me. I also think about the separate parts of her that are gone. Claire and Miles, especially, I will miss. Claire was lovely and Miles was brave. Now those qualities are buried in Karen, but I'll never see them in their individual forms again. Treating Karen has been the most important and deeply fascinating experience of my professional life. We'll both be mourning.

Karen calls the next morning from the motel. She says she's been up off and on all through the night. Memories are flooding her, but she says she's all right. She doesn't want to talk; she's too tired. She's trying to write down what she remembers, but it all comes too fast. I ask her to do the best she can and to call me in two days. She agrees.

Two days later I receive her call, and Karen says the memories are slowing down. She says she hasn't lost time since she saw me, but she's exhausted. I wonder if this has really worked. We confirm our next appointment in a couple of days. I tell her she can call me at any time if she needs to.

When she comes back to see me, she walks slowly, head erect, and looks at me with eyes full of weariness and relief. Her face is drawn and she sinks heavily into the chair.

"I feel better today," she says, smiling weakly. "I don't know why I minded having alters. I've been remembering the interesting, funny parts of them—not the problems they created." Karen's eyes become moist. "I feel like I'm stranded on an island. I'm starting all over again. What's the next step? I feel like I've been in a coma for so much of my life."

"Are you mourning their loss?"

"I don't know how to grieve." She pauses and gets a sly smile. "I should dress in black and go to a cemetery and watch people." We laugh. "That was like Miles," she says.

"I miss Miles, too," I say.

"Yeah. Last night I came home from grocery shopping and my husband asked me what took me so long. I said I was having sex in aisle twenty-one. It just popped out." I laugh again with her. Then she looks at me with some sorrow. "You got to know them all in a different way," she says. "When they integrated, I wanted to get to know them better. I never could really see them, except for the brief time while they integrated. Then they were gone."

"It is hard to think of them being you," I say, "but I know they're in there."

"Yes, I know. I'll drink chocolate milk, which is not my favorite, but a part of me likes it. I have these new memories, but I don't yet fully remember everything."

"Synthesizing all these experiences into an integrated whole is our next task."

"I hope so." Karen shakes her head. "I remember so much more about each part since Holdon integrated, especially the male parts. Did you know the male parts could never go to the washroom? They had no penis. So one of the girls had to come out if we wanted to pee. Miles especially wanted to be male. For years he and the other boys bandaged my breasts to flatten them. Some of the parts had allergies. I didn't know! Holdon held all the information." She takes a handful of paper from her bag. "I don't know what I wrote, I just kept writing; I couldn't write fast enough."

I take the pages and tell Karen to call me in a couple of days. As soon as she leaves, I start to read.

April 29, 1998

The Merging of Holdon
(Last Alter)
Dear Dr. Baer,

It's 10:45 p.m. and what a day it's been. With your help, I finally am one. I can't imagine what my future holds and I hope I can keep a positive attitude. I am terribly afraid of taking my next step, whatever it may be. I am so very thankful you'll be there to help me along the way. For now, I'd like to write about how I am doing so far. The memories are starting and I don't want to forget my feelings on merging Holdon.

I didn't wake up this morning: Holdon did. I found myself already checked in at the Hampton Inn. Although I was a bit annoyed at losing time, I knew arranging this day was important to Holdon. Holdon must really have cared about me.

As I drove to your office, I kept trying not to think about how important today is. But in the car, I felt the sudden impact of it and I was scared to death. I wasn't sure I could go through with it. I sat outside your office for a half hour trying to get up the nerve to go in.

I was afraid I couldn't live without multiplicity. I finally decided to go in realizing you wouldn't let anything go wrong. No one forced me into this integration; I wanted it. It's time. Today is the day! Holdon is ready. The final one.

Driving to the hotel after integrating Holdon, I had a new experience. I daydreamed. Never before have I experienced driving somewhere, with the time passing, while I thought about something else. In the past, if I lost my focus, I would simply lose time.

About 8:00 p.m., the memories started. I'd receive about 30 minutes of memories, fall back into a deep sleep for 20 minutes and awaken to receive more memories. This pattern continued throughout the night.

After talking with you by phone, I recalled the actual integration.

For a moment I wanted Holdon to say, "Let's wait for another day." Even though I knew it would be difficult, I accepted Holdon to merge within me. Memories came flooding to me all day long.

I recalled all the names and ages of all the alters and their purposes. I have all Holdon's feelings towards you, therapy, healing, and his hopes and dreams for the future. I recalled many of the conversations Holdon had with you, and his sense of loss of his relationship with you. I am saddened by it. I feel Holdon's calm and patience. I gained his love of driving, especially at night, when everything is quiet and beautiful.

Many new memories are filling in the gaps. I started to recall which alter handled which episode of abuse. I'm amazed how they switched in and out so that each only had to handle a portion of an abusive episode. They really covered for me. I don't know why I feel so sad. I lost them and I can't seem to understand they are all with me now, all throughout the day. Why can't I make this connection? I wish they could all stand up in front of me so I could thank each one personally.

I don't lose time now and I honestly feel much better about myself. I went to the store today, and everyone who greeted me, I knew them. No need to pretend until some other part came out to rescue me.

Do you think I appreciated them enough? I hope they knew I cared. I guess I don't really know how to express my feelings about this. How could I possibly thank those within me? I'm whole now. I can feel it. I'm myself.

By May 13, *Karen is sleeping better and the memories are* coming less spontaneously, but more now through triggering events, such as when her mother called and asked her if she'd remembered it was her father's birthday and would she drive her to the cemetery. Holdon had predicted she'd be recalling memories if she were reminded of something associated with them, and that seems to be the phase she's moving into now. She's also been getting memories in the form of "reports," such as a sudden explanation of the rationale for how the interstate highway signs are numbered. There's no emotion in these memories, just facts Holdon acquired.

Karen is also remembering instructions to the children and

conversations Holdon had with the other parts when he'd hold the conferences in the evenings. Many of the memories have no emotions attached to them, so she's not sure how she's supposed to feel about these events. Have the feelings been erased? I suggest that perhaps that was how Holdon was: full of facts and not very emotional. She never asked how things got done—who cleaned the house, made her kids' lunch, did the shopping. Now she can remember how she did it. But she feels there are many things yet to remember. A lot is still missing.

Near the end of the session after Holdon's integration, Karen falls silent and looks a little embarrassed. I ask what's wrong, and she says she feels awkward, but can't put her finger on it. Then she laughs and says she's got it. She's not used to talking to me herself for a whole session. I think back and realize that for the past several months, she's been talking to me for only the first ten or fifteen minutes of every session. This one must seem very long, indeed.

At the end of May 1998, Karen comes to see me and I can see changes in her. What's different? It's hard to pinpoint. She seems like more of a person. There's a new richness in her body language, more inflections in her tone. The changes are subtle but striking.

"I continue to experience new memories daily," she says. Even her smile is more complex. "I'm amazed by how much I have to relearn. I know that inside I have the answers, waiting to be rediscovered." Karen smiles warmly at me. "I've missed so much of my life, but I feel I've been reborn."

"You're in the aftermath of a most remarkable process, Karen, but there's still work to do synthesizing all the parts so you can truly be yourself."

She looks pensive. "I remember an alter saying long ago that my life would begin at thirty-eight. I'll be thirty-nine in a few days and I'm setting a new goal of feeling complete by the time I'm forty. This will give me another year to get used to feeling whole." She pauses to gaze out the window. "It's very hard," she continues, "dealing with life's ups and downs without dissociating. I don't ever want to forget the alter parts inside me. They made me who I am, and am becoming." She stops again and closes her eyes. Slowly she turns and looks at me. "I so much want to elaborate on how I'm feeling, but I'm so tired."

"It's okay; we can continue next time," I say. I look at her, feeling a kind of awe. She's an incredible human being.

She smiles at me. "Next time, then. I'll have so much to tell you."

EPILOGUE

In the middle of August 1998, Karen and I take a ride. It's late afternoon, and the summer day's heat is beginning to wane as the sun settles lower in the sky. Karen's old neighborhood is only a few miles from my office, but through city traffic, it takes thirty minutes to get there. We'd talked about my seeing where she grew up and where all the childhood events she's told me about took place. I wanted to see for myself.

We exit the highway and head south. The area is Hispanic now. When Karen's grandfather moved there in 1937, it was German, Polish, and Irish. We turn and drive east and straight to her house. The house is a three-story brick structure with nothing to distinguish it. It fits in with the other houses on the street. And while no two houses are the same, taken together, they form an assembly of inexpensive dwellings from the first half of the century, built to house workers for the neighboring factories and stockyards.

Karen and her family lived in the basement apartment, and her grandparents occupied the first floor. Above them was the attic. We double-park out front and Karen peers at the windows. The beige paint is peeling and the previously painted red brick shows through underneath.

"With the paint peeling around the windows and door," says

Karen, watching the house, "it looks wounded, like a bloodied face with tears."

Karen points out to me the ice cream parlor across the street and the funeral home down at the corner. We drive on and turn left. There is the Protestant church around the corner from Karen's house. She took refuge in the stairwell leading to the church basement when she wanted to escape from home. The pastor from the church could hear her father bellowing, especially in the summer when there was no air-conditioning and everyone left their windows open. He'd unlock the chain-link gate to the alley knowing he might soon find Karen hiding at the bottom of the stairs. Sometimes he'd talk to her and bring her cookies and milk.

Three blocks from her house is the Catholic school and church. The school is a three-story redbrick building from the early 1900s. Past the school, huddled between the school and the church, is the rectory.

"I'd walk from school to the door of the rectory, there," says Karen, pointing. "You could go to the church basement from the rectory by that passageway." Karen indicates the enclosed walkway from the rectory into the church. "Once inside the church, there's a stairway that leads to the basement."

I can tell this isn't easy for Karen. She says she hasn't been back here for several years, and everything looks smaller and dirtier. The triggers in this place are strong, and I can see Karen replaying the events of the past in her mind as we visit each scene.

We turn along the park. She shows me the lagoon and the benches where she'd sit. That's where she'd find her brother Jim, if he'd run from the house. The protective wall around a statue is where Karen would hide if she could escape her father's rages. It's at the far corner of the park, as far away as she could get from her house and still be in the park.

We continue to drive around her neighborhood, doubling back north. There's a bar on every street corner, a funeral home every two blocks, and small storefronts that were once groceries, bakeries, or hardware stores. What once were thriving small businesses are now either run-down or closed. Two blocks from Karen's house is the photography studio where pornographic pictures and films were taken of Karen and the other children. It's now a hair salon.

We head back toward Karen's house and turn up the alley behind it. As we reach her garage, she points out to me the gray, corrugated, metal-and-wood lean-to shed, the shandy, where she was hurt so many times. We pass again the funeral home and the garage entrance, leading to the embalming room, where Karen was tortured for her father's and his friends' amusement.

As we drive back around the front of her house, we draw glares from some of the young men who live on her street. They don't recognize us and we've been casing their neighborhood. It's getting a little creepy for me, so I suggest to Karen we go back. She's had enough, too.

Before we get on the highway, we pass the old entrance to the chemical factory. The street leading to it passes under a wide, low bridge that carries commuter and freight railroad tracks. It's dark under the bridge; Karen says the lights on either side, which provide only dim illumination for the street, are new. When she came here as a girl, it was always very dark and it terrified her. I imagine there should have been a sign at the entrance: *Abandon hope all ye who enter here.* We drive in, under the bridge, and on the other side there's only a large expanse of concrete, fenced off now. The factory is gone. Looking at the vacant site, Karen points out where the parking lot was, and the route they took to go to the back entrance of the building.

Later that night Karen has a nightmare. Her house comes alive. The windows are eyes and the door is a mouth, and it's sucking her inside. She resists, but the pull gets stronger and stronger, and she finally succumbs. I come looking for her, but she's become a part of the walls, a part of the fabric of the house, and I can't see her or hear her. With my help, she finally frees herself from the house. She wakes feeling disgusting and unclean and takes a long shower.

As the months pass, Karen struggles to loosen her mother's grip, to squelch her relentless demands for money and favors. In the past, when Karen lost time, she'd alternately appease her mother and refuse her. Since Karen's become whole, she's done the same thing. The difference is she doesn't dissociate what she's done. Within her are still the traits that were Sandy and Miles. Sometimes she has Miles's strength to withstand her mother's bidding, and sometimes, especially when her self-esteem is low, she plays Sandy's part and can't say no. Karen makes incremental progress, but it's taken years for her to mature past her childhood pattern of paying for her mother's love.

Concurrent with Karen's conflicts with her mother is her striving to part from her abusive husband. Tearing herself free from her contemporary abuser is, she knows, a necessity if she's to distance herself from all forms of abuse. This journey involves trips to the emergency room, police reports, her husband's arrest, and his three-day stay in Cook County jail. I ask my best friend from college, an attorney, to help Karen. For a nominal fee, he works with her, and on Halloween 2001, her divorce is final. Her husband continues to try to manipulate Karen, begging for money and services, and he sometimes succeeds, but she continues to separate herself from him and the relationship he typifies. He rarely pays the court-ordered child support.

Karen's part-time work eventually progresses to full-time employment as a receptionist at a nonprofit organization. Her instant empathy and uncanny understanding of the clients' problems compel many individuals to arrive early to talk to her, for a presession session. Although she's competent and reliable, always performing the extra, unasked-for task, she's terrified of making mistakes and being yelled at. She still seeks me out for help, and I try to get her to experience work more as an ordinary job than as a daily Inquisition. Interestingly, her major professional strength is multitasking.

Integration has not erased the effects of years of physical and mental abuse. Since Karen's full integration in April 1998, we've continued to work together another eight years. Our time has been spent strengthening Karen's resilience and tendency to despair in the face of the ordinary challenges and disappointments of everyday life. Gratifyingly, I've watched this woman grow and evolve into a caring, kind, and compassionate soul who wants to take her rightful place in the world, free from the effects of her past, and who looks forward to a happy future.

In late April 2006, we set a date for termination of the therapy. It will be June 30. As we work toward that day, we reminisce about all that's taken place between us and within her. She's afraid, but she knows she doesn't need therapy anymore. She already knows everything I'm going to say. She just still likes to hear me say it.

When our last session comes, Karen arrives at my office two hours early. She'd driven around Old Town, where I live, and gotten lost. She found herself at a little park on Sedgwick, with "no swings, no kids, and no interruptions," as she told me, and stayed there thinking about what it would mean to her to be without our sessions.

When she arrives at my house, as she's done so many times before, and sits in her customary chair, everything feels different. We've become a part of the fabric of each other's lives, and it seems incredible this day has finally come.

"I have mixed feelings," says Karen. "Really good and really sad. I know I don't really need therapy anymore, but you're like family."

"Does it feel like losing a friend?" I ask.

"No, not a friend, really; our relationship has always been so one-sided. I've always regretted that."

"I know. The limits on a therapy relationship are meant to make it possible to keep the therapy going. I realize it's been disappointing, but it's brought us to this point, and I'm so happy to see the woman you've become today."

"Thank you," Karen replies, blushing a little. "I've never exceeded our boundaries; I was always attuned to you; I could sense what you'd allow. With all that was inside me, I'm amazed we got through it. The only relief in my life was seeing you, Dr. Baer." Karen's eyes begin to tear. "Every time you said I should call you—that was my safety blanket. It kept me going, every week, all these years. You prevented me from killing myself many times."

"I've been happy to have been the one to take care of you," I say. I feel as if I should say more, but I have more feelings than I can put into words.

"Can I e-mail you, if I have things to tell you?"

"Of course; and if you need to call me at any time, that would be fine, too. I feel it's hard for both of us to let go."

"You were my real father, Dr. Baer; I never really had one until you."

"I feel like I helped raise you. I was certainly a father to Miles, Claire, Sidney, and the others." We sit for a moment. I recall a dream

I had the previous night about Karen. Should I tell her? I wonder. I want to, and without sufficient time to weigh the pros and cons, I decide to go ahead.

"I dreamt about you last night." Karen looks up from her reverie and smiles. "I dreamt it was this morning and I'd double-booked our session, that I'd made an appointment to do something for myself at the same time I was supposed to see you. I immediately canceled the appointment for me so I could keep this much-more-important one with you. I think that's what I've always done—put myself aside to take care of you. I really couldn't help myself."

"I always wondered how you did it. It's the best relationship I ever had. You never let me down."

"Will you be okay when you leave?"

"My friend Jan is waiting for me with coffee, pizza, and tissues. My friends don't see me as dysfunctional at all; they've been supportive. Since knowing you, I know what to look for in friends."

As we make our way toward the door, I wonder if Karen will try to hug me at our parting. I open the door for her and stand next to it. Karen turns away, and glancing back at me briefly, walks past me over the threshold.

"What, no hug?" I ask.

She turns around, surprised.

"*Now* it's okay?" she says, almost scolding.

"Yes."

Karen moves toward me and we encircle each other. I can feel her squeeze me and hold me fast, as I do with her. After too many moments, I release her and she looks up at me, eyes brimming with affection and thanks.

KAREN'S NOTE

Tears still come when I think back through all the years I spent in therapy with Dr. Baer, working together to heal me. As I read and reread this book, his words touched me in an unbelievable way, but what matters most is that, through this journey, I was brought back to life. I surely wouldn't be here without him.

Switching Time is an accurate description of what I suffered and experienced, and Dr. Baer has captured my alter personalities exactly as I recall them. My alters grew to trust him before I did. Usually I'd find myself in Dr. Baer's waiting room, alone, anxious, and wondering how I'd arrived. I had to accept that somehow I was just there. But the moment Dr. Baer opened the door I felt safe. For the first time in my life someone was willing to listen to me, time and again, without judgment. Through eighteen years of therapy I've learned from him about trust, respect, dignity, integrity, commitment, faith, compassion, and love.

Actually, *Switching Time* is a kind of love story. After being hurt so badly all my life, I didn't have the ability to love myself or anyone else. As a woman and a mother this was unbearable. Whether real or fantasized, Dr. Baer's patience, understanding, and unconditional care made me feel accepted and, yes, loved.

My message to all who read this book is to watch with fresh eyes the children with whom you come in contact daily. Do they seem distant—not fully there? If so, have the courage to ask questions and demand answers. When children are victimized, as I've been, they no longer exist in the real world. They turn to the only safe place they know—within themselves. As a child in constant fear, I unknowingly protected my abusers by adapting to their needs. To survive, I became compliant. It's my hope that what happened to me never happens to another child who finds him- or herself in an abusive situation with no one to turn to. I pray no child fears telling someone as I did.

Karen Overhill

January 2007

AUTHOR'S NOTE

Early on in my treatment of Karen, as I became aware that she wasn't one person but many, I suspected I was about to witness a remarkable human drama. Once I received Claire's letter and the nature of Karen's condition was confirmed, I began to keep detailed notes of every session. Though I wasn't certain how—or if—I'd ever use the notes, I felt it essential to maintain an extensive and accurate record of Karen's treatment.

In diagnosing Karen and thinking about how to make her whole again, I read more than twenty books, as well as hundreds of articles and abstracts on dissociative identity disorder. At all times I tried to be supportive without influencing the content of what she might say.

In total, over our eighteen years of psychotherapy, I wrote 622 pages of progress notes, and collected 44 drawings, 49 artifacts (gifts from, and items associated with, the 17 alters), 12 audiotapes, and 2 videos. I also received from Karen 275 e-mails, 60 cards, and almost 5,000 pages of journal entries and letters. This book is a distillation of those materials, and every episode portrayed is documented in the record of Karen's treatment. For me, the most difficult part of preparing this manuscript was trying to decide what *not* to include.

After Karen's treatment for multiple personality disorder was completed and I felt she was capable of informed consent, I inquired about her willingness to have her story told. In response, she told me she hoped that sharing what happened to her would make people more aware of the abuse little girls sometimes suffer, and the warning signs to be alert for. If, as a result of this book, one boy or girl could be rescued from a tormented childhood, Karen felt it would be worth it.

In the six years I spent writing *Switching Time*, Karen was invaluable in checking my descriptions of events for accuracy. In fact, she supplied more than eighty pages of corrections, additions, and amplifications to what she'd already told me. To protect Karen's privacy and the anonymity of others mentioned in the book, I have changed Karen's name as well as the names and identifying characteristics of almost everyone portrayed in this book. I have also disguised some of the places described in the book. As for the few episodes depicted where Karen isn't present, such as the scene in the machine shop where Karen's father intimidates Harry, each is a narration of a story Karen heard over and over again. (For example, the scene in the shop is one Karen's father repeatedly replayed, apparently to underscore his power over people and ability to do with them as he pleased.) Karen's writings have been abridged for the sake of space, and years of treatment have been condensed; but nothing has been added or altered in the portrayal of Karen's experiences or the course of the psychotherapy.

Transforming our arduous work together into this book you're now reading has required the help and guidance of several people. Carole Bidnick, my literary agent, immediately saw the value of Karen's story; that's her gift, and she ushered the book unerringly through sale and publication. Jenny Meyer and Whitney Lee were key members of the team Carole assembled to help *Switching Time* reach a wider audience.

At Crown, Rick Horgan did a thorough and expert job of editing the manuscript and steering it through the labyrinth of the publishing process. Assisted by Julian Pavia, he showed me how to better tell the story while leaving the project's integrity intact. Also making key contributions were attorney Min Lee and publicist Penny Simon.

I want to thank Lori Andrews for showing me what it is to have the identity of a writer. I'd also like to acknowledge Mark Rosin and Caroline Pincus for their editorial help on early versions of the manuscript.

During my coursework at Northwestern University's School for Continuing Studies master's program in creative nonfiction, Brian Bouldrey and Susan Harris were particularly outstanding in their expertise and encouragement.

Lastly, I must thank Karen herself for her courage and help in writing this book. Our journey together is an ongoing one. Our therapeutic relationship has turned into a close and respectful friendship. The time we've spent together has forever altered both our lives. This work—both the therapy and the book—has been a true collaborative effort.

Richard K. Baer, M.D.
January 2007

INDEX

abuse: Baer's views about Karen's, 21–22, 26; and Karen's curiosity about Baer, 65; and Karen's fear that Baer will abuse her, 22–23; Karen's views about, 228–29; and MPD, 92, 94–95; multigenerational, 149; and touching, 305. *See also specific person, alter, or event*

"Album of Selves," 327

alter inside Karen, drawing of, 300

alters: aging of, 147, 161; and "Album of Selves," 327; Baer as father figure for, 341–42; Baer's access to, 95, 100, 102–6, 133–35; capacity for identication by, 246–47; death of, 146; and diagram of Karen's internal world, 157–59; drawing of tree and, 322; emergence of, 143, 315, 324; faces of, 163–65; formation of new, 319–20; hypnosis as means for Baer to meet, 95–97, 102–4; individuality of, 147, 160, 161, 195, 281, 284, 285; and internal world as house, 318–19, 320–21; joint decision-making by, 130–32; joint letters from, 131–32, 145–47; Karen's awareness of, 93, 94–99, 100,

126–27, 133; and Karen's pretense about knowing what others are doing, 174; Karen's views about, 164–65, 331, 333, 334–35; keeping secrets from, 92; number of, 91, 95, 96–97, 105, 116, 117, 127, 128, 130, 161, 165; "re-creation" of old/more, 146, 304, 312; voices of, 320; in woman's body, 331. *See also specific alter or topic*

The Angry One (alter): background and role of, 96; death wish of, 99; face of, 165; and first hypnosis of Karen, 105; and Martin's death, 109; and number of alters, 117, 127; and self-harm, 100. *See also* Karl (alter)

Ann (alter): age of, 116, 140; and allegations of Baer-Karen sexual relationship, 180; appearance of, 232; background and role of, 134, 140, 161, 232, 234, 263; and Baer's Christmas present, 131; Baer's relationship with, 135, 233; calls to Baer from, 216, 217; and church sex, 134; and daily life, 156, 157, 177; death concerns of, 146; face of, 165; and grandmother, 147; guilt of, 197,